Marital Therapy

The Guilford Family Therapy Series
ALAN S. GURMAN, *Editor*

Marriage and Divorce: A Contemporary Perspective
Carol C. Nadelson and Derek C. Polonsky, Editors

Family Care of Schizophrenia: A Problem-Solving Approach to the Treatment of Mental
    Illness
Ian R. H. Falloon, Jeffrey L. Boyd, and Christine W. McGill

The Process of Change
Peggy Papp

Family Therapy: Principles of Strategic Practice
Allon Bross, Editor

Aesthetics of Change
Bradford P. Keeney

Family Therapy in Schizophrenia
William R. McFarlane, Editor

Mastering Resistance: A Practical Guide to Family Therapy
Carol M. Anderson and Susan Stewart

Family Therapy and Family Medicine: Toward the Primary Care of Families
William J. Doherty and Macaran A. Baird

Ethnicity and Family Therapy
Monica McGoldrick, John K. Pearce, and Joseph Giordano, Editors

Patterns of Brief Family Therapy: An Ecosystemic Approach
Steve de Shazer

The Family Therapy of Drug Abuse and Addiction
M. Duncan Stanton, Thomas C. Todd, and Associates

From Psyche to System: The Evolving Therapy of Carl Whitaker
John R. Neill and David P. Kniskern, Editors

Normal Family Processes
Froma Walsh, Editor

Helping Couples Change: A Social Learning Approach to Marital Therapy
Richard B. Stuart

Marital Therapy

An Integrative Approach

WILLIAM C. NICHOLS, Ed.D.

The Guilford Press
New York   London

© 1988 The Guilford Press
A Division of Guilford Publications, Inc.
72 Spring Street, New York, N.Y. 10012
All rights reserved

Printed in the United States of America

Last digit is print number: 9 8 7 6 5 4 3

Library of Congress Cataloging in Publication Data
Nichols, William C.
  Marital therapy.

  (The Guilford family therapy series)
  Bibliography: p.
  Includes index.
  1. Marital psychotherapy. I. Title. II. Series.
[DNLM: 1. Marital Therapy. WM 55 N623m]
RC488.5.N534   1988   616.89'156   88-11179
ISBN 0-89862-102-X

TO ALICE

Preface

My intention in writing this book was to provide practical help for those who wish to learn about marital therapy and to improve their understanding and skill in dealing therapeutically with married couples. It is based on the premise that marriage is a powerful and unique relationship, different in some significant ways from other forms of relating. The man and woman who marry bring together two ways of life—with all the complex meanings, values, and expectations that growing up in two different family patterns and groupings entail—as well as their own specific individual perceptions and needs.

Marital therapy is the form of therapy that challenges the therapist most directly and deeply to keep both the individual and the family systems in appropriate perspective and balance. Over the past three decades I have found it to be—simultaneously—the most difficult, fascinating, frustrating, and rewarding form of therapeutic endeavor. This book will have been a success if something of that flavor along with the fostering of a determination to keep learning about this fascinating and challenging form of human relatedness can be transmitted to the reader.

Personal appreciation is expressed to teachers, mentors, and colleagues—Gertrude Zemon-Gass, Ph.D., with whom I shared offices and clinical problems for more than 20 short years; Aaron L. Rutledge, Ph.D.; and Laura Singer-Magdoff, Ed.D. Each has affected my career significantly, probably most deeply by providing examples and visions that continue to fuel my efforts to comprehend, practice, and teach more effective marital therapy.

Specific appreciation for help with this book is expressed to Alice, with whom I continue to learn about marriage and life and who serves as chief supporter and honest critic; to David, who insisted that I get a word processor; to Bill, who insisted that I learn to use it and guided me past my initial disasters; to Camille, who can teach any therapist about supportiveness; to Ellen M. Berman, M.D., for her perceptive comments and helpful suggestions on the manuscript; and to Alan Gurman, Ph.D., series editor, and Seymour Weingarten, editor-in-chief of The Guilford Press, with both of whom it is a pleasure to work once again.

William C. Nichols
Tallahassee, Florida

Contents

Marital Therapy

Foundations for Marital Therapy

The Nature of Marriage and Marital Therapy

Marriage and family, rather than psychotherapy or the techniques of treatment, form the basis of marital therapy. Marriage is not simply a dyadic relationship like all other forms of pairing, and a family system is not merely another entity to which individual or group psychotherapy can be easily and effectively applied. Although techniques of treatment are important and will receive a considerable amount of attention here, these techniques can be most effectively and responsibly applied when the therapist has a solid knowledge of the relationships and systems that form the focus of therapy. Marriage and its meaning for the partners thus constitutes a major theme of this book, while family systems provide the backbone or framework to which the marriage is attached.

Clinicians must understand the nature of the entities with which they are working. Otherwise, they risk applying inappropriate techniques or using techniques inappropriately. The physician's ancient creed "First, do no harm" applies to the therapist as well. For a clinician to try to perform marital therapy or to apply therapeutic interventions with married persons without an in-depth understanding of marriage and the marital relationship is questionable at best and sometimes harmful.

ASSUMPTIONS

It seems appropriate to reveal one's assumptions at the outset of a book. A major assumption of mine is that marriage is an entity of its own. The veteran English marital therapist Henry V. Dicks (1967) referred to marriage as a social relationship *sui generis*, literally "of its own kind," alto-

3

gether unique and unduplicated. This I believe to be correct: No other social relationship duplicates marriage. To so describe it implies neither praise nor criticism, but simply states a significant fact: The motivations, expectations, and dynamics of a married couple are different from those of unattached individuals who are seen by the therapist in individual or group treatment and from those of a two- or three-generation, hierarchically organized family group.

A second assumption is that therapists should give close attention to the context in which persons live and function. The important issue is determining what is the context that needs to be considered for a given individual. With children, the family certainly is the context that needs to be taken into account. To work with a child as if the youngster were not a family member, dependent in crucial ways on adult caretaking and authority figures would appear to be unwise to most therapists. With adults the context includes their extended family, the nuclear family, and their marriage. My assumption here is that for most married persons the marital relationship is the part of that context that deserves much more attention than it often receives from therapists, that it warrants attention as a primary entity in its own right.

A third assumption is that education and training in individual personality theory and individual psychotherapy are not adequate preparation for practicing effectively as a marital therapist. Extrapolations from such foundations, as valuable as they may be in some ways, are not appropriate for comprehending the context and content essential to the performance of marital therapy. The supposition of many clinicians that it is possible to move from an individual orientation to work with marital partners through a kind of additive process simply does not hold up under careful scrutiny. Marital and family therapists frequently are contacted by persons whose previous efforts to find assistance for relationships problems have been mishandled by individually oriented psychotherapists.

A fourth assumption is that marital therapy is often the most effective and difficult of the clinician's psychotherapeutic undertakings. Years of performing individual psychotherapy from a psychodynamic orientation and additional years of doing marital and family therapy have provided me with several bases for a comparison of modalities. Without denigrating individual psychotherapy, it can be said that working with one person in a psychodynamic treatment relationship is relatively easy when compared with dealing with persons in marital therapy. Once the individual is settled into treatment, tracking with him or her and interpreting and making other interventions is much less difficult than attending to the dynamics of a three-way session. Family therapists who agree with the foregoing may find it less easy to accept the notion that marital therapy is more difficult than family therapy. Nevertheless, it has been my experience that it is when family therapy concentrates on the marital dyad that it becomes its most difficult. Marital therapy involves work with the most complex relationship in the family. Marriage as a voluntary selection process is inherently more complex and less stable than other family relationships. Marital therapy must take into account the initial and ongoing attachment of the partners. This process involves the individual spouses in ways that family therapy with children does not.

The foregoing leads to my fifth assumption—that most family therapy eventually becomes marital therapy, either in an informal, implicit sense or in a formal, explicit manner. Although not all family therapists would agree, the semifacetious statement that "Most family therapy becomes marital therapy sooner or later and if you're smart you get there sooner" is only a moderate overstatement and distortion, in my judgment. This view stems primarily from the fact that the husband–wife relationship is the basis of nuclear family formation; dependent childrens' symptomatic and problematic behaviors are frequently a reaction to parental problems. Dealing with the parents themselves thus is often the most rapid and effective way of ameliorating the child's difficulties as well as of getting at the basic problems embedded within the family structure. Similarly, support for the parents of a problematic child may be indicated because of the stress produced by the youngster's troubles.

All of these assumptions will be addressed in subsequent parts of this chapter and in the book as a whole. The intent here is to sensitize the reader to the great importance of learning as much as possible about marriage.

Effective learning about marriage in preparation for doing marital therapy comes not so much from reading books about marital therapy as it does from immersing oneself in materials from cultural anthropology, family studies, sociology of the family, novels, and anything from literature and the mass media that provides one with an understanding of contemporary marital and family behaviors and relationships. Studying such data and observing and analyzing our own experiences in marital and family living through the spectacles of informed theory provides a framework to guide our comprehension. I am assuming that the reader either possesses or will acquire such a background and shall not attempt to provide it in this book.

THE ESSENTIAL DISTINCTIVENESS OF MARRIAGE

Marriage, as noted, is a distinctive social relationship. The mates are peers from the beginning who are initially unrelated and who typically develop a deeper intimacy as the relationship progresses. Marital therapy is consequently different in some respects from most other types of therapy. Among these differences are a concern with voluntary choice of the partner in the relationship, an emphasis on object relations and marital development, and the necessity of taking into account two different family systems. The very things that make marital therapy different also make its practice more difficult for the therapist.

ITS VOLUNTARY NATURE

Marriage is the lone voluntary relationship in the family. Other family relationships—such as certain stepfamily relationships—share with marriage the possibility of being terminated by divorce, but are not entered into voluntarily in the same way that one moves into marriage. Stepchildren acquire stepparents and stepsiblings as a result of the actions of their parent and the parent's new spouse. Those who become stepparents do exercise some choice in the matter, but this is done primarily in terms of deciding whom they will marry. The children in a stepfamily go along as an accompaniment to the actions of their parents.

Aside from stepfamily relationships, only in-law relationships among the ties existing in families can be ended by divorce. Of course, any given individual can reject, cut off emotionally, or legally disinherit another person in the family, but such actions do not change the fact that the individuals are still related and are still members of the same family.

The fact that individuals have a choice in selecting a mate and in deciding whether to remain in a marriage once they have contracted for it opens the way for ambivalance in the mates. Conflicted feelings about the choice of mate, the satisfactions the marriage is providing, and whether or not to remain are often central factors in the interaction of warring couples.

OBJECT RELATIONS

The concept of object relations pertains broadly to interpersonal relations: Specifically, it refers to the early interpersonal relationships between a child and its primary caretakers. Those early interactions and relationships are internalized by the child and become the model for later intimate interpersonal relationships (American Association for Marriage and Family Therapy, 1983).

Object-relations factors have implications not only for understanding how mate selection choices were made originally, but also for how the relationship has changed and how the partners are held together at the present time. In this context it is important to consider how their needs are or are not being met in the current relationship (Dicks, 1967; Scharff & Scharff, 1987; Willi, 1982, 1984).

MARITAL DEVELOPMENT

A marriage is similar in its development to individual and family development in that there is a marital life cycle that has predictable stages. At each stage there are tasks to be mastered at those times if the marriage is to move from start to finish through the death of one of the partners without experiencing separation or divorce as disruptive intruders. Conversely, the marital life cycle differs from both individual and family development in some important ways. Unlike the individual life cycle, it is not based on biological development except in a very general sense. Neither is it predicated primarily on the development and maturing of children, as tends to be the case with the family life cycle.

THE MELDING OF FAMILY SYSTEMS

Understanding marriage generally involves taking into account the wife's family system and the husband's family system and how they articulate with or blend/conflict with the nuclear family formed as a result of the marriage of the man and woman. Marriages are always tied in some historical ways to the norms of the generation going before the marital partners (Yankelovich, 1981). Using the term "culture" somewhat loosely, it is the culture both of marriage in general and of a marriage in particular that concerns the marital therapist: Marriage and marital issues appear to be most comprehensible when viewed in transgenerational or intergenerational terms.

Understanding the nature, meaning, and dynamics of a particular marriage implies a working comprehension of the relationships of both partners' families of origin. What were things like in June's family? In Jim's? What was the size? What were the communication patterns like? What were the values, the rules? What were the influence patterns? Jim, for example, not only was profoundly influenced by his great-grandfather when he was a young child, but also had his work ethic reinforced through continuing contact with his grandmother, who emphasized such maxims as, "If it's worth doing, it's worth doing right." June's family was "laid back and casual, very relaxed." There were significant differences in spite of the fact that both came from small-town, middle-class families. How do they continue to relate to their families today?

This is not to imply that a therapist must always have such mastery in order to make effective therapeutic interventions, but that such comprehension is essential to understanding the marriage in question. The same statement would be appropriate with regard to understanding a nation, namely, that one must know its history in order to have an adequate comprehension of that country, of its nature and dynamics.

Such comprehension of a particular marriage and couple is not merely a matter of discerning the history of the individuals as they have developed in relation to their families of origin. More than simply adding the relationship history of the partners to what is known about their developmental histories with their respective families is needed. One needs to have a working grasp of what may be termed factors both of content (e.g., beliefs, values, information) and of process (what has occurred) for the individuals and their respective families of origin, as well as of how these affect their current marital and family development and living. Such history is truly "living history." The processes of interaction and influence of members of the family of origin have continued vitality in the present, for better or for worse.

The family-transactional nature of symptoms has long been accepted in the family therapy field, due to the fact that many problems in human behavior that show up in individuals stem from difficulties in relationship events between intimately related persons (Framo, 1972). Thus in order to understand not only individual symptoms and behavior pathology but also the general nature of marital interaction and relationships, it is important to be aware that we as therapists may need to understand some transgenerational processes and interactions. As an example, to grasp adequately Carol's anxiety and depression and Paul's strong need to be in control in their marital relationship, it may be helpful or even essential to comprehend how each of them developed in their families of origin as well as how they maintain the current problematic patterns that they refer to as "problems in relating and communication." Sometimes it is helpful to have an awareness of how their parents and even their grandparents deal (or dealt) with each other, as well as a grasp of how they relate to Carol and Paul.

To expand the example a bit, Carol and Paul's socioeconomic, educational, and religious backgrounds were similar. Each came from a fam-

ily of three children, though their sibling positions were different, Paul
being the eldest and Carol the middle child. Both sets of parents had
made it exceedingly difficult for them to differentiate from their family
of origin: Paul's parents had "parentified" him and now leaned on him
for a variety of kinds of support and practical help, while Carol's parents
tried to keep all of their children involved with them in a sticky kind of
enmeshment, in which they spent large amounts of time together. Her
mother also intruded to try to control minute details of Carol's child
rearing and other behaviors.

One way of trying to depict what is being described here is reflected
in Figure 1. The background of each of the marital partners may be
viewed as consisting of a dual system of genetic transmission and inher-
itance and nongenetic transmission, as well as of a living context of intergenerational relationships, influences, and dynamics.

The figure represents the fact that each of the marital partners developed in a family of origin that had within it several subsystems. Typically, in a nuclear family that had more than one child this would involve the marital, parent–child, sibling, and individual subsystems. The
nuclear family interacts with the society and its culture in complex ways.
It filters most of the cultural values for the family members, particularly
in the case of young children.

The individual's course of physical maturation and personal and social development is graphically represented in the channel with arrows
symbolizing the movement through life, away from the family of origin
toward youth and adulthood and entry into the process of mate selection. There is different and more direct exposure to social and cultural
values as the young begin to move toward differentiation from their family of origin. No easy and simple description of what transpires during
either the later or earlier years of development is possible. The main
point to be made here is that there is a continuity between the family of
origin and its influences, the individual, and the sociocultural forces that
enter into the mate selection process and the marriage and so into the
new nuclear family that is formed and that becomes the family of origin
for the children of the marrying couple.

The figure does not reflect adequately the transgenerational nature
of what takes place across the three generations, or across even four living generations in some instances. Family loyalties (Boszormenyi-Nagy
& Spark, 1973) in which intense attachments and feelings find expression
and meaning are noted with an arrow representing their two-way nature
and vertical dimensions. Each member in a family expects fairness and
reciprocity. We all carry our own internal "account book" in which we

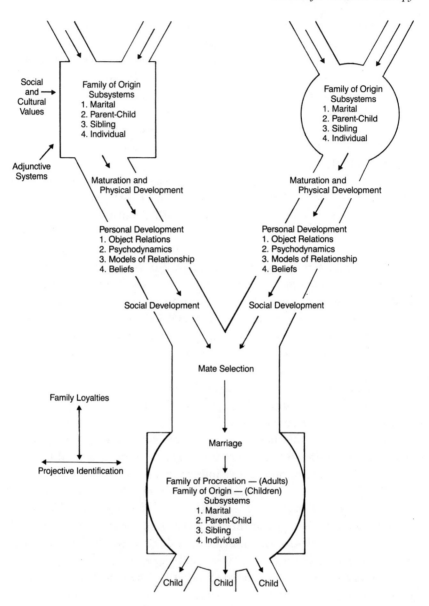

FIGURE 1

Tributary model. Ellen M. Berman has developed a similar tributary model for understanding marital dynamics. Cf. Berman, E. M., Lief, H. I., & Williams, A. M. (1981), in G. P. Sholevar (Ed.), *The handbook of marriage and marital therapy* (p. 5), New York: SP Medical & Scientific Books.

have a balance sheet of what is owed to us by our parents and children and what we owe to them. An important implication of this for marriage is that as strong attachments to the mate develop, some persons may begin to feel caught in a conflict in which they must make a choice, because by attaching strongly to the spouse they are being disloyal to their parents. Those who feel they are caught in such a "zero-sum game" may reject the mate in order to break the tension. Similarly, projective identification, an important object relations concept viewed here broadly and somewhat simplistically as a tendency to project one's needs onto the mate and to become identified with the mate as an expected fulfiller of those needs, is depicted by the two-way horizontal arrow.

The bottom part of the figure shows the new marriage and family forming its own subsystems and sending the children out to take their own places in the world. It should be recognized that this is a general depiction: not all marriages produce children; not all marriages last; not all children grow up in a family.

MARRIAGE AND OTHER RELATIONSHIPS

Returning to the general theme of the distinctiveness of marriage it is also worth noting the ways that marriage differs from other forms of paired relatedness. Although there are similarities between couples such as those involving two people who are living together in a committed heterosexual or homosexual relationship and married couples, there are some differences as well. The gestalt of a married relationship is not the same as that of live-in relationships that are not bound up in the social and legal ties of marriage.

Differences in terms of what is expected from a marital partner and a marital relationship and what is expected from a partner to whom one is not married may be marked and extensive in my observation. What Skynner (1976) has called "models of relationships" is one of the factors contributing to the differences. Models of relationships are a special kind of object relatedness formed through what one has absorbed in the exposure while growing up and reaching adulthood to marriages primarily in one's family of origin. As the concept is used here, models of relationships refer to more than simply images of what marriage looks like; they also contain a strong emotional feeling about what marriage is supposed to be.

Clinically, it is possible to observe again and again an increase in the intensity of feelings as well as in the specificity of expectations once a relationship has crossed the line to become socially and legally a marriage. The "piece of paper" and the things that go with it symbolically and emotionally, as well as socially and legally, do make a difference. As O'Neill (1977) notes, marriage is not as open-ended as living together; it implies commitment, and the ceremony involves a personal acknowledgment that the partners are entering a new state in life. There is more to be observed among married persons than simply the matter of feeling that one is "caught" or more deeply enmeshed in a relationship with another person by virtue of being pronounced husband and wife by some duly constituted official or recognized representative of the state. Rather, one witnesses among the married an increase in the sense of obligation and privilege, sometimes even ownership, that comes when the roles of man and woman become those of husband and wife. The marital state embodies the expectations that accompany the models of relationships and conceptions of marital tasks and roles that have been absorbed by virtue of living in one's original nuclear and extended family and in the society as a whole, via its images and portrayals of marriage. Without belaboring the point, it suffices here to say that it is an observable clinical fact that marriage holds expectations and meanings for many persons that are not necessarily present in an unmarried coupling, regardless of the duration of the unmarried relationship.

Another related point that is often overlooked in discussions of similarities and differences beween marriage and other forms of coupling concerns the fact that extended families of spouses sometimes regard the married couple with far stronger and more explicit expectations than they place on unmarried members of the family who live in a cohabiting relationship. The connections with the family of origin of the partners that are established by marriage are different from the relationships, identifications, and expectations prevailing when a man and a woman are simply living together. Members of the respective families inevitably seem to feel differently toward "Joan's friend" than "Joan's husband, my son-in-law" or "my brother-in-law." Typically, it seems that the feelings—positive or negative—regarding a former in-law who has ceased to be a relative by virtue of divorce are stronger than affective reactions regarding a former live-in companion of a member of one's family.

The marital relationship also differs from other family relationships not only in that it is voluntary but also in that the voluntariness is reciprocal. The relationship may be started and ended by either partner. Whereas both partners need to strive to cooperate and work together in order to continue the marital relationship in most instances today, one spouse may choose to end it unilaterally. This option became even more widely available with the advent of no-fault divorce.

MARRIAGE, PERSONALITY, AND CULTURE

Marital therapy deals both with individuals themselves and with the relationships between individuals and family systems and subsystems. Individuals in marital and family therapy are perceived differently than they are in individual psychotherapy, as I have noted. The main thrust of family therapy generally, including marital therapy, is toward dealing with the individual in context. As Framo (1972) and others have pointed out, the family is the most immediate, lasting, and appropriate system to include as a unit of study and treatment when trying to understand and work therapeutically with a person.

SOCIOCULTURAL FACTORS

The family approach orients the therapist much more strongly in the direction of taking sociocultural factors into account in dealing with persons than does most traditional personality theory. As soon as marriage is included as a relevant concern, one must begin to pay attention to cultural forces. Although they are related to the biology of the human being insofar as sexual attraction and mating are concerned, the forms that attractiveness, mating, and living as a married couple assume are strongly shaped by culture. The same thing could be said about human personality formation as well, but it seems accurate to state that personality theorists generally emphasize factors related to human biology and individual functioning much more than do social scientists and clinicians concerned with marriage.

Especially when we look at marriage and family life and the parts that they play in affecting the behavior of individuals do we find that the range of factors involved is much more complex than those to be considered when looking primarily at physically based factors such as the biological foundations of behavior and symptomatology. If we assume that individual pathology, or to be more precise, behavioral pathology that shows up in individuals, comes primarily or totally from physical sources, we have a comparatively narrow range of factors to consider. Even then the matter is still far from simple. We can, for example, make certain assumptions about human organisms that can be applied to all members of the species. As sociologists are fond of pointing out, the same physical symptoms indicate the presence of an acute attack of appendicitis in human beings around the world, because we share a common biological makeup. The same thing certainly cannot be said with regard to behavioral pathology; behaviors have quite different meanings as we shift from one society or culture to another. Whenever we must take social organization and culture into account, the picture becomes considerably more complex: The units with which we are then working are less easily compared and more difficult to understand at least in part because more factors must be taken into consideration.

While it is true that personality is formed as a result of a complex interplay of the combined effects of nature, culture, society, and factors unique to a given individual (Kluckhohn & Murray, 1956), many psychotherapy practitioners and theorists pay more attention to nature and idiosyncratic factors than to society and culture. Marital and family therapists are more likely to err in the direction of underemphasizing individual factors. Parenthetically, it is probably not accidental that much of the thrust for the development of family therapy came from groups or persons influenced by cultural anthropology (e.g., Gregory Bateson and associates, and Don D. Jackson, who was associated with Harry Stack Sullivan during his training days at Chestnut Lodge).

MARITAL THERAPY DEFINED

Marital therapy, as indicated above, is part of the larger field of family therapy: Although marital therapy, classical marriage counseling, the child guidance movement, and research into the family and schizophrenia all developed somewhat differently, all have nevertheless coalesced into the revolutionary approach to human problems generally referred to as family therapy (Nichols & Everett, 1986). Requests and demands for professional assistance with marital problems began to arise in the period following World War I. For the first time in history there emerged an expectation that formal, professional help could be used for dealing with the difficulties between spouses.

Professional work with marriage arose from relatively unsophisticated beginnings. Much of the early work consisted of efforts to help married persons and couples preparing for marriage. Today's marital therapy eventually evolved from this and other auxiliary efforts, including attempts to work with married persons in various forms of intensive psychotherapy. Marital therapy now treats both problems and symptomatology carrying individual diagnostic labels as well as clearly identified relationship problems.

The limits of the areas to which marital therapy may be applied as a treatment of choice have not been established. In early marital therapy approaches, the focus was on the interlocking pathology and neurotic interaction between spouses. How one partner carried the pathology or symptomatology for the other partner was emphasized. Today, however, some "strictly individual" disorders are treated through marital therapy, including agoraphobia, depression, and narcissism, along with some long-established family therapy concerns such as schizophrenia, eating disorders, and alcoholism (Jacobson & Gurman, 1986).

Psychotherapy has been concerned with the treatment of human dysfunction and disorder, difficulties that can be regarded as essentially affective, cognitive, or behavioral in nature. Sometimes the designation "nervous and mental disorders" is used, especially in statutory regulations. Using such concepts, the practice of marital and family therapy can be formally defined as the diagnosis and treatment of nervous and mental disorders, whether affective, cognitive, or behavioral, within the context of marital and family systems. Marital and family therapy involves the professional application of psychotherapeutic and family systems theories and techniques in the delivery of services to individuals, marital pairs, and families for the purpose of treating diagnosed dysfunctions (Clark & Nichols, 1983).

This formal definition says nothing about the techniques to be used. It simply states that such therapy involves the professional application of psychotherapeutic and family systems theories and techniques. The definition does deal specifically with the focus of the treatment. Context is particularly important. Returning to earlier themes, marital therapy works with individuals in terms of the marital, family, and other significant contexts in which these individuals are embedded. The personality attributes, functioning, and difficulties of the person are deeply intertwined with family ties, including very importantly the attachments with the marital partner. There is a great deal of truth in the observation that "If you wish to understand an individual's personality, you have to know the spouse as well and view them together as one personality, one whole." For the marital therapist to deal only with techniques of therapy and to ignore the nature and functioning of marriage would be similar to the surgeon giving attention to surgical techniques and ignoring the nature and functioning of the human body. For both practitioners, the interrelationship of the various parts of the system in question—be it a body or a marriage—must be of central concern.

The reference to family systems in the definition carries the implication that marriage is truly a family affair. As Spark (1977) has pointed out, marriage needs to be approached from a vertical-intergenerational perspective as well as from a peerlike, horizontal viewpoint. It is more than a relationship between opposite-sex peers who have chosen each other in a relatively open-choice manner. As a subsystem of a nuclear family, the marital relationship typically can also be viewed as essentially a relatively open subsystem in relation to the contemporary world. It is an understandable empirical observation that the influence of family-of-origin members wanes to the extent that those individuals come to represent lessened salience as authorities and objects of emotional attachment, as they "psychologically die" as sources of primary importance and emotional priority for the marital partners. Although some marital cases can be dealt with effectively without involving each spouse's family of origin, the clinical assessment of the therapist may lead to the conclusion that such systematic intervention is needed in many other instances.

The conceptual approach taken by the therapist, rather than the number of persons seen, determines whether therapy is marital and familial or individual in nature. Although some of the early family therapists refused to proceed unless all members of a family were present for a session, it soon became evident to many clinicians that family therapy could be done with only a portion of the family physically present. Similarly, marital therapy or other therapeutic work that affects the marriage can be done with only one of the partners available to the therapist. Conversely, having both partners present does not insure that the treatment will not be conducted as individual psychotherapy. Again, it is the orientation assumed and implemented by the therapist that determines the kind of treatment that occurs.

The main focus of this book is essentially on conjoint marital therapy in which one therapist works with both marital partners simultaneously in three-way interviews. This does not mean that the approach never involves interviews with individual spouses and flexible combinations of interviewing (c.f. Nichols, 1985a). Rather, it means that conjoint treatment, primarily through three-way (triadic) interviews, is the approach that is the point of reference in this book, unless it is specified otherwise. Other forms such as a collaborative marital therapy in which two therapists work with the partners separately and compare notes and marital couples group therapy have been used, and most have their strengths. Nevertheless, both clinical experience and some attention to outcome research studies have bolstered the case for conjoint marital therapy as the major modality of choice among those approaches available to the marital therapist.

Chapter Two

The Marital Life Cycle

Two individuals who enter into a marriage launch a marital cycle that goes through several predictable phases. They must complete certain marital tasks if those phases are to be negotiated satisfactorily. This chapter focuses on describing a complete marital life cycle that produces children and lasts until the union is disrupted by death; divorce is addressed in Chapter 10.

Couples who remain childless/childfree typically go through the same stages as those who produce and rear children, except for those circumscribed directly by the parenting aspect. Their tasks would be expected to be influenced more exclusively by other factors, such as the passage of time, than are those of couples with children. This chapter applies in a limited way to cohabiting couples. Cohabitation not only appears to be primarily a childless life-style, but also it does not often entail a life-long or long-time commitment (Blumstein & Schwartz, 1983; Clayton & Voss, 1977; Spanier, 1983).

THE MARITAL LIFE CYCLE

The idea of a marital life cycle is more metaphorical than purely descriptive, implying that marriage carries some underlying order in its development. Although each marriage has its singular aspects and is thus essentially unique, all lasting marriages go through some of the same sequential phases and require the achievement of certain common marital tasks. Solving such marital tasks is not done once-for-all-time. Rather, the solutions are in continous change, varying in relation to the needs of the couple and the stage or season of the marriage (Berman & Lief, 1975; Levinson, Darrow, Klein, Levinson, & McKee, 1978; Wynne, 1984).

Marriage, in an important metaphorical sense, can be viewed as unfolding over the years. That unfolding is neither smooth nor easy to accomplish and understand. Embodied in the process are progression as well as sameness and static conditions, stability as well as change, and continuity as well as discontinuity. The therapist has the task of trying to comprehend the relationship between these opposite and different factors in order to help effect appropriate adjustments and changes.

MARITAL AND OTHER LIFE CYCLES

Marital partners must deal with their own individual development in addition to their shared marital and family tasks. Similarly, individual, marital, and family development and life cycles all are important to the understanding and work of the therapist. Relating them systematically is difficult. For example, the individual, marital, and family life cycles all are involved in the processes of oscillation between the periods of closeness and periods of distance that typically occur in many families. Combrinck-Graham (1985) noted that families can be expected to change shape three times during the life cycle of the individual; with the birth and adolescence of the child, with the birth and adolescence of the child's children, and with the birth and adolescence of the child's grandchildren. She also pointed out (Combrinck-Graham, 1985) that these oscillations between centripetal (pulling inward for intimacy) and centrifugal (letting go and differentiating/individuating) processes provide family members with repeated issues to work on within the universal closeness–separation issues of family life and human development.

One attempt to relate cycles has been made by Berman and Lief (1975), who put individual and marital life cycles into a single framework. Their efforts to put marital stages into the categories used with individuals seem to make individual development the major basis for the schema. As much as possible, the discussion that follows will be restricted to marital development and functioning.

Marital development as such is different from individual development in that it is not so closely tied to human biology. Rather, it is much more dependent on its relationship to sociocultural factors than to biological conditions for the course that it takes. Biology does play a role, of course, in that mating and marriage occur after reproductive abilities have been attained. Reproductive capacity is generally considered a necessary but not a sufficient condition for marriage, which typically occurs many years after such ability has been gained. Similarly, one cannot say that individual development occurs wholly independent of sociocultural factors, but merely that such factors tend to carry less weight in the individual context than do those more specifically related to biology.

Marital tasks are more numerous and complex than individual tasks; contrary to Erikson's (1950) familiar eight-stage individual schema, there is no central and essentially unique task for each stage of the marital life cycle. The nature of the marital relationship is such that several central tasks are to be found in all stages, though it should be noted that these marital tasks do resemble Erikson's individual tasks in that the foundations for a particular task laid down in an earlier chronological period may be built on later. Thus, the communicational abilities established in the early part of the relationship between spouses often constitute the basis of communicational skill in later stages of the marriage. Conversely, there may be deterioration or regression in task maintenance, much as there may be regression in an individual's maintenance of a sense of autonomy that at one time had been firmly established.

MARITAL STAGES AND TASKS: A DEVELOPMENTAL-CLINICAL FRAMEWORK

For clinical purposes the marital life cycle can be divided into five stages, similar to those that we have used elsewhere for the larger family life cycle (Nichols & Everett, 1986). These stages are as follows:

1. Formation: mating and marriage;
2. Expansion: parental beginnings and subsequent years;
3. Contraction: individuation and eventual separation of youth;
4. Postparental stage;
5. Other stages: marital break-up, single-parent living, and remarriage.

As has been mentioned, the fifth stage, constituted of marital break-up, single-parent living, and remarriage, is addressed in Chapter 10; the first four constitute the focus of this chapter.

CATEGORIES OF TASKS

As a couple, the marital partners have, roughly speaking, two categories of tasks to accomplish at various stages of the relationship, starting during their mate selection interaction and continuing throughout their marital life cycle. One category pertains to tasks focused on matters that lie inside the boundaries of the marital relationship and the other to those lying outside those boundaries.

These distinctions between tasks internal and those external to the marriage are made with the awareness that important areas of overlap and influence exist between the interior of the marriage and the outside world. Goldner (1985) has argued accurately that the inequalities between men and women in the world of work significantly affect their power relationship and roles within the family. Work and family life have been separate and unequal and women dominated family life solely as a "counterpoint" to male dominance in the outside world, for example. Despite some overlapping areas, there is some practical, heuristic value in referring to internal and external tasks. This is done here with the understanding that although couples may deal with such tasks in a variety of ways—traditionally, creatively, inequitably, or equitably—the tasks are a joint responsibility, however they are discharged in the two spheres.

Both sets of tasks need to be accomplished sufficiently well or "good enough," as noted, to provide for both the internal and external adequacy and effectiveness of marital relationship. Internally, dealing with the tasks should be done in such a fashion as to provide sustaining satisfaction for the partners and a suitable atmosphere for the development and maintenance of healthy individual selfhood and growth. Externally, the marital relationship requires sufficiently appropriate and effective discharge of the tasks to ensure maintenance of a workable marriage. These are part of the meaning of marital tasks by definition.

Internal Relationship Tasks

Within their relationships marital partners need to deal with core issues of commitment, caring, communication, and conflict/compromise, as well as to attain and maintain an acceptable degree of intimacy and a workable balance of power. The central internal marital tasks described here are posited from clinical observation, empirical research, and theoretical materials. They take different forms at different stages of the marriage, but they can be generally defined as follows. *Commitment* refers to how and to what extent partners value the relationship and to their intentions with regard to its maintenance and continuation. *Caring* is used instead of the ambiguous term "love" to refer to the kind of emotional attachment that ties the partners to one another. *Communication* refers to the ability to communicate verbally and symbolically, to share meanings.

Conflict/compromise pertains to the ability to recognize and deal with the disagreements that are inevitable in any intimate human relationship.

Intimacy in enduring human relational systems, according to Wynne (1984), has four major overlapping processes, or patterns: attachment/ caregiving, communication, joint problem-solving, and mutuality. Optimally, they follow one another in becoming the major focus and top issue in the relationship. Intimacy is thus epigenetic in nature, one stage building on the preceeding stage. As Wynne emphasizes when intimacy does occur, it is "a subjective corollary of mutuality" (p. 300).

This understanding of intimacy is importantly related to the power relationship between the partners. Stock (1985) has explained the situation as follows: An approximately equal balance of power is required in order for true emotional intimacy to occur, since intimacy, status, and power are interrelated. Men, typically higher in status, have tended to look outside the relationship to the world of work and its concomitants for their rewards. Women traditionally have looked to males for status, power, and intimacy. (Theodore Reik once summarized this kind of situation as "Women love men, and men love work.") The attainment of intimacy between individuals of different status requires the assumption of equality. "Moving downward" often is threatening to males, who may fear a loss of power. Females see that they can only gain by entering into a relationship of mutuality or complementarity.

External Relationship Tasks

As a marital couple the partners have the task of forming and maintaining appropriate relationships with other individuals, systems, and family subsystems. In the early days of relationship formation, the partners need to begin establishing a "firm enough" and yet "penetrable enough" set of boundaries around their relationship and between themselves and friends, families of origin, and, in some instances, occupation or career. They need to start experiencing what it would be like to have the exclusive kind of relationship that is customarily expected of love affairs and marital relationships in Western society, while changing their old relationships with other persons and systems. The key appears to be the establishment of an appropriate balance between "inside" and "outside" the marital relationship.

Later, if they have children, appropriate boundaries between their marital subsystem and the parental (parent–child) and sibling subsystems within their nuclear family need to be set and maintained with appropriate degrees of strength, flexibility, and permeability. Once the children have become a part of the picture the partners are faced with the delicate task of maintaining an adequate balance among three generations: their own, their parental (or the grandparental, as it is often labeled, for convenience), and their children's. The dimension of power also is involved in the couple's efforts to fulfill the external marital couple tasks.

Balancing Roles

There is one additional marital task or perhaps set of tasks that does not fit easily under the rubric of either internal or external tasks, but involves both dimensions, as well as both the individual and the marital areas. How do the spouses balance their roles? The husband typically has the dual roles of work life and family life. Increasingly, women have the task of balancing the two roles as more and more married women work outside the home for pay. The dual dual-career issue of balancing his work/family roles and balancing her work/family roles has become a reality for more than half of the married couples in the United States. By 1986 more than half of the professional positions in the United States were filled by women, meaning that a very large number of women were in real and technical terms following career paths instead of merely working at a job.

Not even the fact that the woman works outside the home appears automatically to bring greater equality inside the home. Some recent research showed that working women still perform more than five times as much domestic work as their spouse. Men tend to begin to do more domestic chores only when their wife's income begins to approximate theirs (Model, 1981). There is also some evidence that physical tensions and wife abuse increase in some marriages as the wife's income increases (Stock, 1985).

STAGES AND TASKS

The marital life cycle is depicted in Table 1 in an illustrative fashion. the listing of tasks is not intended to be all-inclusive: Other specific tasks probably could be added, and some of those listed as core tasks could be interpreted differently and thus placed under other headings. Efforts have been made to construct a marital life cycle that is both general and as free of class and sexiest biases as possible.

The cycle is intended primarily as a guide for the clinician who is

TABLE 1

The Marital Life Cycle

Stage 1—Mating and Marriage

Core Tasks

Commitment

Developing an initial commitment.

Caring

Discerning whether there is sufficient and appropriate caring to warrant marriage.

Communication

Beginning to establish workable processes and patterns of communication and constructing a shared universe of discourse.

Conflict/Compromise

Beginning to learn how to resolve conflicts and effect compromise.

Contract

Working to explore and clarify expectations and establish a good interactional contract.

Specific Tasks

Establishing a mutually satisfactory affectional-sexual relationship.

Separating from families of origin and developing a couple identity.

Stage 2—Expansion: Parental Beginnings and Subsequent Years

Core Tasks

Commitment

Dealing with external attractions and threats.

Dealing with internal threats, including possible discovery of original or subsequent mismating.

Caring

Reworking caring definitions and meanings.

Communication

Enlargement of range and depth of communication.

Conflict/Compromise

Dealing with "floating" marital task of rebalancing the power relationship in marriage due to shifting of roles.

Contract

Reworking the coexecutive relationship.

Specific Tasks

Making room for an addition and adjusting to the realities of being part of a new nuclear family and not simply a couple.

"Settling into" the marriage.

Learning to fulfill parental roles *as a couple.*

Re-relating to own parents and taking a new place in extended family networks *as a couple.* (Floating task of reworking power relationship with own parents.)

Stage 3—Contraction: Individuation and Eventual Separation of Youth

Core Tasks

Commitment

Maintaining a solid couple boundary and internal bond while coping with the difficulties of rearing adolescents.

Caring

Maintaining closeness and caring in spite of the possibility of divergent interests, individual development, or sameness and boredom threatening marital satisfaction.

TABLE 1 (*continued*)

Communication
Attending to maintenance of intellectual and emotional sharing.
Reexamining assumptions about communication and presumed shared meanings.
Conflict/Compromise
Reconciling personal and marital needs and desires.
Contract
Reworking the expectations and "bargains" of the couple relationship.
Specific Tasks
Letting go of children.
Dealing with the "empty nest" period.
"Settling down" for the remaining years.
Stage 4—Postparental
Core Tasks
Commitment
Supporting each other in attempts to find meaning, satisfaction, and productivity.
Caring
Maintaining a satisfactory degree of closeness in the face of declining physiological
functioning (including potential diminishing of sexual desire or ability) and eventual
loss of partner by death.
Communication
Deepening communication to provide for examination and sharing of the meanings
and reactions in facing loss, loneliness, and eventual death.
Conflict/Compromise
Developing adequate patience and skill to deal as a couple with fears of loss of pro-
ductivity and possible meaning.
Contract
Supporting each other in joint grief work and joint attempts to find meaning and
satisfaction.
Specific Tasks
Realigning relationships to include in-laws and trigenerational or quadgenerational family
network.
Dealing with retirement.

---

doing marital therapy. Special marital life-cycle concerns for the therapist are the degree and manner in which tasks are fulfilled, the problems
that emerge from failures in task fulfillment, and the crises, conflicts,
and dislocations that arise at times of change and transition in the cycle.
Treatment interventions often are aimed at dealing with issues associated
with all of these things.

Mating and Marriage

The process of selecting a spouse typically occurs in the early 20s in
American society, although recently it has taken place later in that de-

cade for an increasing number of young persons. Associating with members of the opposite sex in unchaperoned settings begins during the high school years or earlier for most youngsters. Dating, essentially a post-World War I phenomenon, originally began with unattached young adults and subsequently moved downward into the teenage years.

The "sexual revolution" of the 1960s loosened considerably the traditional normative ties between sexual intercourse and marriage. Living together became a familiar part of interaction between males and females at various age levels, including the young never-married category. Living together before a first marriage or a subsequent marriage for one or both persons is now frequently part of the preparation for marriage; either by design or default it often becomes a prelude to marriage. Convincing evidence appears to be lacking that living together generally constitutes a genuine "trial marriage" or that it is an improvement over other patterns of premarital association and mate selection.

As has been stated elsewhere (Nichols & Everett, 1986), "The process of selecting a mate is not magical or mystical but an expression of each individual's personal needs and development in a particular sociocultural context" (p. 152). One of the more comprehensive theories of the mate selection process has been advanced by Murstein (1976). He has described a stimulus–value–role theory of marital choice: Initially a person is attracted to the other because of physical, social, mental, and/or reputational attributes. If the attraction process "takes" or works successfully, a value comparison stage follows, negotiated essentially through verbal interchange. The final stage basically involves the couple's functioning in compatible roles. By the time the couple begins to negotiate via verbal communication, and particularly after they have entered the role stage, they are involved in the beginnings of relationship task resolution.

It is possible to describe several lists of tasks for the premarital period, if one so desires. As many as eight tasks in the couple's interpersonal preparation for marriage have been given for the engagement period and three for a honeymoon phase (Rapoport, 1964).

What are the relationship tasks during the formative period leading into marriage? Regardless of the patterns of interaction and association followed by the pair, what relationship tasks need to be mastered in a manner "good enough" to ensure the continuation of the woman–man connection?

Generally, it seems to be important to the couple to do a "good enough" job of mastering *some* of the core tasks as best they can be handled at that stage of the relationship. Other core tasks can be accomplished rather poorly and the failure glossed over or ignored at that time.

It is thus quite common to encounter couples clinically who indicate that their communication "was not good from the start. We *never* communicated very well." Their attraction to each other and their need to mate or to leave home were sufficiently strong, however, to cause them to overlook their deficiencies in communication skills. Similarly, many couples fail to develop conflict resolution abilities during the early stages of their relationship and encounter trouble later on when they face problems that are complex and serious enough to require a high degree of such skill. A veteran clinician (Greene, 1970) found that in 50% of the couples he observed, premarital conflicts persisted on into the marriage.

The internal tasks of the pair during the premarital stage include developing an initial *commitment* to each other, discerning whether there is sufficient and appropriate *caring* to warrant marriage, constructing a shared universe of discourse and beginning to establish workable processes and patterns of *communication*, and working toward learning to resolve *conflicts* and effect *compromise*. More generally, the couple needs to work toward the exploration and clarification of their "contract" and their expectations of each other and the relationship.

If the partners are to form an enduring relationship that is mutually valued, they face the early task of establishing a reliable *commitment*. Each must have a workable level of confidence that the other is committed to the relationship and is capable of fidelity. Similarly, it is important to be able to resolve their own doubts about their personal commitment. Can self, partner, and the relationship established between the pair be trusted? Is there congruence between the verbal statements of commitment and the behaviors of the pair? What evidence of doubt and discrepant behavior exist? Have there been crises in the commitment and, if so, how have they been addressed?

Despite what was said above about *caring* being a more neutral and useful term than love, the establishment of both caring and commitment for the young in particular as they contemplate marriage typically depends on whether they feel they love or are "in love with" the potential mate. Love means different things to different people, as both clinicians and researchers have noted. Lasswell and Lasswell (1976) researched six types of love, using ideal or pure types. This means that no single individual will possess such love as it is described in pure or ideal form. Given individuals will manifest portions of one or more types. At this stage, marital partners may find, upon reexamination and reflection that they do not love their partner with the pure eros (romantic love) they thought they did previously but feel more of a pragma (logical-sensible love) for the other person. Their mania (possessiveness and intense dependency) may have given way to some form of storage love (life-long friendship). At any rate, reevaluating the caring aspect of their relationship is an important task.

A significant part of commitment and caring, in particular, is the establishment of a mutually satisfactory affectional-sexual relationship between the partners. This term is hyphenated in order to emphasize simultaneously the separateness and overlap between how the young persons experience and express affection as an entity in itself as well as a prelude to and a part of sexual activity. The clinician's sensitivity to feminine and masculine differences in perception and meaning about affection and sexual relating may be crucial in clarifying feelings and effecting change at later stages in marital interaction. The stereotypical masculine evaluation of sex that minimalizes the importance of affection and the feminine evaluation of affection as an essential prelude of physical lovemaking often contribute to problems. Frequently, such stereotypes must be changed if intimacy is to be enhanced.

An aspect of the process of establishing effective communication that often does not get worked out in the early stages of a relationship is the understanding that communication is not a synonym for agreement. The therapist may need to help a couple understand that they can communicate clearly and yet disagree absolutely. This understanding obviously has implications for helping a couple comprehend how obfuscation in communication may be protective, since attaining clarity could expose differences. At the same time, clinical work can frequently be directed toward assisting a couple to moderate their fear of disagreement and to be more comfortable with the therapeutic effects of being heard and understood, even if not agreed with in the communicational relationship.

Developing a Couple Identity

The process of developing a couple identity is significantly associated with the establishment of boundaries, as well as with the interchange of emotions and behaviors within the interior of the pair's relationship. As noted above, a marital relationship becomes a subsystem in two extended families and, with the addition of children, in the nuclear family system. It is linked by boundaries that both set it off from and attach it to other systems and subsystems, since viable systems and subsystems require semipermeable boundaries that permit appropriate transactions between themselves and other systems.

The couple preparing for marriage have the boundaries task of attaching less strongly to peers and others with whom they had been in close relationship prior to pairing off. They need to attenuate such bonds and establish the primacy of the relationship with each other, making the future spouse the "significant other" in their life. Other relationships need to be altered—or, in some cases, terminated altogether—so that they do not compete with the spousal relationship for primacy.

The individual task of separating from parents and family of origin that began in the teenage years fuses with the marital task of establishing a couple identity, thus becoming part of the marital boundaries work. Couples frequently marry in an effort to establish individual identity and achieve differentiation from their family of origin, though family researchers have pointed out that better choices are made regarding marital partners if boundary issues with one's family of origin have already been clarified (Boss, 1983).

One other aspect of boundary clarification pertains to work and occupation or career. How do the partners each accomplish this and then fuse their individual resolution of work/personal life issues into the marital boundaries task? Is one primarily married to the job or career or to the spouse? In the mate selection stage this issue has important precedent-setting meaning and implications.

Boundary setting and clarification also occupy attention within the developing internal relationship. Sex roles, idealistic expectations, and competition between the partners furnish three salient areas of boundary ambiguity in marriage (Boss, 1983). During the mate selection period these issues are beginning to take shape as tasks that have to be faced if the ambiguity is to be lessened.

The early marital period typically involves some challenges to the couple's task fulfillment. The realities of living and dealing with each other may raise questions about whether their expectations are being fulfilled or are going to be met. A kind of dialectical process can be seen in many marriages, especially in cases where romantic love conceptions play a significant role.

Romantic love, by definition, means that the loved object is idealized. A set of illusions develops in which the lover distorts reality by perceiving the loved one more as she or he wishes that loved one to be than as the loved one is in actuality. Several things lead to inevitable disillusionment. These include changes in the behaviors of the spouse, or in one's perceptions, or a combination of both, along with disappointment over the failure of the marriage or the partner to deliver the unrealistic and often undeliverable expectations. For some persons, illusion leads to disillusionment, to marital break-up. For a dialectical process to be completed, of course, there would not have to be a break-up of the system. Rather, there could be some kind of synthesis within the marital process and interaction, a kind of adaptation in which there would be an acceptance of the fact that things are different than previously expected.

The ideal in an ongoing relationship would be a situation in which the mates' discovery that expectations were not being met would lead to a sharing of thoughts and feelings, an improvement in communication, and a workable solution of any conflict that was present between them. Weathering the often inevitable disillusionment does not always lead to a reworking of the contract between the spouses. Sometimes one or both of the mates will alter their expectations without discussing their thoughts and feelings with the other. This kind of unilateral approach may lead to a strengthening of the marital relationship, as can be the case when unrealistic personal expectations are replaced with more realistic and mature expectations. Conversely, such an approach may simply conceal disappointments or resentments and set the stage for future difficulties, as when the disappointment and related feelings are retained on an unresolved basis.

Other challenges to the couple's task fulfillment during the early stages of marriage are brought forth by the dynamic, changing nature of the marital relationship and the partners' needs. Their task during this period is to ascertain the nature of their commitment when such challenges come and to determine that the commitment is strong enough to hold firm even if original expectations have been changed. The task with regard to caring is to keep it alive and sufficiently nourished and developing to match their changing needs. The partner's communicational abilities need to keep pace with the changing events in their lives and with their developing intellectual concerns. They need, in other words, to maintain a contemporarily useful universe of discourse. With regard to the area of conflict and compromise, the partners have the task of solving enough of the low level chronic and acute difficulties to retain the viability of the relationship. The specific, concrete problems to be met during this period vary considerably with the couple and their situation.

Expansion: Parental Beginnings and Subsequent Years

This stage begins psychologically with pregnancy or, in some cases, with the decision to have a child. Preparation for this stage inevitably starts before it arrives; such early preparation occurs in other stages as well, particularly Stage 3.

The special tasks of this period are related, understandably, to ex-pansion and the concomitants of this process of adaptation. The major special tasks can be briefly stated as making room for an addition and adjusting to the realities of being part of a nuclear family and not merely a couple, learning to fulfill parental roles *as a couple*, both re-relating to his and her own parents, and taking a new place in the extended family network.

As the partners move into the area of childbearing, add a child or children, and thus form a nuclear family, they begin to face the task of relating to a new family subsystem, as well as of dealing with external systems in different ways than they did previously. They encounter the immediate marital tasks of making room in their lives for the family new-comer and adjusting to the realities and reactions associated with being not merely a couple but also a nuclear family. Learning how to fulfill parental roles not only individually but also as a cooperative pair be-comes a marital (and family) task.

The therapist who works with marital couples at this stage must be alert to the reactions of both partners to the advent of a third party into what has been a two-party relationship. Family researchers in the past carried on a healthy debate over whether or not parenthood created a crisis for the spouses (Dyer, 1963; Hobbs, 1965; Hobbs & Cole, 1976; LeMasters, 1957; Rossi, 1968). Clinically, the answer is the old standby, "It does and it doesn't; it all depends." For some marriages there is a threat in the addition of a first child or sometimes a subsequent child to the home. Physical difficulties, strains of caretaking, and other changes sometimes do create sufficient tension and distress to bring about a crisis. Depressive reactions on the part of the mother following childbirth or jealous and immature reactions by the new father engender tension and sometimes crisis, although many couples handle the situation without experiencing anything resembling a crisis by expanding their roles and their abilities to include another human being in their everyday living and intimate circles in effective and "good enough" ways.

Simultaneously with their internal alterations, the partners gener-ally find that the external marital couple tasks have begun to occupy a much more prominent role than they did before the birth of the infant. This is especially true in the case of the first child, the time at which the couple enter a new phase in their lives by becoming parents, which places them in a different position vis-à-vis their own parents. Having been concerned for several years up to that point with differentiating from their families of origin in most cases, they now begin the process of re-relating mentioned above. The marital task involves relating to their own parents and family of origin as parents and taking a new place in the extended family, becoming a link in the generational chain.

Briefly, the boundaries of the marriage and of the new family need to become clearly delineated. The partners have the task of deciding who belongs in the family as well as who does what in the family. Who is in and who is not needs to be clarified as the addition of an infant brings up questions of the roles to be taken by extended family members from each partner's side. If the parents have not been married for an extensive period before the birth, the marriage during this time is still in a process of settling in. Similarly, whether the birth occurs early in the marriage or after an extended period of being married, a rebalancing is needed subsequent to the arrival of the child.

Three of the core marital tasks come in for particular attention during this stage. Commitment may be tested from both within and without the marital relationship. Caring may need to be reexamined and redefined. It must be viewed from a different perspective than it was previously. The marital contract also may need to be reworked. These changes appear to be related more to the length of time that the partners have been married than to their ages.

The commitment of the partners frequently undergoes a testing after several years of marriage. Levinson (1977) in his longitudinal study of men found a peaking of marital problems in the age 30 transition period. Others have made clinical observations in support of the proverbial "seven year itch" (Berman, Miller, Vines, & Lief, 1977) and a 10-year marker as potential scenes for commitment crisis. Whitaker (Neill & Kniskern, 1982) has talked about an eroding of the original emotional attachments after a number of years and observed that some spouses engage in extramarital affairs not because they wish to leave the marriage but in order to "heat up" a relationship that has cooled. Whatever the source of challenges to marital commitment, a reexamination and reworking of the attachments typically is called for after the commitment has been questioned seriously or threatened. For many marriages this process correlates with an ending of the early phase of childbearing and childrearing.

The tasks associated with caring also require attention during this stage. Extramarital relationships are not the only threat to the commitment of the spouses and the expression of caring in their interaction. Failures to deal effectively with closeness or intimacy or expectations in the continuing relationship may find expression in a building of emotional and behavioral barriers between the mates. One frequently sees couples clinically who are living in two different emotional fortresses inside the marriage, each distanced from contact by the width of the walls and the depth of the surrounding moats. Couples that are coping with the commitment and caring tasks effectively are living with an increased degree of closeness, minus the threat of extramarital relationships or divisive internal barriers.

Once again, it needs to be pointed out that these tasks are not accomplished once for all time: The boundaries of the couple and their nuclear family may be closed temporarily against outsiders for a few years and then be subject to being breached once again. Berman and Lief (1975) have pointed to a potential disruption of the boundaries around ages 40 to 42. Life is often reevaluated at that time. Fantasies about outside sexual or romantic interests may increase.

During this period the task of developing together is probably more important for the couple than at any other time in their marital life cycle. If their courses of individual development and interests diverge too greatly, the marital partners are faced with the eventual discovery that there is too little left in common to make their marriage satisfactory to them. Martin (1976) has underscored the difficulty of salvaging a relationship in which the partners have developed along different paths and at differing rates. Specifically, he has termed "subsequent mismating," or mismating after the marriage has been launched, as "the most common toxic process in marital disharmony" (p. 63). In such situations the partners cannot point to things that the other has done to hurt them or affix blame as is possible in conflict-ridden marriages. Instead, they make the sad discovery that without meaning to do so they have developed in such ways that they no longer have much in common as individuals and thus as marital partners. Consequently, each no longer meets the needs of his or her partner for sharing and other emotional-interactive satisfactions.

This task is described as most important during Stage 2 for two reasons. One is the significance it has for couple functioning during the period of family expansion. This period I also referred to earlier as one of "settling in" for the partners. It comes after the resolution of the early tasks including the absorption of the children into a family unit. The second reason that the task is so important during this stage is that its successful management establishes a base for coping with the task of "settling down" in Stage 3. Settling down refers to preparation for coping with the long haul of marriage (Berman & Lief, 1975) that starts for most couples around middle age.

Two tasks connected with a reworking of the marital contract appear during this stage of the marital cycle. One pertains to a reorganization of the relationship itself, while the other deals with external issues that relate to the spouses' respective parental systems.

A "floating" marital task that often appears sometime after the expansion stage has been launched involves the reorganization of how the partners deal with power and expectations inside the marital relationship (Zemon-Gass & Nichols, 1981). The task emerges when a woman begins to take steps to establish her own individual identity after living with a contingent identity as her husband's wife and her children's mother. Developments leading to the emergence of the task within the marital relationship often begin to surface when the youngest child nears kindergarten age, but may arise in some marriages a decade or more later.

A task for individuals identified by Williamson (1981, 1982) not only appears to be something of a marital task as well but also seems to have a floating quality. Referred to as the "termination of the intergenerational hierarchical boundary," this individual task involves reworking the power relationship with one's parents and getting authority issues resolved so that they are "former parents." This task is assigned by Williamson to the 4th decade of life (i.e., to one's thirties), although for some persons, it appears to arise as a task in their late twenties and for others in their forties. Generally, there is considerable variation regarding the time that such a task is undertaken and the extent to which it is accomplished among adults. Whatever the time period in which it occurs, resolution of this task seems likely to be a significant part of growing up. It is related to freeing formerly bound-up energy adequately and appropriately and finding new abilities to commit oneself more completely and wholeheartedly to a variety of life tasks, including participation in marriage.

This stage of the family and marital life cycles can be one of expansion and expansiveness for the couple. Once the commitment issues and floating tasks have been resolved, the children adequately absorbed into a family unit, and work/career paths and patterns firmly established and providing rewards, the partners generally are in a position to regard the future with optimism. Couples for whom things are going well frequently manifest a belief that life is manageable and that everything is under control.

The clinician working with couples whose marriage is at this stage will be concerned not only with the matters discussed here but also with the status of their fulfillment of the complete range of core marital tasks that began in Stage 1 and last throughout the marital life cycle. Are commitment, caring, communication, and conflict/compromise being handled in a "good enough" fashion by the couple? If not, where are the problems and what can be done about them?

Contraction: The Individuation and Eventual Separation of Youth

This stage of the family life cycle and the marital life cycle is character-ized by the movement of the children toward an eventual departure from the family. While they are in the process of getting ready to depart, the parents encounter what is generally agreed to be the most difficult stage in parenting. It covers the new parental experience of dealing with teen-agers and, finally, young adults.

This third stage of the marital life cycle begins as the adolescents in a family start to attach more directly and strongly to peers and others outside the family. Parents are faced with the reality of seeing children who may have been conforming and even docile during elementary school years become alternately hostile and rebellious, moody, boisterous, quiet, uncertain, stubbornly assertive, and, on occasion, their "old, sweet self." Issues of power and control frequently rock families that formerly were comparatively quiet. The parental tasks more than ever become con-cerned with balancing the dependency–independency needs of their chil-dren. This means letting out enough rope to permit the children freedom to explore and cope on their own, while holding the reins tightly enough so that they are not given freedom beyond their ability to use it safely and responsibly.

This period in a real sense "starts before it starts" (Nichols & Ev-erett, 1986) in that preparation for launching the young begins long be-fore the D-Day of their actual departure from home arrives. Psycholog-ically, entering this period may be difficult for the adults. The last 2 decades or so have witnessed a sociocultural phenomenon in which adults have taken over many of the aspects of the teenage and youth subculture in terms of dress and behaviors. The young have responded by leaving those things to the invaders and inventing new dress and behaviors. Many interpretations have been placed on such adult actions, most of which boil down to the idea that adults are trying to stay "eternally young." Whatever the meaning, such behaviors make it difficult for both genera-tions to handle the differentiation of the children.

Whereas the beginning of this stage is difficult to identify, the end-ing is more discernible. It concludes when the children have separated from the family and established themselves on their own. A recent phe-nomenon in which a fairly large number of adult children have returned home to live with their parents after having made an initial physical separation muddies the water and complicate the marital tasks. Con-versely, the parent–child relationship may benefit from the temporary movement of the young back into the home. Some parents and their children gain another opportunity to rework some unresolved aspects of their relationship during such periods.

The developing needs and demands of the adolescent require more flexibility than virtually any other part of the marital and family life cycles. Much parental interaction with adolescents focuses on struggles over where the young go, with whom, and when they come home, go to bed, and study, particularly in middle-class families. These and other issues reflect the developing need and desire of the adolescents to be autonomous. Not only the cooperation of the spouses as parents but also the development of flexibility within their marital relationship is required in order to deal effectively with both the specific and general issues involved in the increasing autonomy of their children. Parental response requires marital adaptation. This is particularly evident in situations in which coping with their children taps into values and norms stemming from their respective families of origin. Such struggles in the present create potential loyalty conflicts between each spouse and their feelings about their own parents and childrearing.

Dealing with the vicissitudes of rearing adolescents confronts the marital couple with the possibilities of either having their relationship strengthened or experiencing the insertion of a wedge between husband and wife. The marital task calls for the maintenance of a clear boundary around the couple and the forging of a solid bond between the partners while they cope with the difficulties of rearing adolescents.

A considerable amount of popular and professional writing on the so-called "empty-nest syndrome" has called attention to the situation that is produced when the children finally leave home. The new set of circumstances in which the adults are once again alone in the home may lead either to more conflict and distance between the spouses or more closeness and satisfaction. Research has disclosed that marital satisfaction tends to increase once the childrearing phase has ended (Rollins & Feldman, 1970). In contrast, popular writers have often emphasized that the departure of the children may reveal a vacuum in the marital relationship that had been masked by the presence of the offspring. In some instances the children had provided sources of emotional fulfillment and attachment in lieu of deficits in the marriage; other situations were cited in which the presence of a child had provided a buffer or a third party who could be triangulated into the marital relationship, thus moderating conflict and permitting the spouses to remain in the marriage despite significant differences and disagreements. Clinical reports have reflected both sides of the picture: either increased closeness and satisfaction or intensified conflict or distance.

A major marital task of this period calls for the partners to keep in touch in their emotional and intellectual growth and change so that divisive divergence does not occur. If adequate attention to this need was given in Stage 2, maintaining closeness will be easier during this stage. The task may be restated as that of maintaining closeness and caring in spite of aging and the possibility of different interests, individual development, or sameness and boredom threatening marital satisfaction. Still another way of describing the task is in terms of regenerating the marital relationship as a dyad (Carter & McGoldrick, 1980).

Certain individual tasks have a significant impact on the marital relationship at this stage. The masculine version tends to occur around 40 or in the early forties. It is popularly connected with a so-called "midlife crisis" for many men. Briefly stated, the task pertains to dealing with questions such as "Who am I and where am I going?" The part of this task that deals most directly with the marriage involves asking, in one form or another, "What do I owe my wife and wish to give her? What do I wish for myself?"

One feminine version, as noted, is more likely to occur earlier but may take place in the late thirties or even in the forties. It starts with the familiar questions "Who am I?" and "Is this all there is?" This questioning is a "floating" marital task. It also deals most directly with the marriage through the queries "What do I owe my husband and wish to give him?" and "What do I owe myself and wish for myself?" The specific marital task calls for reconciliation of personal and marital needs and desires. It pertains to commitment, to making choices between continuing in the marriage or pursuing the individual's own interests. Such interests as work or career, attraction to a new love object outside the marriage, seeking one's own self-fulfillment apart from attachment to the spouse, and others may compete with one's commitment to the mate and marriage.

There is clinical evidence that some—perhaps a growing number of—men and woman have similar questions around both the age 30 and age 40 decade markers. Changes in roles including the assumption of careers and the delay in childbearing by some women into the late thirties can be expected to lead to a lessening of attitudinal and crisis differences between men and women.

A process of disillusionment that is common for males during the midlife transition has been described by Levinson (1986). The outcome can be varied, ranging from feeling that one has suffered an irreparable loss to becoming free to be more flexible and thus able to view others in a less idealizing fashion. In some respects, this process, as described by

Levinson, is very similar to the disillusion suffered by both partners in the early months or first year of marriage. Midlife for women has its difficulties, but it can also be a period of unanticipated pleasure and perhaps even power for many females (Baruch & Brooks-Gunn, 1984). As the combination of male disillusionment and female experience of new pleasures and new power occurs, the couple and the clinician are faced with the need to strike a new balance for the marital dyad.

The Postparental Years

The postparental stage is typically the longest in the marital life cycle. For a few couples who marry later than the average or have their children later, this period comes when they are beginning to move toward the latter part of middle age or even toward old age. For most, however, it comes when they are in middle age and have a good many years of life expectancy remaining. This stage is essentially a phenomenon of the 20th century; there was little or no postparental period for most couples prior to this century, since a couple of years before the last child left home, one of the spouses probably would have died (Glick, 1955).

For older partners or those chronologically farther along in their individual life cycles, major challenges to their security as a couple come from the necessity to cope with loss and potential loss, as well as with physiological decline and aging. Some significant marital difficulties arise from major age discrepancies (e.g., the clinically familiar situation of an older husband and a much younger wife who have a young child or young children).

Losses for couples in this stage typically are associated with children becoming adults and pursuing their own lives and interests outside the parental home. Friends and family members, especially from the partners' families of origin, may also be lost through death, as well as through the lack of contact brought on by geographical distance and involvement in their own increased family responsibilities and investments.

Such losses make it necessary for the partners to deal adequately and appropriately with their individual and joint grieving processes. Simultaneously, the losses encourage the closing of marital boundaries and increased reliance of the partners on each other. This process is further complicated by the fact that the losses foreshadow the eventual loss of one's spouse and the prospect of being left alone without a marital partner. Beyond those possibilities and fears lie a concern with one's own death.

Immediate tasks in this stage pertain to realigning relationships in order to include in-laws and grandchildren and taking an appropriate role in a three-generation or four-generation network of family relationships. The partners in such instances soon face the task of taking on grandparental roles.

The commitment and caring tasks during this period call for the maintenance of a satisfactory degree of closeness in view of declining physiological functioning. This includes a potential diminishing of sexual desire or ability on the part of one or both spouses and the eventual separation from the partner through death. Additionally, the mates have the task of supporting each other's attempts to continue being productive and finding meaning and satisfaction in the face of their declining abilities (Berman & Lief, 1975).

Conflict/compromise tasks tend to be brought forth also by the threats to one's ability and life. The specific task for this area and stage is the establishment of patterns of power management that are suitable for the couple's changed and changing situation.

The last major readjustment or rebalancing of the marital relationship as such is typically brought forth by the retirement of one or both spouses from the external work world. The familiar picture of a working male retiring and being in the way of his housewife spouse is being replaced in many instances by a different pattern in which the employed husband, who is typically a few years older than his wife, retires first while she works for several more years.

Chapter Three

An Integrative Approach to Marital Therapy

Applied mathematics, handmaiden of the sciences. Pure mathematics, may she never prove useful.

These intriguing words, quoted in a display outside the mathematics department where my father-in-law, a distinguished mathematician, served as professor and department head, caught my eyes many years ago. Gradually, they came to make sense to me as he shared with me some of the philosophical and practical issues facing the mathematician and physicist. There I encountered the problems in logic posed by Bertrand Russell and others long before I was acquainted with Gregory Bateson as anything other than a South Seas anthropologist.

EPISTEMOLOGY

The epigram from the mathematics department display still provides guidelines whenever issues of theory and epistemology are raised. Whenever we get into epistemology—defined here as a concern with the origins, nature, methods, and limits of knowledge (AAMFT, 1983)—we are likely to move into a realm in which there is concern with purity. There are theoretical concepts that are not necessarily useful, that are divorced from our everyday reality as we experience it. There is a need for "pure" research that has no immediate practical value. On the other hand, as accurate, intriguing, and mind-stretching as epistemological concepts may be, we face the need daily for working theories that may contradict "pure" theories, but that make sense of what we perceive and prove useful in our living.

39

Liddle (1982) has referred to the therapist's "epistemological declaration." By that he means one's own individual, idiosyncratic declaration
of what one knows, how it is known, what and how one thinks, and
what one includes and how one makes clinical decisions. With a respectful bow in the direction of our contemporaries who are concerned with
what I shall term "pure theory," I have to move on to making practical,
operative sense of what is encountered in human marital situations. This
chapter is part of my epistemological statement.

THEORETICAL INTEGRATION

I am concerned with integrating theory to the extent that I am able to
integrate it for marital therapy. I call my approach "integrative" rather
than "integrated" in order to reflect the reality that the process of integration in marital therapy is far from complete. The work of integrating
is continuous, never ending.

Integrate in simple dictionary terms refers to making whole. One
creates a whole by adding or bringing together parts of something into a
unity. Integration is different from sycretism, which refers to making an
unsystematic and uncritical combination of features from diverse sources.

ECLECTICISM AND FORMALISM

The term *eclecticism* is sometimes used to refer to efforts to bring together
various elements into a coherent system. Eclecticism is defined more precisely in theoretical system building as "the selection and orderly combination of compatible features from diverse sources" and the effort to
find valid elements in various theories and to combine them into a harmonious whole (English & English, 1958, p. 168).

Two ends of a continuum are sometimes posed in the area of theory
and theory building. Eclecticism is on one end of the line and formalism
on the other. Formalism seeks to maximize rational order and consis-
tency. It produces competing schools and theories. Formalism leads also
to tightness of organization and rigidity. The eclectic finds formalism so
rigid and dogmatic that it runs the risk of distorting the realities that one
seeks to comprehend. Eclecticism is looser than formalism.

Eclecticism is often used as a kind of wastebasket term. Those in
the therapy field who describe themselves as eclectic sometimes do not
operate from a coherent theoretical perspective. On the contrary, they
often have pulled together a smorgasbord of ideas and concepts from

various places and have not integrated concepts to the extent that they could be blended. Hence, I prefer to call myself an integrationist and my work integrative.

Pragmatism is a major concept in my efforts to secure an ongoing integrative effort. Does it work? Or, better, do the theoretical and conceptual ideas that I am using reflect the practical and clinical realities that I observe when I work with people? Do the concepts that I am attempting to integrate help me comprehend what I observe so that I can make informed interventions? (I am not implying that all interventions are based on theory and on rational comprehension. Certainly, there is, or should be, plenty of room for intuition and existential elements in marital and family therapy. For that matter, it is rational to follow intuitions where doing so has been successful in the past.)

Again, do the concepts help me to understand what I observe? Certainly, they shape what one observes. The concepts by which one observes the phenomenological world significantly mold what one sees and how it is interpreted. Concepts thus provide both a framework for observation and a set of definitions for what is seen.

Integration, in my judgment, requires that the clinician try to maintain a feedback system in which data from two ends of the line—concrete clinical situations and theoretical/conceptual ideas—inform and alter each other. Both clinical situations and conceptual frameworks interactively work together in an ongoing fashion. Similarly, empirical findings on the family, marriage, and human personality must be included in an informed approach to dealing with marriage and marital interaction. Research certainly has its limitations, but it also deserves to be allowed to inform the clinician. Both inductive and deductive reasoning are involved in the attempt to work toward an integrative form of marital therapy. Deductive refers to an approach in which one moves from a general principle to specifics as that principle applies to a specific case. Inductive reasoning leads one to look at a specific case and to take or discern from that case the relevant general principles.

A MIDDLE-RANGE-PLUS FOCUS

The integrative approach described here has an in-between focus. Rather than trying to formulate a grand theory of marital/family therapy and human interaction or dealing simply with a collection of clinical hypotheses, I am concerned with putting together what can be characterized as a middle-range-plus approach. Middle-range theories in research have been defined as those falling between all-inclusive systematic attempts to build a unified theory and those dealing with everyday minor working hypotheses (Merton, 1968). I am concerned with whether the approach is useful when I walk into a room with a couple, but I am also concerned that the approach incorporate as much theoretical understanding as I am able to include appropriately from broader theoretical materials pertaining to marriage and the family, to marital interaction, and to therapy.

Perhaps a few thoughts on what is meant by theory in general would be useful at this point. Theory has been described somewhat operationally as referring to the assumptions, concepts, and practices held by clinicians in their everyday work, as a point of view and a way of simplifying reality (Liddle, 1982). That operational definition is basically compatible with what I am calling a theoretical approach.

A reasonably comprehensive theoretical approach to marital therapy needs to deal with the reciprocal nature of several forms of interaction. These include the reciprocal nature of the relationship not only between the spouses but also between the persons and the environment. Seagraves (1982) has made the point that theory should encompass the behavior of the person, the effect of that behavior on others, and how the person thinks and feels. An adequate appreciation of the reciprocal nature of the interaction among these various elements puts the clinician in a position to recognize that treatment interventions can be made effectively at various points and with different elements.

My approach involves the recognition that clinical work for all except perhaps the most mechanistically oriented therapist involves a considerable amount of artistry. Although it is too simplistic to criticize theory as being unnecessary or undesirable because it is thought to hamper the spontaneity and creativity of the therapist (Whitaker, 1976), it is also unnecessarily restrictive to hold the view that theory alone without the use of intuition and the creative "use of self" is adequate for the clinician and the clients.

MAJOR STREAMS OF THEORETICAL UNDERSTANDING

Several different streams of theoretical understanding are included in this integrative approach. Each of those chosen—systems, psychodynamic object relations, and social learning theories—provides helpful and complementary elements. This is not to deny that successful therapeutic interventions can be made unilaterally from each approach, but as a theoretical base for clinical work each has shortcomings and limitations as well as strengths. None is viewed here as universally applicable as the orientation of choice for all marital therapy cases. The well-informed marital therapist, in my opinion, needs to be familiar with the ways in which each of these approaches contributes to an understanding of human functioning and difficulty. Each provides guidance for therapeutic interventions with marital distress and discord. It is to be hoped that the therapist can blend their strengths appropriately for comprehension and use the implications and interventions derived from them flexibly in working with cases.

The major aspects of those theories that help to explain marriage and marital interaction and provide a basis for intervention can be delineated as follows. A theoretical foundation for marital therapy needs to deal with the context in which personality and marriage are developed and function, with intimate attachment processes, and with motivation and how persons learn. Systems theory seems to provide the best available explanation for understanding the relevant contexts of personality and marital interaction; and adaptation of general systems theory is thus used as one of the major foundations for a theoretical approach to marital therapy. Similarly, an adaptation of psychodynamic psychology's object-relations theory provides help for dealing with how a man and woman choose and remain attached to each other. Social learning theory, again as adapted for marital therapy, provides important supplementary assistance, especially with regard to learning and change.

SYSTEMS THEORY

Systems theory provides the chief contextual explanation for the conduct of marital therapy. The family, of course, is the primary contextual system in which individuals are formed and function. Other systems are important, as are how they interact with the family and how the family acts as a buffer and communicational link between them and the individual. The marriage itself is a system or, more appropriately, a subsystem of the family system.

Systems theory has been described as being concerned with how people organize and how they communicate. Systems theory as such focuses on current behaviors, communication, and roles (Friedman, 1980). Systems classically have been described as a set of elements standing in interaction (von Bertalanffy, 1968). Simply put, the term refers to something put together in such a way that whatever affects one part also affects other parts. We are using a systems perspective when we view things as making up a pattern (Steinglass, 1978).

ORGANIZATION

The idea of systems implies that things are organized. Key ideas within the concept of organization are wholeness, boundaries, and hierarchies (Gurman & Kniskern, 1981).

Wholeness

Wholeness pertains to conceptualizing patterns rather than reducing entities to their constituent parts in a reductionist fashion. Rather than looking at marital interaction and seeing only that "Daniel has a bad temper" or that "Estelle is a nag," one sees the whole pattern of interaction. The irritability, temper outbursts, nagging, irritability, nagging, temper outbursts, irritability, and so on are seen as a repetitive pattern in which the spouses are mutually and interactively involved.

Boundaries

The concept of boundaries refers to who is to be included within a given system and the quality of the interactive process and feedback that occurs in relation to other systems (Nichols & Everett, 1986). Those who are members of a given family system have certain rights, privileges, and responsibilities that are denied others outside that system. Communications within the family systems contain certain private information and meanings that are not supposed to cross the boundary, for example. Minuchin (1974) has described family boundaries as being disengaged, enmeshed, and clear. Clear boundaries presumably help the marital relationships to function effectively.

Hierarchy

Hierarchy refers to the fact that systems have several different levels. Living systems have seven, ranging from the simple to the more complex: cell, organ, organism, group, organization, society, and supernational systems (Miller & Miller, 1980). The marriage, which is composed of two individual subsystems, is itself a subsystem of the nuclear family, which consists of a man, woman, and their child/children. The nuclear family, in turn, is a subsystem of an extended family system.

COMMUNICATION

In the family systems perspective all behavior is considered to be communication. Verbal and nonverbal communication are both very important. "One cannot *not* behave," as Watzlawick, Beavin, and Jackson (1967, p. 48) have put it. Hence, one cannot *not* communicate. Patterns of communication not only help to shape the behavior and functioning of family members but also provide clues to the relative openness–closedness of the system in its interaction with other parts of its environment. Systems, in order to exist and function adequately, must have functional communication and interchange with their necessary environment; they must live in accordance with the principle of communication (Sullivan, 1953). They cannot be either too closed or too open and continue to function in a healthy manner. There must be continued inside–outside and internal communication and "fine tuning." Communication and feedback processes can help to maintain a steady state condition in which the disequilibrium that produces growth and development and the continuity of the system are adequately balanced.

OTHER SYSTEMS CONCEPTS

Other systems concepts that are useful in an integrative approach to marital therapy are equifinality, circular causality, nonsummativity, and change.

Equifinality

The concept of equifinality indicates that the same results can be secured by starting from different points and by using different means. There may be, for example, several different paths and procedures by which noxious marital interaction can be altered. The pattern of nagging and temper explosions of Daniel and Estelle can be approached from more than one beginning point and dealt with in several different ways. It is not necessary to deal with "A" first to get to "B" to get to "C" to get the system changed. Neither individual psychotherapy with Daniel for his temper and Estelle for her level of self-confidence nor negotiation/mediation with the spouses would be the only route to change. To put it

another way, change could be brought about by working with both partners, or with either partner as a system representative, and by intervening at the point at which the irritability is building, the nagging increasing, or at some other juncture.

Circular Causality

Causality does not operate in a linear, A causes B fashion. Feedback
processes operate in systems so that there is a shared influencing of various parts of the actions that occur. Once again, does Estelle nag because
Daniel is irritable and engages in temper outbursts, or is Daniel short-
tempered because Estelle crowds him, and so on? The answer is, of
course, "both/and," as it is with most behavioral patterns in a human
system. There are important clinical implications associated with the
concept of circular causality. Among them is the fact that one does not
have to search for "the cause," but can intervene from any one of several
starting points and be successful in effecting change. (This holds true
even when a therapist is using a behavioral model. That is, even though
one spouse may be furnishing reinforcers for the undesired behaviors of
the other, the converse can be found, and the interventions can be launched
from more than one starting point with good possibilities for positive
outcome.) It is not necessary to use a mechanistic, reductionistic model
in which a given condition is assumed to have been derived from a specific prior cause that must be treated and altered in order to effect change.

Nonsummativity

The marriage as a whole is different from the sum of its parts. Marriage
is not understandable merely through summarizing the attributes or
characteristics of the individual marital partners. To describe Jack as an
individual and Mary as an individual is not the same as describing the
pair of them in relationship and interaction. Summing up the parts does
not provide the whole picture; that can be done only looking at the picture as a whole.

   To use an analogy, a house is made of nails, lumber, electrical wir-
ing, and other materials, but to say that one's house is composed of so
many nails, so much lumber, and so on does not describe the house.
Rather, it is necessary not to look at the parts and sum them up but to
pay attention to "the pattern which connects" (Bateson, 1980, p. 3) in
order to appreciate the structure. Similarly, the clinician must give heed
to "the pattern which connects" and not merely to the bits and parts of

the behavior of a marital couple. The marriage as a whole is different from the sum of its parts.

Change

Change in a system has been referred to as first order change and second order change (Watzlawick, Weakland, & Fisch, 1974). First order change pertains to those alterations in a system that leave the fundamental organization of that system unchanged. A symptomatic marriage could thus be said to undergo first order change whenever it adapts in response to a therapeutic intervention but does not cease its symptomatic functioning. Daniel, for example, may no longer "blow up" at Estelle, but substitute a "cold war" for the "hot war" by treating her with cool irony. Estelle no longer nags but "gets under the skin" of Daniel as strongly as ever by ignoring him. Formerly the marriage was symptomatic in one way, but it now is symptomatic in another way.

Second order change refers to alterations in a system that change the fundamental organization of the system. When a marriage adopts a different form of organization and ceases its symptomatic interaction in response to therapeutic intervention, second order change is said to occur (AAMFT, 1983). If Daniel and Estelle manage to change so that they are no longer dealing with each other in negative and nonproductive ways and are living in comparative harmony, basically free of symptomtic behaviors, second order change has occurred.

Second order change is generally considered to be superior to first order change by family therapists. Furthermore, on occasion there is the implication that change should be permanent, once it occurs. Gerald Zuk's (1986) metaphor of dipping into a stream is helpful. Perhaps by the act of dipping into it one succeeds in diverting its course, knowing full well that modest expectations must be held for some cases and that it may be necessary to intervene again in the future. Change is change is change, and the change itself probably will change. Attempting to freeze change into anything resembling permanent categories is a futile business.

DERIVED THERAPEUTIC INTERVENTIONS

Viewing couples and marital interaction from a systems perspective gives us as marital therapists some important therapeutic advantages. We can focus on change and on effecting change through alteration of the context in which the marital partners live and function as a family subsystem. We are not compelled to search for roots and historical causes, although we are free to deal with the past as well as with the present aspects of the situation. We have the possibility of intervening at several different points in the family system: We can work with one partner, with both marital partners, and/or with the extended family. If we deem such an approach useful, we can involve not only the couple and the extended family but also other members of their social network (Speck & Attneave, 1973). Structural changes through reworking the boundaries—by clarification or strengthening, for example—can be helpful. Focusing on processes, such as improving communication, can be beneficial in many instances. We can focus on the total system or its parts, its structure or its processes, or all of these.

The flexibility afforded by a systems approach is found also in the techniques that it makes available to the therapist. When the goal is change, and change in a system, one is not restricted to a limited number of techniques such as uncovering, reconstruction, dream analysis, confrontation, interpretation, and a few others. The techniques that can be used literally "fill a book" (e.g., Sherman & Fredman, 1986). They range from sculpting, genograms, family rituals, and reframing, to various paradoxical maneuvers, and other interventions. The major issue in my judgment, is whether we behave responsibly, and use the range of available techniques with appropriate knowledge and ethical concern.

Taking a systems approach also enables us to serve as a systems consultant (Wynne, McDaniel, & Weber, 1986). This not only has the advantage of making it unnecessary to adopt a pathology framework—something that also is possible with other orientations—but also enhances our ability to place the responsibility for change appropriately on the system itself.

OBJECT RELATIONS

Systems theory is very helpful in family therapy as such. It provides a useful framework for understanding and/or changing family interaction. It can help to explain how current marital interaction is occurring and some of the things that must be done or can be done in order to change the interaction. It appears less helpful, however, in explaining certain things such as how and in what ways reciprocal attractions occur in voluntary relationships. Therefore, I find it helpful to supplement the family systems orientation that is the backbone of the integrative marital therapy approach described in this book with object-relations theory.

The concept of object relations has been referred to as the bridge between individual systems and the family system (Slipp, 1984). Using object-relations theory helps to deal with some of the kinds of problems Duhls and Duhls (1981) evidently were referring to when they said that one "cannot kiss a system." In broad terms, object-relations theory attempts to deal with certain aspects of human relatedness, development, and motivation from infancy onward. How does the infant experience its environment and discover that it is in some respects separate from its environment though related to it in vitally important ways? How does it begin to distinguish between fantasy and reality, between inside and outside, between self and not-self?

In order to understand the complexities of object relations, it is important to ask a number of overlapping questions. How does the infant relate to the primary nurturer? How does it discover that it is separate from that person (object)? What are the consequences of such discovery? What are the processes involved? What are the implications of the early experiences with the nurturing one and other close figures for later intimate relationships, including those of adulthood and marriage? The patterns of relating and the internalized residues of the early experiences, as developed subsequently, provide the basis for later intimate relationships. object-relations theorists generally agree that this occurs. But in what ways does it happen?

Object-relations theory has been described by Guntrip (1969) in terms of our need to retain our experience in order to maintain continuity with the past and thus to have a basis for present functioning and relating. We do this by carrying things in our minds as either memories or internal objects. "Good" objects and experiences are carried as memories. Our outer experiences of pleasure and satisfaction meet our inner needs. Thus we have no conflict and can have confidence in our ability to continue to possess the real object both in the present and in the future.

"Bad object" situations are handled differently. A person whom we need becomes a bad object by ceasing to love us, disappearing, or dying, or doing something else that we experience as frustration or rejection. That person or object is internalized in a more fundamental and vital sense than is a memory. The person experiencing the frustration or rejection is emotionally identified with the internalized object. We thus construct an inner psychic world that replicates the original frustrating and unhappy situation. Linked to the bad object, we continue to feel deprived and unhappy and have a temptation to project the bad object back onto someone in the external world.

Two of the more important basic processes in object relations are introjection and projection. Both are essentially unconscious processes.

In the act of introjection the person transposes objects and their intrinsic qualities from the outside to inside her or his psyche. Introjection is different from identification, which is based on a desire to model oneself after the object and, in effect, to be the object. Projection is the opposite of introjection. In that process, one "casts out" undesired parts or qualities of oneself and places them onto another person or persons in the external world.

Two major patterns of introjection concern the marital therapist. One is the pattern of parental introjection in which we form libidinal (instinctual craving) attachments and make introjects from parental figures, no matter what the parents are like in real life (Guntrip, 1969). Note that the attachments pertain not only to the primary nurturer or mothering object but also to the paternal figure. Sonne and Swirsky (1981) have emphasized the importance for the infant of having the father as a love object and as a love object of a different gender from the mother. The child is required to deal with an awareness of different genders and to attempt to locate itself in relation to the parents in the marital dyad, thus creating an internal triangular representation in itself. The other major pattern is family introjection, the attachment to the family system as a whole or to some significant part of it such as the marriage or a sibling subsystem (Framo, 1965).

FAIRBAIRNIAN OBJECT RELATIONS

An adaptation of what may be termed the English object-relations approach provides some of the best explanations available for comprehending certain important aspects of marriage and marital interaction. No other approach helps to explain persistent attachment in the midst of unsatisfactory and unhappy marital interaction or failures in attachment as coherently as these adaptations of object-relations theory seem to do. Specifically, the object-relations approach developed by W. R. D. Fairbairn (1952, 1963)—following earlier leads by Melanie Klein—offers a theoretical explanation of the communal existence of marital partners that does much to inform the therapeutic approach to marital interaction.

Fairbairn based his theory on the nature of dependence upon other persons rather than on the drive theory of earlier psychoanalytic psychology. Human organisms from birth onward are seen to be primarily object-seeking, rather than driven, as in Freud's theory, by a need to alleviate somatic tensions and seek pleasure. An individual's major need is not merely to discharge tension but to be involved in social interaction and relationships. Both the capacity to enter into and develop intimate human relationships and the origins of psychopathology have roots in the stage of infantile dependency. The quality of the early object relations determines to a significant degree the integrity of the ego of individuals when they become adults.

The ego in Fairbairn's theory is a personal self, not merely a psychic apparatus or psychic structure (Guntrip, 1969). For Fairbairn the ego did not develop out of conflict as in early psychoanalytic thought but was present from birth. He described ego development as proceeding from an original state of infantile dependence based on primary identification with the nurturing object through a transitional stage into a state of mature or adult dependence. The original primary identification with the object is abandoned in favor of the mature dependence mode in which the self is differentiated from the object. In my interpretation the state of optimum adult functioning is best described as one of reciprocity and interdependence.

MAJOR RELEVANT CONCEPTS FROM OBJECT-RELATIONS THEORY

Five major concepts from object-relations theory have direct implications for marital therapy. The first four—splitting, projective identification, collusion, and ambivalence—pertain to how an individual relates to another individual. The fifth—models of relationship—refers to how an individual has internalized parts of his or her family of origin and the implications this has for marriage.

Splitting

The concept of splitting is foundational in Fairbairn's theory. The splitting of an object into two conceptual entities—one "good" and one "bad"—does not occur when the human infant is totally satisfied. The object that satisfies the infants needs can be dealt with consciously, and representations of it can be retained by the infant in memory. There is, thus, in Fairbairn's understanding, no reason to split an essentially satisfying and good object.

Fairbairn (1941) delineated two risks of the infant in relating to the nurturing one: loss of libido and loss of the good object, both of which have implications for the infant for its later object relations. The first risk, discharging libido into an emotional valcuum (i.e., risking attachment and getting no response) was seen as leaving the infant with a sense of inferiority and worthlessness, thus producing a schizoid affect of futility. Extreme results here would be reminiscent of the "marasmus" or wasting away described by Spitz (1945) in a study of hospitalized infants who did not receive sufficient tactile and emotional care. The risk of being rejected and losing the good object as a result of expressing aggressive feelings toward the nurturer produced feelings of depression in the infant, according to Fairbairn.

When faced with an unsatisfying object, the infant splits the object that it faces. Splitting takes place as follows: The human infant, possessing an ego from the beginning, seeks to express its libido or instinctual need by attachment with a love object. When the infant's craving is not accepted by the mothering one, an intolerable situation results. When the nurturer creates frustration, that nurturer is split into two objects by the infant psyche, a bad or unsatisfying object and a good or satisfying object. The good object, as noted above, is dealt with consciously and retained in the memory of the person.

The bad object is another matter: Unable to control the bad object in the external world, the infant then internalizes it in an effort to achieve mastery over it as an internal object. That is, the infant represses the bad object and takes it inside where there is some hope or possibility of controlling it.

The infant, in Fairbairn's conceptualization, is thus faced with an internalized object that it regards ambivalently. Another intolerable situation exists as a result of this internalization. Unlike the satisfying or good object, the bad object is both tempting and frustrating. Internal splitting then occurs, and the original bad internalized object itself becomes two: a needed or "exciting" object and a frustrating or "rejecting" object.

One outcome of this deprivation and frustration, as mentioned, is the depressive reaction, which comes from the eliciting of the infant's aggression toward its libidinal object (the nurturing one). Another is the schizoid reaction, which comes from the eliciting by his or her internalized bad objects of the hunger needs of an infant toward the nurturing one. Fairbairn saw both as fundamental responses to internal bad-object relationships. The exciting object and the rejecting object become the fundamental forms of internal bad objects. They remain parts of the ego, although they are split off from the central ego. Because of the functioning of the internalized bad objects, the schizoid is always being made hungry, provoked, and pushed into withdrawal, as is the depressive always prodded into anger. These patterns last over the years as the person deals with external real persons as if they were the same as her or his internalized bad objects (Guntrip, 1969).

The internalized objects are invested with a significant amount of strong feeling. Objects embued with a large amount of hate and the accompanying guilt feelings are felt by the person to be inside one's self. Where there is continuing rejection on the part of the parental figure(s), the person comes to feel that such feelings are also held by the object toward her or him. Thus, there begins a cycle of introjection–projection that many individuals carry into later life as a prototype for intimate interpersonal relationships.

Comprehending how conflicting feelings that spouses may feel toward their mates are related to conflict between feelings, images, and expectations held consciously by the central ego and those stemming from subsidiary egos can be exceedingly helpful in dealing with certain kinds of marital problems. A person may consciously regard her or his spouse as embodying certain desired values while being attracted to or frightened by an unconscious perception that the mate possesses contradictory traits.

Some splitting presumably occurs in all human beings. Our experiences have not been uniformly positive. All of us have limitations on our ability to trust and to love another object or person. We have not always received the love or emotional support that we needed. When we have put out feelers or given to others, they have not always reciprocated— but most of us do not need to carry schizoid and depressive reactions to this lack into adulthood.

Projective Identification

Projective identification is first of all a primitive defensive mechanism and probably the earliest form of empathy, the ability to put oneself in the place of the other. It also is an interactional style within marital and/ or family relationships. More than simply the projection of unacceptable parts of one's own personality or feelings may be projected onto another person. Projective identification may also be concerned with making projections onto the ideal object in an attempt to avoid separation from the object, or with making projections onto the bad object in order to gain control of the source of perceived danger (Segal, 1964). Since it does involve internally transposing part of oneself onto another, projective identification may produce anxiety in its author by arousing the fear that the object of one's projection will respond with projections of his or her own or that parts of oneself will be grasped and controlled by that object (Segal, 1964).

Several other concepts are used by clinicians and researchers to refer to essentially the same phenomena as those covered by the idea of projective identification. Wynne (1965), for example, has described the mechanism of "trading of dissociations." Dicks (1967) says that the partners treat each other as if the other were the original frustrating object. In this mechanism a deeply unconscious "deal" is struck by which the fixed view that one member has of another family member is unconsciously swapped for a fixed view of her- or himself by that family member (e.g., I will regard you as nonaggressive if you will perceive me as nonsexual). Each person is dealing with a part of the other that the other cannot acknowledge is present. Such reciprocal interaction in the family of origin can be, of course, powerful "basic training" for similar patterning of interaction in marriage. Mechanisms of defense and adaptation referred to as externalization also may take the form of projective identificatory behaviors.

It is important to recognize that projective identification is not always problematic or pathological. Zinner (1976) has noted that projective identification can occur along a continuum. At one end of this continuum may be distorted and perhaps even delusional perceptions of the object, while on the other end may be a healthy empathic connection with the subjective world of the object. Whether one's projective identifications are pathological or healthy depends in large measure on the ability to use the mechanism for approximating shared experience in an empathic fashion instead employing it as a means of externalizing conflict (Zinner, 1976).

Collusion

Projective identification requires a reciprocal action on the part of one's object: The other must accept the projection and act in accordance with it if projective identification is to be part of an ongoing interaction. This is what occurs when projective identification becomes part of the process of mate selection and ongoing marital interaction. In object-relations terms, such a relationship does not begin and continue unless each spouse is willing at an unconscious level to accommodate by accepting and identifying with the projective identification from the other.

Projective identification is more than simply a process of projection, although some (e.g., Grotstein, 1981) would say that they are the same thing. Projection refers to externalizing a feeling, attitude, or other aspect of one's psychic processes onto another person or external object. In projective identification, the term "identification" refers to a person's identification with his or her projected part as experienced within the object. We relate to the projected part of ourselves in the other person as we would to the self-part if it were within ourselves and attempt to involve the other person (object) in collusively behaving in the way in which we perceive him or her (Zinner, 1976). For example, if I regard another person as if she were a "bad mother," I attempt to pull her into dealing with me in negative ways. Consequently, I respond to her as if she were treating me badly. Participants in projective identification are involved in a collusive process and relationship in ways that are not present in simple projection.

Each partner "carries" something for the other in a collusive process of splitting and projective identification. For example, a man who is "kind, sweetly reasonable, and somewhat dependent" may be married to a woman who is "angry, excitable, and bossy." She does not have to be kind or reasonable as long as he will carry those feelings for her, and he does not have to be angry or assertive as long she carries those feelings for him. The denied split-off "bad" parts of oneself are carried by the other so long as the unconscious agreement prevails. This means that one does not have to become comfortable with the denied and projected parts of oneself while the collusion lasts.

Additionally, there is continual shaping of the mate through the collusive process as the marriage continues (Slipp, 1984). Greater degrees of predictability for the mates typically develop as the relationship evolves. The partners begin to feel more comfortable and trusting as the responses of the other confirm their object-seeking endeavoors. Similarly, the efforts of the other to induce one to play a particular role or set of roles increase the predictability of the relationship (Boszormenyi-Nagy, 1965).

Dicks (1967) has illustrated how the process of unconscious marital collusion operates in many marriages. There is a kind of unconscious "bargain" struck in many pathological relationships, in which each partner perceives the other as promising that old problems will be worked through, old hurts redressed, and—as an even stronger reassurance—that nothing will change. Mate selection in such situations is based on a mutual signaling system. Unconscious signals or cues convey the dual message that the other has the capability for engaging in the joint working through of unresolved conflicts or splits in one's personality, while simultaneously guaranteeing the paradoxical message that such conflicts will not be worked through with that person (i.e., that nothing will change). The latent interaction is initially concealed by idealization, most of which is conscious. To the extent that both continue to play their roles, a kind of rigid and pathological relationship continues.

Dicks' (1967) adaptation of Fairbairn's theory to marriage has been particularly helpful in illustrating how "can't live with and can't live without" relationships—which he refers to as "cat and dog" marriages—work, and how and why they continue and are resistant to therapy. Such marriages contain at a conscious level the partners' expectations for an ideal union, expectations that are aimed at keeping bad feelings out of the marriage. An unconscious joint effort or collusion denies that there are troublesome inner realities and maintains a shared resistance to change. Reality testing in the marriage often exposes the unreality of the idealization and permits frustration and regressive demands to surface. If the repression holds and there are other inner resources and adequate living conditions, such marriages are frequently enduring. While there are genuine needs for growth and integration that help to keep the marriage going, the tensions due to this repression may appear in psychosomatic difficulties, in depression, or in difficulties in the children.

Dicks (1967) has also described collusion in terms of patterns in which the partners treat each other as if the mate were the earlier object and thus regressively coerce or persuade them to respond to childish revenge and favor maneuvers. This often functions in "back and forth" pattern, as if the bad object were being tossed to and from between the partners. Rejecting qualities are attributed and evoked from each partner by the other. In some instances each partner acts both as the parent model and the child reacting against the parent.

Willi (1982, 1984) has developed a psychoanalytically oriented marital therapy approach centered around the concept of marital collusion. Not only clinically but also through research he has been able to demonstrate some of the effects of splitting, projective identification, and collusion. He found with a European clinical population that both women and men present different personalities depending on whether they are seen alone or with their mate (Willi, 1982). When he gave Rorschachs to men and women alone, he found no typical masculine or feminine form of perception and interpretation. But when he gave couples a Rorschach together and they had to agree on a common interpretation of each card, he found some important differences. The men tended to maintain the overall view and to show a greater tendency toward emotional control and realism than the women, while the women tended to bow to the men's views. Willi's (1982) suggestion for marital therapists is that they can simplify their task by concentrating on the common unconscious (common denominators) of the couple. What may be termed the "complementarity" of the couple is exhibited in the partners' tendency to play out their basic difficulties (disturbances) in relation to marriage through contrasting roles. One partner may engage in regressive behavior, for example, and the other in overcompensatory actions.

Ambivalence

Frustration in the infant and young child brings forth emotional reactions that generally are quite strong in nature, so that handling the rage that often emerges is not a simple matter. Mahler and associates (Mahler, Pine, & Bergman, 1975) believe that with the emergence of love the infant or small child simultaneously feels rage toward the nurturing individual who both nurtures and frustrates. Fusing the feelings of hate and love into ambivalence toward the mothering one thus forms the basis for dealing effectively in intimate relationships. Dicks (1967) points out that from infancy onward, mastery of the resultant ambivalence is a major key to human relationships. With adults the capacity for ambivalence toward a loved object is a sign of stable interaction and stable intimacy (Davis, 1983). Failure to master such tasks as the fusing of love and hate and the development of the possibility of ambivalence toward intimate figures results in some of the pathological relationships that appear in therapists' offices and elsewhere.

Models of Relationship

Marital relationships are deeply affected not only by one's earliest experiences with the nurturer and subsequent reaffirmations in experiences with other individuals, but also by the internalization of portions of families and family relationships. Skynner (1976) has used the term "models of relationships." One takes in or internalizes models of the behavior of others, which then can be used as a kind of program that can be reproduced, within certain limits, by the internalizer. The internalized model can also be used as the basis for responding appropriately when it is perceived in others, which is a kind of object relations that is more extensive and broader in context than the identification with the parts of a mothering one or even with a whole person. As Skynner (1976) and others (e.g., Davis, 1983) have noted, children internalize a model of each parent, a model of the affective interaction between spouses, and a model of the parents as a system.

These models are different from those that have been acquired through the hearing of verbal descriptions of behavior. Rather, they were obtained through the direct experience of seeing the behaviors of others and identifying with them as a whole. That experience makes such models of relationship much more powerful than the ideas and attitudes one has acquired about marital roles from hearing about them piecemeal. These models are alive and dynamic in the sense that the attitudes, tendencies, and beliefs that children have absorbed through observing and experiencing the interaction of people are continually recombined into new syntheses (Skynner, 1976).

Probably the most important aspect of Skynner's models of relationship is they are also internalized models of children's parents as a couple, rather than as mere separate individuals. Once again, we have an explanatory concept to deal with the question of how married persons may act with their spouse in ways that are inconsistent with their behaviors outside the family. Skynner (1976) sees this happening in cases where denial and repression may keep split-off parts of relationship models inoperative except in the marital relationship. They function in relation to one's spouse but not elsewhere. Roles previously witnessed in models of relationship may be played interchangably at times, with first one partner and then the other taking a regressive role, for example. This is reminiscent of Dicks' (1967) idea that projections are "tossed to and from" between the marital partners.

Skynner (1976) also makes the point that marriage always involves an attempt at healing and finding oneself again. This is consistent with the truism in mental health generally that "the basic thrust of the organism is onward, toward health and growth." This is true even though the effort may be a tragic or cataclysmic failure. Even repeated marriages in which "neurotic" elements seem to predominate in the choice of mate and in the subsequent marital interaction appear to be explicable in terms of continuing efforts to find a suitable object relationship, rather than in terms of accident or drive theories calling for tension release.

Marriage also, according to Skynner (1976) and consistent with Dicks (1967) and others, may serve as a defense against growth when the partners each rely on the personality makeup and defenses of the other to keep things as they are. In such relationships, the partners are seeking primarily security and comfort—that is, as much meaning and enjoyment in relationship as possible without significant alteration of the status quo. The relationship affords as much growth as they feel able to seek or as much change as they feel able to tolerate.

Social relations, of which marital relations are a prime example, are viewed here as transactional in nature; systems rather than individuals are the focus of attention. One understands individuals by viewing them as a system of action in themselves as well as part of larger systems of action. Action organizations involve a subject and an object, while transactional systems involve feedback processes and reciprocal behaviors. The subject (or one who acts) and the object (one acted upon) swap roles periodically with subject becoming object and (former) object becoming subject. The determinants of one individual's actions may be rooted in the self-delineation needs of the other: We choose the other as our object on the basis of our intuitive assessment of the ways in which they might turn to us as the object of their needs (Boszormenyi-Nagy, 1965).

OTHER OBJECT RELATIONS MATERIAL

The object relations work of others besides Fairbairn also contributes significantly to a dynamic theoretical underpinning for marital therapy. There are similarities in their concern with the strong impact of need satisfaction and need deprivation on the human infant and the role of anxiety in early experience. The family of origin should supply the infant and child with conditions and responses that satisfy its needs for the time and for surmounting the natural needs of its developmental phases. Appropriate responses by other human beings provide a reciprocal intimate human relatedness that affirms the validity of the infant's object-seeking efforts. During that process the youngster has its loveableness affirmed and begins as well to comprehend how to deal with its own upsetting and disconcerting impulses. With respect to anxiety, the original and earliest form experienced by the infant is separation anxiety (Fairbairn, 1963). Anxiety, of course, continues to be a major factor in human adaptation and functioning.

Sullivan

Harry Stack Sullivan (1953) also viewed anxiety as the most important factor contributing to the individual's difficulties in living and as the chief disruptive force in interpersonal relationships. Such anxiety is rooted primarily in the dependent condition of the human infant on a mothering person, and compounded by the abnormally long period of physical (as well as emotional) dependency of the human young on adults for their very survival. One uses what Sullivan termed "security operations" in order to cope with the conditions of living.

Sullivan saw human organisms as essentially social in nature: Unless anxiety interferes, he thought, human actions are positively aimed toward goals of collaboration with other human beings and toward mutual welfare and security. Sullivan similarly theorized that what he called the self-system of the infant comes into being, because of the necessity to avoid or minimize anxiety and to secure necessary satisfactions without arousing anxiety.

Mahler

Mahler's work (Mahler *et al.*, 1975) on the psychological birth of the human infant provides the marital therapist with some additional guidance in comprehending object relations and marital interaction. The separation-individuation process, as she terms it, runs from the 4th or 5th month of life to the 30th or 36th month. During that period the infant establishes a sense of separation from and relation to a world of reality outside itself. The core of the process consists of securing a sense of separateness of one's own body from the external world as that world is experienced through the infant's experience with its representative, the mothering one who serves as the infant's primary love object.

The separation-individuation phase is preceded according to Mahler and colleagues (1975) by an early life phase of primary narcissism. That early phase has two subphases. First comes a stage of "normal autism," an objectless phase in which the infant is not aware that there is a mothering agent. Satisfaction of its needs presumably is experienced by the infant as coming from within its own orbit. A symbiotic stage begins around the 3rd month of life. There the infant is in a psychological symbiosis in which it dimly perceives that the satisfaction of its needs comes from a need-satisfying object (the mothering one). The object is perceived as a part-object, the source of satisfactions, rather than as a whole object (whole person). Spitz (1965) has termed this a "preobject" phase of development for the infant.

At the peak of the symbiotic stage the process of separation-individuation begins. Gradually, the infant turned toddler moves from need-satisfaction relating to object relationships. Mahler and associates (1975) distinguish four subphases of separation-individuation: differentiation, practicing, reapprochement, and separation-individuation. The differentiation subphase begins the infant's "hatching" from the common symbiotic orbit that it shares with the mothering one. During the practicing subphase, from 7 to 10 months to approximately 15 to 16 months of life, the youngster is absorbed in its own narcissistic pleasures, busily exploring the world around itself, and becoming increasingly aware of its separateness from the mothering one and the need for her (or his) acceptance and renewed participation in its life. This is a subphase marked by extensive emotional "refueling" actions by the developing infant.

During the rapprochement subphase the toddler's awareness gradually increases that he or she is physically separate from others and that the love objects (mother and now father) are separate individuals. This subphase lasts from about 16 months to approximately 25 months and includes a "rapprochement crisis." The renewed approach behavior on the part of the toddler toward the love objects is very significant in laying the foundations for subsequent mental health or psychopathology. During this subphase the toddler avoids intimate bodily contact and engages in "shadowing and darting away patterns." Danger signals here are significant increases in separation anxiety. The kind of acceptance or rejection, availability or nonavailability of predictable and benign love objects establishes patterns of trust and feelings of reliability, or feelings that love objects are not reliable and trustworthy—to put the matter in simple terms.

A certain degree of object constancy is attained in the separation-individuation subphase. The formation of mental representations of the mothering one that are psychically available to the toddler makes this possible. Given such mental representations, the child becomes able to stay away from the mothering one for some periods of time and remain able to function.

Kernberg

Otto Kernberg (1974), whose orientation differs in major ways from that of Fairbairn, has described a continuum of configurations of ability or capacity for object relations that provides both mutual satisfaction and love and sexual (genital) relating. Along with each configuration, Kernberg has provided an example of personality organization that fits with the configuration.

Adapting Kernberg's ideas and those of others, I have constructed a series of "levels" that provide the marital therapist with some assistance in divining and predicting the abilities of given individuals for marital interaction and sexual intimacy (genital relationships).

This schema is generally helpful but has little to say about specific object choice. The levels of differentiation delineated here are compatible with the ideas of Bowen (1978) and others who claim that marital partners generally have achieved the same level of differentiation from their respective families of origin. This observation is essentially correct: As noted earlier, it is necessary to look at both partners in order to understand either one adequately. To recognize that both partners are differentiated to approximately the same degree can be very helpful in understanding marital functioning and pathology in particular.

TABLE 2
Effects of Personality Organization on Affectual-Sexual Relating

Level	Major Characteristics	Examples of Personality Organizaton
1	• Almost no capacity for closeness and tenderness • Same limits on sexual relating	Schizophrenic
2	• Limited capacity for closeness and tenderness • Sexual promiscuity (heterosexual or polymorphous perverse)	Narcissistic (Moderately Disturbed)
3	• Primitive idealization of object • Clinging dependence on loved one • Some capacity for sexual relating	Borderline
4	• Capacity for stable and deep object relations without capacity for full sexual relatedness	Characterological Neurotic
5	• Capacity for stable and deep object relations and tenderness integrated with capacity for full sexual relatedness	"Normal" (in a developmental sense)

A point that generally is overlooked with regard to the homogeneity of differentiation or individuation by marital partners is that what appears in the office of the clinician some years after marriage has been contracted may not be the same as the state that existed at the time of mate selection and marriage. An observation that the partners are at approximately the same level of differentiation when seen by the clinician should not serve as the basis for assuming that the identical levels existed for each of them when they married. Once they have married, individuals are not necessarily frozen at the same level permanently, or even for a few years. One partner may continue to grow while the other becomes fixated or even regresses. The partners may or may not have been functioning at similar levels of differentiation when they married, although in most instances they probably would have been functioning at basically the same level.

At the time of marriage, there was probably sufficient differentiation from their family of origin for each of them to make at least a minimal attachment to the other. They may have misperceived at both conscious and unconscious levels the stage of differentiation that actually existed in their partner and in themselves. Sometimes individuals may think that they are ready to make an attachment and commitment outside of their family of origin, only to be "grabbed" as it were by feelings of fear or guilt at "deserting" their family for a new object. Consequently, they retreat from the marital relationship and become reabsorbed into their family of origin. The physical separation from the family combined with the emotional attachment to the spouse and the legal/social acknowledgement that they have made an extrafamilial commitment may be sufficient to cause the person to realize that they cannot make the break. This realization sometimes is relatively slow in coming, arriving after the initial idealization of the mate has worn off.

Fortunately, the key issue for clinical work is not what prevailed at the time of marriage, but what prevails at the juncture at which treatment is sought. While it is likely that the partners were functioning at approximately the same level of individuation at the time of marriage, it is not all that important from a practical point of view.

Additional understanding is provided by Balint's (1965) idea that adult capacity for intimate relating, specifically the experience of expression of sexuality, requires the individual to be able to regress. This fits with my own notion that giving—including giving up and letting go—in sexual relationship and intercourse involves the capacity to let go with abandon. The utopia of genitality involves an ability to merge with the loved one, to let go of boundaries, to become temporarily psychotic in the sense of using "regression in the service of the ego" (Kris, 1934). Such contact and activity involves engaging in a kind of temporary symbiotic relating reminiscent of one's early and primitive experience with the mothering one.

The term *temporary* is exceedingly important in this instance: One is able to regress temporarily; autonomy is not lost on a permanent basis. As Boszormenyi-Nagy (1965) has described the process, the relationship consists of a human dialogue in which there is a reciprocal alternation of moves by the participants that serves as a safeguard against a symbiotic merger. In my view, adequate autonomy in the individuals, combined with the strength of the boundaries around themselves and their self-systems, permits temporary symbiosis and merging with minimal threat to their autonomous existence. Such persons have attained the level of object constancy in their own individual development, an achievement perhaps close to what Boszormenyi-Nagy means when he speaks of mature love as being a true dialogue rather than a fusion. Being able to form the temporary merger thus provides the participants in the love relationship with the requisite "emotional refueling" and recreative experience to continue functioning in a reasonably autonomous and mature interactive fashion.

Symbiosis is different from a host–parasite form of attachment. The relationship in symbiosis is one in which each partner provides for the other something that the other lacks (Goethals, Steele, & Broud, 1976). The original mother–child symbiosis provides the biological-interactional prototype of the kind of sharing that many adults seek in marriage. The mother–child pair seem to function as a common psychobiological unit in which the egos of the two are related through highly permeable boundaries. Although the infant presumably fantasies that it wields virtually unlimited power over the mother, the reality is that she actually has the physical and decision-making power (Ehrenwald, 1963). The marital symbiosis, to the extent that it is formed from time to time, is a temporary blending of two adult peers. When this process works well, it does not involve forcing either spouse into a dependent position or into helplessness, but pertains to meeting the other's needs without the autonomy of either person being threatened (Giovacchini, 1976).

Symbiotic relating can be of two major types. Giovacchini (1976) has described a character object relationship and a symptom object relationship. The former consists of total involvement on the part of the partners and is necessary for stability in the relationship. Symptom object relationship, on the other hand, has to do with partial involvement; only one facet of the spouse's personality is attached to in an effort to maintain one's psychic stability. Sally may be attracted to Ed's strength and be needy for a strong person to protect and care for her while she is simultaneously fearful of getting close to him. Thus she clings to him while giving very little emotionally. She uses a variety of symptomatic and pathological behaviors in order to guard against getting involved in deep intimacy.

DICKS' SUMMARY OF MARRIAGE

Since Dicks' (1967) attempts to deal with marriage and marital interaction from a Fairbairnian object-relations approach remains very significant, a summary may be helpful at this point. Dicks describes marriage as a social institution (accepted by the partners at a conscious level), a system of interpersonal relations (an "integrate," dependent on an overall balance of satisfaction over dissatisfaction for both partners), and a marital interaction system with three major levels or subsystems.

The three major levels or subsystems are internally related and change in importance over time as they help to maintain the cohesion of the marital dyad as it passes through different phases of the marital life cycle. These subsystems also can vary independently. Dicks terms cultural norms and values the "public" subsystem, noting appropriately and accurately that at the social level (e.g., social class, educational level) mates generally are selected on the basis of homogeneity—that is, "like marrying like."

The "central egos" of the partners, the second subsystem, function on the level of personal norms, conscious expectations, and judgments that have come from the background of object-relations experiences and social-learning experiences acquired by the mates prior to marriage. To the extent that it works well, this subsystem is identical with Fairbairn's "mature dependence" stage of development.

The third subsystem is one in which unconscious transactions are going on between the partners in an effort to secure object-relations satisfaction. This is where the repressed or split-off parts of the central ego function. Their dynamic presence influences the integrity of the central ego's perception of its object needs and the course that it takes in seeking the object and maintaining satisfying relations with it. They also influence the central ego's potential conflicts in perceiving and seeking its object needs. Dicks maintains that the deeper unconscious ties of the mates should be understood by assuming that they are concerned with establishing joint ego boundaries around the pair. Once again, he emphasizes that the hypothetical model of a central ego from which ambivalent and painful emotional relational aspects have been divested permits us to understand why individuals can grow up to be socially and intellectually competent beings while remaining impoverished in their intimate object relationships.

Such marital pathology may find expression in, for example, a marriage in which one partner uses a depressive defense, suffering depressive anxiety and guilt reactions. A split prevails in which a spouse idealizes the partner's personality and wishes to preserve that loved person as good. On the other side of the split, therefore, the spouse perceives himself or herself as bad, taking the frustration and hatred generated in the relationship onto himself or herself. Excessive displays of contrition, self-abasement, and restitution become part of the effort to make things up to and to deserve the partner. There are many other patterns to be found: According to Dicks (1967), the clinician needs to learn to assess the contributions from each subsystem of each partner toward the integrate of the pair.

DERIVED THERAPEUTIC INTERVENTIONS

One of the more significant treatment issues in terms of object relations in marital therapy is the discovery and successful use of methods of reintegrating (or perhaps integrating) the individuals as individuals so that good and bad objects can be experienced together. The individual, in other words, requires help in bringing dissociated parts of the self together so that the partner can be related to in current and reasonably realistic terms rather than on the basis of object-relations distortions. He or she needs to build an inner world that corresponds reasonably well to the external world in which he or she is participating so that it is not necessary to attempt to coerce or otherwise draw the marital partner into patterns of interaction based on unresolved interactions and relationships from the past.

Three ways have been described for intervening in marital situations in which projective identification and accompanying distortions are significantly operative. Greenspan and Mannino (1974) indicated that therapists can either (1) interpret the unconscious fears that bring about such defensive reactions or (2) confront straightforwardly the misperceptions of marital partners and help them to discover behaviors in each other that they had not previously perceived, thus providing a corrective perceptual experience. The third approach, advocated by Framo (1981) and others, involves the use of family-of-origin sessions in which adults are seen with their parents and other family members. Such an approach carries the problems back to their original sources and allows the adults to see the parents and siblings as they are, thus providing the opportunity to alter the internalized perceptions from the past.

SOCIAL LEARNING THEORY

The third stream contributing to an integrative approach to marital therapy comes from social learning theory. This tributary finds expression under the heading of behavioral marital therapy. Behaviorism began in individual psychotherapy and was subsequently expanded to include marital and family therapy, where behavioral orientations toward marital problems have become a significant aspect of professional work with marriages for approximately the last 2 decades. Direct confrontation and alteration is the approach that is most directly associated with the last of the three contributors to an integrative approach to marital therapy.

Behaviorism has at its core the assumptions that behavior is learned, that the most important source of human motivation is social reinforcement, and that strong, continuing behavior is maintained by intermittent reinforcement (Liberman, 1970). In contrast to psychodynamic psychology, behaviorism views symptoms as learned responses that are not adaptive rather than as symbolic reflections of underlying or unconscious conflict. The overt and visible behaviors rather than the intrapsychic processes of the person are thus the focus of behaviorism (Weiss, 1978).

This approach, in brief, emphasizes the environment and the importance of learning in therapy. The goal is to define the problem clearly in overt behavioral terms and to develop problem-solving solutions that are mutually acceptable to both the clients and the therapist (AAMFT, 1983).

Two kinds of conditioning theory have contributed to behaviorism: classical ("respondent") conditioning and operant ("instrumental") conditioning. Put simply, classical conditioning emphasizes the behaviors that are elicited by preceding stimuli. Operant learning is basically concerned with the consequences of the behavior, that is, with the conditions that follow the behavior and the presence or absence of rewards in response to the behavior. The two approaches overlap to a significant degree.

Operant conditioning has been more prominent than classical conditioning in the application of learning theory to marital problems. Among its major contributions has been its emphasis on the role of the external environment in determining behavior. Attention to the findings from the laboratory work that produced operant learning principles compels the clinician to pay heed to the behavior–environment relationship and to the antecedent stimuli and consequences that affect or even control marital behaviors (Margolin, 1985). Operant conditioning has been joined by applications of social exchange theory (Thibaut & Kelley, 1959).

Social exchange theory, sometimes referred to as behavioral exchange, is essentially a quasi-economic theory applied to human relations and, here specifically, to marital relationships and interaction. It is assumed that the behaviors of the spouses can be understood through focusing on the social behavior of each partner. This behavior is considered to be primarily a function of the consequences each partner provides the other for the behavior in question (Jacobson & Margolin, 1979). Specifically, it is concerned with costs and benefits: A relationship is considered satisfying if the benefits it provides exceed the costs of being in it, the reward/cost ratio thus determining the amount of satisfaction gleaned by a marital partner (Weiss, 1978). Social exchange theory provides one model for analyzing how relationships are affected over the long haul by behavioral exchange (Margolin, 1985).

Viewed in another way, social exchange theory is primarily a cognitive rather than an affective model. Each person's basis or standard for evaluating the satisfactoriness of the rewards provided by the partner is internal. One judges the adequacy of the rewards in terms of a combination of past experiences and one's perception of the gratifications that could be secured from being alone and unrelated or from being in other, alternative relationships (Jacobson & Margolin, 1979). It is important to recognize that social learning theory not only takes into account the strong and pervasive effects of the environment on behavior but also the private individual thoughts and reactions of the individual (M. Nichols, 1984). Another way of stating this is that social learning theory involves a focus on both cognitive processes and the reciprocal relationship between the environment and the person (Seagraves, 1982).

Behavioral approaches to marital problems are significantly concerned with the things that maintain positive and negative behaviors. Practically speaking, the clinician focuses not only on the symptom but also on helping the mates to learn more effective and productive ways of causing behavioral changes in one another and thus in their relationship. Changing the contingencies by which a person elicits positive responses from his or her partner has been described as the basic learning principle providing the power for behavioral marital therapy (Liberman, 1970). This involves using such techniques as communication skill training, problem-solving skill training, and contingency contracting (O'Leary & Turkewitz, 1978).

Another important learning principle is modeling (sometimes called imitation and identification). An esteemed person, such as the therapist, manifests behavior that is desired and adaptive, and the client then imitates the behavior. Approval (positive reinforcement) helps to sustain the new desired and adaptive behaviors on the part of the client(s) (Liberman, 1970).

The major contribution that social learning theory makes to marital therapy well may be the emphasis that it places on the reciprocal nature of the marital relationship. Interaction and cause-and-effect are viewed as being reciprocal. The broad meaning or implication of reciprocity is that the partners tend to reward each other at essentially the same rates. As Jacobson and Margolin (1979) have pointed out, when the partners accept this model they are made much more aware of and sensitive to their own contributions to the difficulties, and behavioral change suddenly seems possible. Reciprocity also implies that change on a partner's own part will bring benefits to her or him through change on the part of their spouse.

Contingency contracting has been described as the technique most widely used by behavioral marital therapists. An expression of reciprocity, it has been used by these therapists in two general ways. Early marital therapists and others (e.g., Lederer & Jackson, 1968) used a *quid pro quo* kind of contract, in which one mate agrees to do something in exchange for a different behavior (presumably of the same value) by their partner. This approach has not met the high hopes that some therapists held for it in the early days of its use. A second kind of contract is the "good faith" contract introduced by the Oregon Group (Weiss, Hops, & Patterson, 1973). In the good faith contract the behavior of one person is not dependent on the actions of the spouse. For example, a wife may be rewarded with an afternoon at the movies after cleaning the house. The husband may have a Saturday afternoon off to play tennis as a reward for trimming the hedge or straightening up the garage. Research at the University of Oregon (Wills, Weiss, & Patterson, 1974) has given empirical support to the use of the concept of reciprocity.

One of the more important aspects of the development of behavioral marital therapy has been the shift from a strong reliance on technique to an emphasis on principles of social learning theory. The point of view here is that marital therapists must give careful attention to the empirical findings of social learning theorists and to the principles that they have derived and established.

A major shortcoming of the behavioral approach has been its lack of attention to the role played by individual pathology in marital discord (Seagraves, 1982). Seagraves (1982) has suggested that behavioral, psychoanalytic, and systems approaches are all struggling with the issue of how to deal legitimately with the relationship between internal mental events and external behavioral events. The struggle has not been made explicit in all three or even acknowledged by adherents of those models. Gurman (1982) has indicated that behavioral marital therapy will fall short in its efforts to become integrated with other approaches to marital therapy if it does not acknowledge that family members must become integrated as individuals in order for family systems to operate adequately. He has gone farther in advancing the opinion that if behavioral and object-relations models are to secure rapprochement, behavioral approaches must facilitate the process of assisting family members to reintegrate parts of themselves and of other family members that have been repudiated.

Gurman has also suggested two ways in which behavioral interventions can assist individuals to become integrated and function as whole persons in intimate relationships. First, problem-solving training and communication training have the potential of assisting directly with correcting or alternating unconscious splitting and collusion. Second, proclivities for using projective identification can be decreased through teaching clients to use positive reinforcement techniques as a means for increasing desired behaviors in other family members. He points out that commu-

nication and problem-solving skill deficits are essential to the maintenance of unconscious collusion and projective identification. Explicit attention to teaching interpersonal skills directly challenges collusion and
contributes to helping individuals to relate as whole persons. Additionally, and very importantly, Gurman indicates that behavioral changes
initiated by the therapist must be sensitive to the idiosyncratic and unconscious meanings that family members attach to those modifications of
behavior. Putting things in very simple terms, he is enunciating the principle that change efforts launched by the therapist must fit with the individual, unconscious agendas of the persons with whom she or he is
working in order to be effective.

DERIVED THERAPEUTIC INTERVENTIONS

It is difficult to write a separate section on therapeutic interventions derived from behavioral approaches to marital discord and human problems that can be treated through marital therapy. The foregoing discussion on social learning theory included an illustrative and fairly extensive
description of behaviorally oriented interventions.

Perhaps it is most appropriate merely to reiterate that the major
contributions of social learning theory in my opinion are the emphases
on learning—including how persons may relearn—and reciprocity in relationships. The ideas of reciprocity and fairness call for involvement by
both partners in efforts to secure change and to engender cooperation
with each other and with the therapy. The therapist's ability to tailor
interventions to the mentality and needs of the couple is greatly enhanced by the tenets of social learning theory. One can design a great
variety of behaviorally oriented interventions on the basis of the particular needs and outlooks of the clients.

INTEGRATION IN PRACTICE

As noted above, the effort to secure a workable theoretical perspective
for working with marriages and marital interaction starts with what I
encounter in clinical settings and with what I find in theoretical and
empirical research materials on marriage and marital interaction. How
and in what ways do I bring these together in clinical practice?

The answer to this question is not unlike the response to the old
query, "How do porcupines make love?" That is, "Very carefully"—
though that is too facile an explanation. In reality, one does not bring

together all of the concepts that explain marital interaction in an easy and complete manner. We have used the metaphor of "lumps in the oatmeal" (Nichols & Everett, 1986) to reflect the idea that the various concepts that one encounters and uses in therapy do not necessarily blend into a homogeneous whole that contains no disjunctive and disconcerting lumps or bumps. The smooth blend could be obtained only at the expense of omitting important data and distorting some of the realities that show up in practice, research, and theoretical work. Integration is an ongoing process.

Chapter Four

Marital Therapy: General Issues

When does one decide to use marital therapy with clients? When is it the treatment of choice? What is it used to treat?

Marital therapy, as noted, is a form of family therapy. It treats marital conflict and individuals in context. Dicks (1967) has indicated that marital conflict occurs on three levels: social and cultural norms, conscious personal expectations, and unconscious activities of self-images and object images. Marital therapy covers not only marital difficulties as such but also a variety of personal, "individual" problems and pathologies. It has thus emerged as one of the most powerful approaches available for dealing with a wide range of clinical problems (Gurman, 1978).

The marital and family therapy perspective views conflict as originating outside the individual rather than stemming solely from intrapsychic conflict. This does not mean that the individual is not affected and does not require change, but the widening of diagnostic understanding from an individual model to a family transactional point of view embodies a broadening of treatment concepts to include efforts to change important contexts (Framo, 1972; Robinson, 1979).

The family system that includes marriage is, once again, the most important and accessible context for treating individuals. This does not imply that all problems that emerge in marriages and married individuals stem totally from family causes or may be subject to second-order change through clinical work. For example, what Goldner (1985) in a discussion of feminism and family therapy has called "maternal centrality and paternal marginality" (p. 35) is related to the world of work; since the industrial revolution the male has had a superior position in the "outside world" and the female has been in an ambiguous role of having much family responsibility and inferior status and power. There are limits on what may be changed through a therapeutic approach without altering other parts of the context such as the work world and the society and its culture.

WHEN AND WHEN NOT TO USE MARITAL THERAPY

Over the past several decades a number of clinicians have attempted to establish indications and contraindications for the use of marital therapy. What follows is an illustrative rather than an exhaustive treatment of the reasons and situations for using or not using marital therapy, of these indications and contraindications for its use.

BACKGROUND

Marital therapy in part arose from the psychoanalytic tradition. Working with couples in conjoint sessions began first with nonmedical professionals, and there were other branches of the development besides the psychoanalytic (Nichols & Everett, 1986). Within the psychoanalytic framework, marital therapy began with the work of C.P. Oberndorf, who presented a paper on the topic before the American Psychoanalytic Association in 1931 (Oberndorf, 1934). Over nearly a quarter century he had treated some married partners separately by means of psychoanalysis. His concern was essentially with the neuroses of the individual spouses.

Complementary neurotic reactions between mates was the focus of Mittelman's analytic work with marital partners. Mittelman's pioneering work, which was first presented in 1941, led to the conclusion that every neurosis in a married person is deeply anchored in the marital relationship (Mittelman, 1944). Mittelman (1948) later reported successfully treating several couples, using either psychoanalysis on both partners or psychoanalysis for one partner and briefer psychotherapy for the other.

Martin and Bird (1953) were reporting on the advantages of what they called "the stereoscopic technique" by the early 1950s. This was a form of collaborative treatment in which one therapist saw the wife and another the husband in individual treatment, and then conferred with each other periodically. Some of the advantages given were a saving of time for the patient through more rapid recognition of the patient's distortions of reality by the therapist, opportunities for scientific research in private practice by the clinicians, and continuation of training by the exchange of ideas between therapists. Disadvantages for the therapist were seen as the additional time required to meet and plan and the added task of working out a collegial relationship. For the patients, a disadvantage was the addition of the therapist–therapist relationship on top of the therapist–patient relationship.

Clinical reports in which psychoneurotic spouses were treated separately but simultaneously indicated that the complicating transference reactions feared by psychoanalysts did not necessarily emerge (Thomas, 1956). Concurrent treatment of "a latent schizophrenic and his wife" by the same therapist was being described by the late 1950s (Jackson & Grotjahn, 1959). The therapist and his consultant concluded that no treatment would have been effective without therapy for the wife because of the nature of the marital relationship. Concurrent treatment by the same therapist was also felt to increase the efficiency of the therapeutic work.

Neither transference nor countertransference, long considered barriers by the psychoanalytically oriented, were proving to be significant sources of difficulty in conjoint work with couples. Whitaker (1958b), along with others, was suggesting that direct therapeutic work with couples or families limited transference problems. This was because a realistic reactivation was occurring rather than a transferred one with a therapist in a one-on-one analytic situation. Interpretation and other kinds of interventions could be aimed directly at the interlocking patterns of the spouses when they were seen together.

Whereas some early therapists began working with neurotic couples and moved to treating marital pairs in which at least one partner was psychotic, Whitaker (1958a, 1958b) and colleagues went the other way. They considered conjoint treatment of couples appropriate when there was a fragile marital relationship, immaturity, interlocking pathology, and paranoid trends. The partners were always seen together in an effort to avoid increasing paranoid issues. One partner was used as a non-professional attendant for the psychotic mate.

An optimistic view of the potential for conjoint marital therapy was taken by Watson (1963) in an influential paper. He considered conjoint treatment an excellent way to retard major and reality-disruptive distortions and destructive neurotic processes, as well as being especially well suited to "acting-out" characterological problems. Watson noted that conjoint marital therapy had been used with grossly psychotic couples and with those facing both unusual reality problems and mundane difficulties, but he was still cautious about spelling out indications and contraindications for the use of conjoint marital therapy.

By the middle of the 1960s the literature was beginning to be filled with reports on various kinds of approaches to treating married persons.

Gottlieb and Pattison's (1966) review of the literature showed that most objections to the treatment of couples came from a priori considerations—specifically "unnecessarily narrow commitment to psychoanalytic theory"—rather than from practical clinical sources.

By this time Sager (1966b) could describe seven forms of dynamic treatment used with married couples in efforts to change both individual psychodynamics and the dynamics of the relationship. These were: (1) successive psychoanalysis of the husband and wife; (2) concurrent or separate but simultaneous treatment of the spouses by the same therapist; (3) conjoint therapy in which one therapist sees the partners together; (4) collaborative treatment in which separate therapists for the spouses confer periodically; (5) four-way sessions in which the spouses and their separate therapists meet together occasionally; (6) various forms of group couples therapy and other group therapy; and (7) family therapy in which the focus is on the couple rather than on the child or children.

Indications for marital therapy given by Sager were broad but limited in number. The couple's awareness that they have a marital problem was seen as an indication, while the lack of desire of either partner to maintain the marriage was viewed as a common contraindication to using marital therapy. When a situation involving discomforting symptoms for one or both mates perpetuated or exacerbated those symptoms, marital therapy was deemed appropriate. Sager's most important personal contraindication was described as his occasional inability to prevent destructive use of the session by one spouse against the other.

Sager (1967, 1976) has continued to describe marital therapy as a modality that is valuable for the treatment of individual difficulties as well as marital problems. Accordingly, he believes that a considerable amount of therapeutic leverage for dealing with individual symptomatology and its etiological sources is provided in conjoint marital treatment. The therapist can use indications of repression, distorted perceptions, defense mechanisms, transferentially based actions and feelings, and unrealistic expectations of the spouse for work with the individual.

Operating from a very different perspective than the psychoanalytically oriented therapists who shaped and dominated early marital therapy, Haley (1963) offered five indications for using marital therapy. Conflict in marriage was viewed by him as stemming from disagreement about the rules for living together and about who is to establish the rules, and efforts to enforce incompatible rules. The indications for marital therapy that he offered were: (1) when individual therapy has failed; (2) when individual therapy cannot be used; (3) when a sudden onset of symptoms in a patient coincides with marital discord; (4) when therapy is requested by partners who are unable to resolve their distress or conflict; or (5) when there are indications that a patient's individual improvement will result in divorce or the appearance of symptoms in a spouse.

By the middle of the 1970s conjoint marital therapy had become probably the most common modality of marital therapy (Berman & Lief, 1975). Gurman (1973) in an early review of research literature found improvement in two thirds of the cases treated by marital therapy. That rate essentially matched the results from eclectic therapies with adult neurotics. Results were even better in later studies of treatment outcome. Subsequently, use of conjoint marital therapy and conjoint group marital therapy appeared to be clearly established as superior and desirable forms of treatment when compared to other approaches. Individual therapy for marital problems was found to be ineffective and sometimes harmful (Gurman & Kniskern, 1978b).

CONTEMPORARY MARITAL THERAPY

Marital therapy today is routinely used with a wide range of disorders generally considered individual in nature, as well as with problems specifically labeled marital or interactive. Current literature illustrates clinical work with clients whose difficulties are described at widely scattered places in the current *Diagnostic and Statistical Manual* (DSM-III: American Psychiatric Association, 1980). Some clinicians use marital therapy as the treatment of choice, others as one of the indicated therapies, and still others as an adjunctive treatment. The range and number of difficulties for which marital therapy is used continues to expand. The disorders described below are among the individually diagnosable conditions treated today by means of marital therapy.

Agoraphobia

Hafner (1986) has indicated that agoraphobia in maritally dissatisfied women is best treated in a marital context. Others have also centered on the marital relationship as the source of symptoms and focus of treatment on both an outpatient (Goldstein & Swift, 1977) and an inpatient basis (Holm, 1982). Hafner's perspective locates the origins of the difficulty in the choice of marital partner. Some findings have suggested as well that many such husbands react negatively to their wife's symptomatic improvement (Hafner, 1977). Changing the marriage thus provides alteration in the agoraphobic needs and behaviors of the symptomatic spouse. Hafner also has explained the "overvaluation of behavior and drug therapies" in treating agoraphobia on the basis of certain biasing artifacts in research projects.

Alcoholism

Marital/family orientations have become very prominent in the treatment of alcoholism. The idea of an alcohol-dependent person and a codependent or coaddict spouse has become familiar to many therapists. The recognition of a circular relationship between marital interaction and alcohol problems has developed over a long period of time. A common stance today would be that marital conflict alone seldom causes alcohol problems but often contributes to their maintenance once they have appeared, while alcoholism itself does produce marital conflict (O'Farrell, 1986).

A common treatment approach involves the teaching of problem-solving skills and a focus on interpersonal relations as they are manifested in marital and family living (Cadogan, 1979). Attention is given also to modification of consequences and dealing with cognitive issues (irrational beliefs) in working with alcoholic marriages (Paolino & McCrady, 1977).

Research reviews (Gurman & Kniskern, 1978a; Jacobson, 1978) provide some support for group marital therapy as the treatment of choice for alcohol-problem marriages. The reviews also suggest that it may be superior to the individual treatment of the alcoholic marital partner.

Depression

Marital interaction and the marital relationship do not have to be etiological factors or to "cause" depression in order to be useful in its treatment (Coyne, 1986). Marital therapy is successfully used as the treatment modality for "neurotic" depression of long duration as well as for shorter term reactive depression episodes.

Greene and colleagues (Greene, Lee, & Lustig, 1975) described the use of marital therapy as part of a treatment regimen for manic depressive illnesses. They used it in the treatment of 100 couples in which one or both partners had suffered psychotic episodes. Others (e.g., Mayo, 1979) have found that conjoint marital therapy, though difficult, is often more effective than individual psychotherapy with such disorders.

Eating Disorders

Marital and family therapists have become familiar with the use of family therapy in the treatment of eating disorders (anorexia, bulimia, and combinations) in children and adolescents, particularly at the Philadelphia Child Guidance Clinic (Minuchin, Rosman, & Baker, 1978). More recently, attention has been given to the treatment of eating disorders

through marital therapy (Foster, 1986). Some indications and contraindications and assessment and treatment strategies have been outlined by
Foster (1986).

Narcissistic Disorders

These difficulties, like most of the others discussed here, are generally
considered quite hard to treat. Marital therapy only recently has been
used as a major treatment approach with them, and is still not likely to
be used as the sole therapy modality by most therapists. How therapy
is conducted with narcissistic cases depends on whether the therapist
addresses the symptom, the personality, or the system (Lansky, 1986).

Schizophrenia

The severity of the schizophrenic disorders poses special problems for
clinicians. Attention to the possibility that marital difficulties may be
primarily a response to stresses produced by the illness in one of the
partners has been comparatively rare, even though all such couples probably could be helped by some marital therapy (Anderson, Reiss, & Hogarty, 1986).

A phase-oriented approach (Wynne, 1983) in which therapists start
with a "least pathology" assumption (Pinsof, 1983) appears to be the indicated path. Such an approach is based on the idea that one helps couples to deal with immediate problems causing or perpetuating the illness
before assuming that there are pathological marital relationships and trying
to deal with marital pathology. Initially, the therapist tries to help the
partners with information, support, and the development of coping skills.
This is similar to the approach others have taken with parents of a
schizophrenic individual (Lantz, 1986). After these steps have been taken,
additional marital therapy may be employed as its use is deemed appropriate. Specific goals for added marital therapy depend on the effect of
the disorder on the couple and their wishes for additional change (Anderson, Reiss, & Hogarty, 1986).

Sexual Disorders

Sex therapy is different from marital therapy. Sexual dysfunction that
does not involve pathology in the marital system probably is best treated
by specific goal-directed forms of sex therapy, active treatment that has
been well established as a useful form of intervention (Kaplan, 1974).

Reciprocal and circular relationships between marital discord and sexual dysfunction are seen frequently in therapeutic practice. Sager (1974) has described some guidelines for ascertaining when to try treating the sexual dysfunction directly through goal-specific treatment and when broader marital therapy should be used. Although the briefer sex therapies may be used with problems of sexual desire (Kaplan, 1979), more broadly based marital therapy is also useful (Heiman, 1986) and may be the approach of choice. Marital therapy in this instance would explore all of the pertinent systemic issues, including the general relating of the partners.

Children's Problems

The relationship of problem behavior in children and family disorder has been one of the central issues of family therapy (Nichols & Everett, 1986). A systemic relationship exists between many cases of problem behavior and marital difficulty. The relationship is such that the amelioration or elimination of the marital discord may cause the cessation of the child's problems or prevent them from occurring (Oltsmanns, Broderick, & O'Leary, 1977).

Careful assessment by the clinician may lead to the decision to start treatment directly with the marital couple; it is sometimes not necessary to see the children at all. This is the case when it is apparent that the child's problematic behavior is clearly reflective of marital discord and the child's fear that marital break-up could cost her or him the presence of a parent. Even so, the problematic behavior should not be so deeply rooted within the behaviors of the child or have caused such practical, social consequences that failure to see the child would have untoward outcomes.

Paranoid Reactions

Some clinicians have regarded paranoid reactions as untreatable through conjoint marital therapy, which indeed may be the case for certain extremely malignant forms. It has been possible, however, to treat a paranoid individual on an outpatient basis with the assistance of medication and the aid of the spouse as a supportive figure. Florid pathology including active paranoid ideation is not necessarily a contraindication, unless it focuses on the spouse. Such outpatient treatment over an 18-month period not only enables one person to remain at home, but also is accomplished at much less financial cost than would have been involved in a

2- to 4-week psychiatric hospitalization, which would typically need to be followed by outpatient psychotherapy.

WHEN NOT TO USE MARITAL THERAPY

There appear to be two major contraindications for the use of marital therapy. One is the refusal or inability of the couple to engage in marital therapy, an example of which is the presence of such strong paranoid tendencies or hostility on the part of one or both partners that they cannot stay in the same room without engaging in destructive and nonproductive behaviors. With some couples it is necessary to work with the partners individually at the beginning of therapy to prepare them for conjoint work. The other example of a situation not conducive to marital therapy is the absence of a commitment to the relationship or an unwillingness to consider changing. One of the major issues here is the manner in which the spouses are attached and the assessment of the likelihood of their continuing the marriage once the malignancy has been modified.

The other major contraindication to the use of marital therapy is the clinician's lack of familiarity with marriage, marital interaction, and marital therapy, or lack of ease with the approach. It seems indisputable that clinicians do best with modalities with which they are familiar and to which they have a strong commitment. Enthusiasm alone will not make an effective therapist, but lack of knowledge and absence of commitment to an approach certainly undermine its use. The clinician who is convinced that psychoanalysis is "the" most effective and "deepest" form of psychotherapy, for example, may not be able to work at maximum effectiveness with other approaches.

VARIOUS TREATMENT APPROACHES

Today several treatment modalities are employed under the general heading of marital therapy. The more commonly used of those modalities are discussed below.

CONJOINT MARITAL THERAPY

Conjoint marital therapy as used here refers to treatment in which one therapist meets with a couple in a three-way session. Therapy in which two clinicians, cotherapists, meet with the couple also is often referred to as conjoint marital therapy, but this is not the reference when the term is used in this book. If my intention is to talk about cotherapy, that specific term will be used.

Cotherapy is sometimes hailed as offering unique advantages over treatment by a single therapist, among which is the possibility of modeling different roles, especially when a male–female cotherapy team is used. Neither my experience nor outcome research (Gurman & Kniskern, 1978a) provides support for using cotherapy in conjoint marital therapy, except perhaps in special instances such as training therapists. The added cost of using two therapists for conjoint marital therapy does not appear justified in either private practice or agency settings, although the subsidization of that approach to treatment for research and perhaps training purposes may be justified.

Conjoint marital therapy is probably still the major form of marital therapy used by clinicians. There seems to be no good reason to think that things have changed in the decade or so since Berman and Lief (1975) highlighted it as the most frequently used form of marital therapy.

MARRIED COUPLES GROUPS

Couples groups composed of pairs of marital partners are still widely employed and, according to outcome research (Gurman & Kniskern, 1978a), are an effective approach to dealing with marital discord. The rationale, dynamics, and process of using couples group therapy have been described by Kaslow and Lieberman (1981). Some therapists prefer to use this approach as the major form of therapy; Framo (1983), for example, has described his mode of dealing with marital difficulty as that of routinely putting couples into married couples groups. His statement to them is, "You can accomplish anything in the [married couples] group that you wish to accomplish in therapy."

My own observations and work with such groups indicate that they have shortcomings as well as strengths. One of the deficits is associated with the fact that groups often focus on either generic concerns or on the problems of some but not all couples in the group. Not infrequently, the outcome is one in which the concerns and problems of couples are not addressed directly or specifically. Unless the motivation of all couples is high and the skill of the leader(s) outstanding, such omissions are likely to occur.

FAMILY-OF-ORIGIN SESSIONS

This technique typically involves one or two therapists meeting with a client and the members of their family of origin. Framo (1983) has described a pattern in which cotherapists meet with the client and his or her nuclear family for 2 hours on a Friday night and 2 hours on the next morning, as a supplement to married couples group sessions. Other therapists use family-of-origin sessions in connection with conjoint marital therapy. A variant of this approach that frequently proves helpful is an occasional meeting of the therapist with a sibling of a client or with the entire sibling subsystem of a client's family or origin. Such family-of-origin sessions often require careful planning and the opportunistic use of occasions in which members of a client's family of origin are in town for holidays or family visits.

COMBINATIONS OF TECHNIQUES

Individual or family-of-origin sessions may be used along with conjoint marital interviewing or in connection with married couples group therapy. Some therapists routinely use a combination of weekly individual sessions with each partner and a conjoint meeting with the therapist and both partners (Murphy, 1976). This approach has the obvious disadvantage of being expensive and time consuming for the clients. It is most likely to be used by clinicians who view human difficulties as stemming primarily from intrapsychic sources.

There are two major situations in which individual therapy may be helpful as an adjunct to marital or even indicated instead of conjoint marital therapy. One consists of those occasions in which preparation is needed to get individuals ready to participate in marital therapy. This may take several forms. Partners may be so entangled and hostile, hurt, or fearful that they require individual treatment to secure catharsis or support in order to progress to the stage where they can work effectively and cooperatively in conjoint therapy. Sometimes they may be so confused and ambivalent that they require sessions apart from their mate in order to sort out their feelings and resolve their questions and ambivalence to the extent that they can participate in conjoint work. An example of the latter situation might be a case in which an individual felt it necessary to resolve an extramarital relationship before moving on to work on the marriage.

The other major time at which individual therapy may be helpful is when marital therapy uncovers individual problems that do not significantly involve the mate. The difficulties may have to be ameliorated or resolved before marital therapy can proceed satisfactorily. Individual problems may in some instances be uncovered during the course of marital therapy but postponed until that treatment has been concluded. The key issue in either case is that the problems do not require the participation of the other spouse in the treatment.

ADJUNCTIVE MODALITIES

Modalities that are adjunctive to the central techniques of marital therapy include various types of skill training such as relationship enhancement efforts and communication facilitation. The enrichment programs in particular seem to hold promise in the preventive area (Gurman & Kniskern, 1978a). The designation "adjunctive" also can be used to refer to the assistance provided to couples by self-help groups such as Alcoholics Anonymous, Al-Anon, and, more recently, the Children of Alcoholic Parents programs. There are literally scores of self-help groups that may be useful to the marital and family therapist in working with and helping clients.

BEHAVIORAL AND NONBEHAVIORAL
ORIENTATIONS

Both behavioral and nonbehavioral therapies have demonstrated effectiveness in dealing with therapeutic problems; each approach has its strengths. Behavioral approaches offer precise intervention techniques and testable models (Gurman & Kniskern, 1978a). Jacobson (1978) found a significant amount of research support for the effectiveness of behavioral approaches and skill training, but his review of the literature did not disclose that behavioral approaches were more effective than other types.

No single approach or school of marital/family therapy is clearly superior to other approaches on an across-the-board basis. Systems therapies, for example, are the treatment of choice for dealing with certain problems and reaching certain goals, such as treating anorexia and decreasing hospitalization rates for some patients, among others (Gurman & Kniskern, 1978a).

The need to integrate various orientations has been addressed by several clinicians (e.g., Gurman, 1982; Pinsof, 1983). Illustrations can be found of increasing effectiveness as a result of integrating approaches. The use of "insight" approaches alone for dealing with out of awareness (unconscious, preconscious) feelings and experiences is not a particularly effective way of treating marital discord. On the other hand, when insight is combined with active efforts to make connections between the clients' inner experiences and overt behavior and to recast and modify the overt behavior, effectiveness increases markedly (Gurman, Kniskern, & Pinsof, 1986).

Probably no issue in the general therapeutic field illustrates the need for integration more clearly than marital collusion. This concept refers to an interplay between the intrapsychic and the interpersonal, between the individual and the system, that poses a major set of difficulties for the clinician. Between the spouses there is a mutual acceptance of internal images that have been projected from the other mate (Dicks, 1967); marital collusion, in brief, is an unconscious agreement to interact in a way that is gratifying to both partners. Dicks (1967) also pointed to the fact that the collusion contains an unspoken agreement not to change.

The processes of splitting and projective identification in the object relationships of the partners can be modified by behavioral interventions. Communication and problem-solving training can be helpful in altering the splitting of objects, with positive reinforcement techniques being used to increase desired behavior in a spouse and thus reduce projective identification tendencies. The integration involved here would bring together psychodynamic object relations, systems, and behavioral theories and therapy. It would include the recognition that the marital partners as individual subsystems of the family need to be reintegrated (or integrated) for the system to work well (Gurman, 1982).

SOURCES OF REFERRALS

Both the sources of referrals to the therapist and the focus of the request for treatment may be important issues in the launching and outcome of marital therapy. These will be examined briefly at this point.

FOCUS OF REFERRALS

The origin of the referral to the therapist may have significant implications for client understanding, motivation, and treatment. Referral sources may be classified under the headings of self-referral and other-referral: Did the partners decide for themselves that they needed to see a marital therapist? Did they select the clinician or did someone else provide the name? Did someone else determine that they should consult a marital therapist? Did the source recommend a particular clinician, give them a list of therapists, or leave the search completely up to them? If the case is self-referred, what do the marital partners understand to be the purpose of the referral? If the partners were other-referred, what was conveyed to them about therapy and the therapist by the referring party? In either instance, what do they expect from the clinician?

Self-referrals based on a joint husband–wife decision may signal a stronger motivation for therapy and a greater determination to follow through on change efforts than most other-referrals. Couples referred because others such as parents think that they need help may or may not be convinced that they actually do need assistance. Court referrals because of family violence or alcoholism may not carry sufficient client motivation to make the partners good treatment prospects. The coercion of legal authorities may be enough to get the couple to the therapist but not sufficient to cause them to be cooperative once they arrive. Clinicians need to determine what kinds of parameters are required in order to have an adequate basis for working with such couples.

Cases referred by attorneys often may be better suited for mediation or divorce therapy than for marital therapy. Such cases require explicit attention to the expectations of the clients regarding the role of the clinician. Occasionally, contact with the attorney regarding her or his expectations may be wise. Does the attorney see the clinician's role as that of advocate? Is the therapist expected to be available to provide testimony?

When clients are referred by others does the clinician have any responsibility to the referral source? Does this source expect a report, or some particular result or outcome? Are those results expected within a specific time frame? If so, how realistic are the expectations?

FOCUS OF THE REQUEST

What is the specific focus of the clients' request for help? Is it a request for individual treatment, child therapy, parent–child relationship therapy, total family therapy, or specifically for marital therapy? Each of these may, of course, reflect a particular view of what is needed, and thus may signify different motivations.

Requests for individual therapy and child treatment especially may be based on the idea that the problems reside in an individual. Requests for individual help where marital difficulties are mentioned need careful examination, since they sometimes stem from the notion that one individual is responsible or mainly responsible for marital difficulties. The idea needs to be conveyed to the prospective client that even if such were the case, two partners are affected by what has and is transpiring, and so both partners should be included in efforts to change the situation.

Many therapists do individual treatment as well as marital/family therapy. For cases in which individual psychotherapy is used, there are in my judgment important practical and ethical reasons for seeing the spouse for at least one session. Psychotherapy of a married person can affect the marriage adversely, but the marital relationship does not have to be damaged needlessly. A session with the spouse who is not in treatment can provide her or him with information concerning what to expect as a result of the partner's therapy. Both spouses deserve to be informed so that it is possible for them to give informed assent to whatever they agree to do. Clinicians who follow this pattern also may find that resentment, fear, suspicion, and hostility on the part of the "left out" spouse tend to be minimal or nonexistent. Routine refusal by a clinician to have contact of this kind with the spouse of a client because of a fear of transference contamination certainly appears to reflect not only an overly strict and rigid interpretation of psychoanalysis but also a low degree of confidence in the strength of the client–therapist relationship (Gardner, 1976).

Requests for help with parent–child problems may take three major forms: a caller may ask for personal help in dealing with a child (e.g., "It's between Debby and me"); the request may be for an appointment for the spouse and a child (e.g., "My wife and our daughter just don't get along"); or the focus of the request may be for help for both partners in dealing with a child. Any of these may be an indirect request for marital assistance, as, similarly, may any of them reflect a complaint that actually foreshadows more basic marital problems. The same points hold true with regard to requests for family therapy.

Some requests are made specifically for marital therapy. The proportion of one's requests for help that specify marital assistance is probably closely related to the reputation of the therapist. If it is known that one works largely with couples, for example, the incoming referrals and requests are more likely to be for marital cases than for individual or child treatment.

Whatever the sources of the referrals and the initial request for help, the expectations of potential clients need to be clarified at the outset. Often this can be done over the telephone when the request for an appointment is made, and decisions about whom to see can be made at that time. The clinician may suggest that both partners rather than one come in, for example, or that the couple come in without the child or children.

Clarification of the clinician's role also can be effected with other professionals by providing information and clarification about appropriate referrals and helpful referral procedures when another professional person makes contact about giving their name to potential clients.

A concluding point here is that marital therapy may evolve out of any one of several initial types of referrals or requests for help. It also may arise out of therapy that starts off with another focus. Child therapy, family therapy, or individual therapy cases may after a period of time develop a request or manifest an obvious need for marital therapy.

COMPLAINTS AND PROBLEMS

Clients contact therapists with complaints, complaints that may not be identical with the problems that disturb the couple. Often clients do not know the sources or the precise nature of their difficulties and discontent when they first appear at the therapist's office. The vagueness of their difficulty, as well as their inability to alleviate their discomfort on their own, may be parts of their presenting complaint. What clients present does furnish them some motivation for contacting a clinician and an initial content focus for the interview. Exploration of the complaints may lead to the elucidation of other facets of what has been presented or to the discovery of more basic and important problems.

Systemically oriented marital/family therapists will be looking at the presenting complaints or symptoms in terms of the relationship system that they believe functions to maintain symptoms. Attention will be given to individual symptomatology but with the recognition that an individual's symptom is reflective of systemic dynamics. It is essential to regard a marital complaint as involving a total situation. As Russell and colleagues (Russell, Olson, Sprenkle, & Atilano, 1983) have pointed out, the systems perspective holds that change possibilities are greatly increased by involving the members of intimate relationship systems in plans for intervention. At the very least, following this principle implies that it is important to secure some common understanding among the therapist and the two marital partners about the things troubling the marital pair and thus engaging all three in a cooperative effort to effect change.

We use individual diagnoses because individuals are important and because such categories as relate to the individual are conventional in the general psychotherapy and mental health fields. This kind of diagnosis is used here with the understanding that they label only a part of the total complex of pertinent dynamics and difficulties. To classify a condition as an "anxiety reaction" or a person as "paranoid" may mean that we are labeling only a symptomatic part of larger and more pervasive family dynamics and transactions.

No taxonomy of marital problems exists. Efforts to classify marital problems over the years have been limited, so that what we have are some descriptions that fit some cases in some ways but not in others.

Individual difficulties may correlate with certain kinds of marital problems but not necessarily be related to them in a cause and effect (linear
or circular) manner. Nevertheless, it is still helpful to try to understand
the various classifications of marital relationships, normal and abnormal,
that are available, and to use their guidance in working with couples.

CLASSIFICATION OF MARITAL RELATIONSHIPS

Attempts to classify marital relationships have been organized into three
rough groupings by Fisher (1979). Some groupings are based on individual dynamics, others on conflict and power dimensions, and still others
on broad types of "normal" relationships in the marriage.

INDIVIDUAL DYNAMICS

Most of the early classificatory attempts were drawn from an assessment
of the individual dynamics of the two spouses. Complementarity, the
way the two sets of dynamics fit together, is generally a key emphasis in
such classificatory schemes. Some examples of this kind of classification
are discussed in the following paragraphs.

Mittelman (1944) described five complementary marital styles. The
patterns include one aggressive and dominating spouse and one passive
and submissive spouse; one emotionally detached partner and one emotionally needy spouse who seeks emotional support; two intensely com-
petitive mates, each of whom is afraid of losing the other; one extremely
considerate partner and one weak, helpless mate who becomes more needy
and depressed when the need for an omnipotent spouse is not fulfilled;
and partners who alternate in sequence of assertiveness and helplessness.

An extremely unequal relationship in which one spouse (the master)
encourages or requires the incompetence of the other (the doll) has been
described as the "doll's house marriage" (Pittman & Flomenhaft, 1970).
The doll, who is usually the wife, is subservient; the other spouse is
uncomfortable with any manifestation of competence on the part of the
doll.

Four pathological marriage patterns have been delineated by Martin
(1976). All have significant amounts of interlocking pathology. They are
the "lovesick" wife and "cold, sick" husband (hysterical wife and obsessional husband) marriage, an "In-Search-of-a-Mother" marriage (hysterical husband and obsessional wife), the "Double-Parasite" marriage (hys-

terical–hysterical or dependent–dependent), and the paranoid marriage (e.g., the *folie à deux*, paranoid, and conjugal paranoid patterns).

Three patterns described as "classic partner types" (Wile, 1981) essentially fit in the pathological category, being the clinical patterns of withdrawn partners, angry partners, and demanding–withdrawn partners. Spouses in the first pattern fear intimacy and try to avoid conflicts and controversial issues by chronic withdrawal. Explosive couple interaction is the hallmark of the second pattern, while the third involves a pursuer–distancer polarization. Problems in the third pattern include anger, self-criticism, and a sense of incompatibility.

Seven "behavioral profiles" or partner types have been described by Sager (1976). These consist of ways that marital partners have of relating to their mate. Such behavioral profiles are not fixed and rigid; most partners may manifest characteristics from different profiles or may move from one pattern to another within a given day. The determinants of the profiles are multicausal and cannot be precisely explained on the basis of present knowledge. These profiles, according to Sager (1976), are not necessarily how persons think they behave or what they think they want, but how they actually behave. Although the profiles require more research testing, he believes that they have considerable clinical value. Essentially, they provide a kind of heuristic schema for observing marital behaviors and transactions.

The following are the seven behavioral profiles or partner types:

1. *Equal partners.* This individual behaves as an equal partner in marital interaction and desires an equal relationship (whether or not the spouse has the same desire for equality).

2. *Romantic partner.* This person acts as if he or she is incomplete and requires a romantic partner in order to be whole.

3. *Parental partner.* This type involves a master (essentially an authoritarian and controlling parent stance carried to an extreme). The husband in Ibsen's *The Doll's House* is the prototype, and includes a rescuer subtype who typically establishes a temporary complementary relationship with a "save-me" type during a crisis.

4. *Childlike partner.* This is a profile of a person who wishes to be taken care of, but who actually may wield the power in the marital relationship. The counterpart of the parental profile, this person exhibits the "save-me" subtype mentioned above.

5. *Rational partner.* This type is strongly defended against admitting that emotions may affect her or his actions and tries to form a logical, orderly relationship with the spouse.

6. *Companionate partner.* The basic wish of this type is a partner with whom to share daily living. A person of this type exhibits behaviors that are aimed at escaping being alone. This type typically can tolerate closeness.

7. *Parallel partners.* Avoiding an intimate relationship is the goal of this type's behaviors. The partner is expected to accept the independence and emotional distance that such a marital relationship entails.

Sager describes a large number of partnership combinations that may be found, such as the equal-romantic, romantic–rational, partner–partner, childlike–childlike, and others.

CONFLICT AND POWER

Several different marital patterns can be grouped under the heading of conflict and power. Gehrke and Moxom (1962) focused on the marital relationship and did what they called "relationship counseling." Out of their work they outlined five patterns based on the content of marital conflict. Those patterns, as adapted, are: (1) gender role conflict in which the spouses tend to reverse (traditional) roles and to take somewhat ambivalent stances; (2) sadomasochistic conflict in which the male's negativism toward females is heaped on his submissive wife; (3) detached–demanding conflict between two dependent partners who demand parenting from a mate who will require nothing in return; (4) oral, dependent conflict between two dependent, basically helpless individuals whose oral needs are quite primitive and strong; and (5) neurotic illness conflict in which a husband who feels inadequate attempts to meet all needs of a helpless appearing wife with pervasive somatic complaints.

Lederer and Jackson (1968) defined marital power relationships as symmetrical (equal power), complementary (dominant–nondominant), and parallel (rule-based and varying between symmetrical and complementary). They further described four types of relationships based on the power dimension: (1) stable-satisfactory (explicit agreement about control of specific areas); (2) unstable-satisfactory (temporary, transition during time of change); (3) unstable-unsatisfactory (incompleted transactions and continued maneuvering for control); and (4) stable-unsatisfactory (a withdrawn, cold, pseudomutual front, with a concealment of instability). Each of the four types has two subtypes to which Lederer and Jackson gave catchy labels such as the Weary Wranglers and the Heavenly Twins. A key factor in this classification is an exchange of behavior between the partners that leads to a relatively workable relationship.

Stierlin (1981) has delineated two patterns that couples use in attempts to deal with conflict and relating. One is a centripetal pattern in which the moves are inward and the other centrifugal in which the focus is outward. Those patterns are particularly prevalent among middle-aged couples who are dealing with the separation of adolescent offspring from the family (Stierlin, 1981).

An example of a pathological centripetal couple is described as a marital pair who show indications of strain, fatigue, and irritation with each other, but deny to the clinician that there is any problem with the marriage, smile at each other, and use endearments. It eventually emerges that their sex life is nonexistent, but the absence is attributed to work pressures, worries over children, and bedtime migraine headaches. Such couples express only positive, harmonious, and loving feelings (Stierlin, 1981); the tendency is to "stick together."

Extreme centrifugal marriages typically end in separation or divorce. Some centrifugal couples remain together "for the sake of the children, who need us," but find their satisfactions outside the marriage. Careers and extramarital affairs rather than the spouse tend to claim their respective interests and emotional investments (Stierlin, 1981).

These patterns show up in general family functioning (as in the Beavers Systems Model: Beavers, 1977), as well as in parental handling of adolescents and in the marital interaction. Unlike some of the other classificatory approaches mentioned above, the centrifugal and centripetal patterns are held to be matters that require a multigenerational treatment approach. The clinician needs, in other words, to look toward altering the relationships and unresolved issues between the marital partners and their own parents (Stierlin, 1981).

"NORMAL" RELATIONSHIPS

Patterns of marital relationships also have been described from "normal" or nonclinical populations. Research with middle-class or upper-middle-class samples at different stages in the marital life cycle has provided information on patterns of marital forms or styles.

Ryder and his colleagues (Goodrich, Ryder, & Raush, 1968; Ryder, 1970a, 1970b) focused on the early marital period, finding four factors that discriminate for the early (first 4) months of the marital relationship: closeness to the husband's family, closeness to the wife's family, marital role orientation, and marital problems. These factors can be related to issues discussed in the marital life cycle (e.g., marital boundaries, intimacy, power).

Working with that sample of young couples, Ryder (1970b) discovered 21 patterns of marriage. He cautioned that it should not be assumed that other patterns could not be found or that those discovered would occur with any particular frequency. Nearly a third of the sample was not classified. Husbands could be differentiated on the basis of effectiveness ("potency") in the marriage and impulse control or restraint. Wives were classified on the basis of dependency versus counterdependency, positive versus negative orientation toward sexual activity, and marriage versus nonmarriage orientation.

A more precise typology has been offered by Cuber and Harroff (1966), who were primarily interested in sexual behavior and studied middle and upper-class couples that had been married 10 years or longer. The types that they noted were based on interviews with more than 200 men and women who had never considered separation or divorce. Those lasting nonclinical marriages showed five distinct patterns or life-styles.

The configurations are placed on a continuum from a conflict habituated style on one end to a totally integrated relationship on the other. The conflict habituated marriage is marked by omnipresent tension and conflict that are largely controlled rather than acted out by the partners. The devitalized marriage, falling in between the two extremes, is one in which the excitement of earlier years has not continued and has been replaced by middle-aged reality. The next marital style, the passive-congenial, is one in which the partners expect little from their marriage, seeming to make limited emotional investment in it. Togetherness and vital, real sharing characterize the vital marriage, in which the relationship provides much of the essential meaning of life for the partners. The last style, the total marriage, is similar to the vital but more inclusive; there is in this pattern a genuine sharing of everything. Cuber and Harroff found the total marriage to be rare and the vital a decided minority.

A NOTE ON MARITAL CLASSIFICATION

None of the approaches to classifying marriages made to this time is perfect. Those made by researchers have their values and their limitations. One of their strengths is that they give the observer a sense of perspective about marriages and sometimes call attention that might otherwise be overlooked. Classifications made by academicians sometimes seem abstract and oversimplified (Ryder, 1970a). Hence, they may apply to many couples to a limited degree but not fit a particular couple to the extent that they appear realistic and helpful for practical interventions. Ryder (1970b) has made an additional point: Beyond some given level, the more we know about a marital couple, the less adequately such classifications will apply, because we will discover elements that do not fit.

Clinical characterizations have the value of being useful for dealing with the particular couple that is being described. On the other hand, clinical descriptions may be too limited and may not allow for differences so that they can be applied to other couples (Ryder, 1970a).

IMPLICATIONS

All of this would seem to support the idea that therapy should be carefully tailored to the conditions and needs of the particular individuals and couples facing the therapist. General categories and classificatory schemes certainly have value for the therapist, since applying general therapeutic concepts and intervention patterns to couples may provide successful outcomes in some instances. Research and clinical findings cited earlier in this chapter indicate, for example, that some treatment modalities seem to work more effectively with given sets of conditions and syndromes than others.

The point remains that all therapy seems to be partly an art and not merely a technological endeavor. Therapists need to follow the lead implied by Ryder's statement about discovering discrepancies the more one learns about a couple. The major clinical implication in my judgment is that we need to keep both the general and the specific in mind and to make an assessment that aids us in determining what kinds of treatment will suit a particular couple with particular needs.

Conjoint Marital Therapy

Chapter Five

Assessment and Alliance

"This is _____. I got your name from _____. My ____ [wife or husband] and I are looking for some help with our marriage."

Fill in the blanks or even change the wording slightly and fill in the blanks and you have the typical opening lines for the first scene of Act One of marital therapy today.

THE FIRST INTERVIEW: THE TELEPHONE

The nature, politics, and technology of professional practice are such that marital therapy typically begins with a telephone call from a potential client to a therapist. Traditionally, professionals were not allowed to advertise or solicit clients. Recent actions by the Federal Trade Commission have made it possible for professionals in the United States to advertise, so that now telephone yellow pages, newspapers, radio, and television provide opportunities today for practitioners to offer their services to clients more directly. Nevertheless, professionals still do not use lists of prospects and call potential clients soliciting "business," but respond to requests for help and professional service initiated by potential users of their expertise.

(Not all cases that end up as marital therapy start with a request for marital help. As has been noted, some open with a complaint about a child-centered problem or as a request for family therapy. After some initial work around the situation manifested by the child's behaviors or distress or with the total family on other issues, the treatment may be restructured as marital therapy. For the sake of convenience and simplicity, this discussion is limited to instances in which direct requests are made only for marital assistance.

The initial contact starts a series of negotiations which are designed to test out the readiness of therapist and client systems for working together. Can adequate conditions of motivation and trust be established? Some of this exploration is explicit and some implicit: The therapist is asking internally and perhaps even aloud such questions as "Do they want to change?" "What do they think is involved, one visit or what?" The clients may be thinking, "What is this all about?" "What is this person all about?" "Do I wish to do this?" Both the therapist and the clients are grappling with trusting the other.

Whether the telephone contact is a pretreatment stage or the beginning of therapy is a matter of some debate among clinicians. Regardless of how it is labeled, the initial telephone contact between prospective client and therapist is exceedingly important. Although it is not always possible in some institutional and agency settings for the initial negotiations to be handled directly between the help seeker and the help provider, such a pattern is highly desirable in my opinion and is assumed in this section. It is in many respects the first interview, leading either toward a structured therapeutic situation or perhaps to a referral or a decision not to pursue treatment.

Briefly, if it takes the first course, things typically proceed as follows: Once the amenities have been dispensed with, essential questions answered on both sides of the transaction, and details of scheduling an appointment adequately settled, therapist and clients are ready to get together for a face-to-face meeting.

The face-to-face interview that I schedule is—to paraphrase and adapt from Sullivan (1954)—the initiation of a relationship of primarily vocal communication in a triadic group that is more or less voluntarily brought together, on a continuously unfolding expert–client basis, for the purpose of elucidating characteristic patterns of interaction that produce difficulties or satisfaction for the clients and of securing some benefit for them as a result of that elucidation and their work with the expert professional. To put things in more simple terms, in the typical expert–client relationship, the clients go to the expert with certain expectations that the professional will provide assistance from her or his knowledge and skill to the troubled marital couple.

The relationship that is established is consequently primarily an unbalanced one. Clients seek the help of a clinician who is expected to be able to help them deal with their problems. Ideally, clients bring their problems and desire for help, while the therapist comes with his or her expertise and commitment to the therapeutic task of helping them. In actuality, things do not always proceed so straightforwardly or simply.

Potential clients do not always approach the clinician with a unified set of expectations and pristine motivations. At the very least, they may have a considerable amount of confusion and ambivalence about what they are seeking.

The first interview conducted by the clinician thus generally takes place over the telephone and involves only one of the marital partners. From this contact both therapist and prospective client begin to form the impressions that determine the subsequent course of their dealings. It is a screening and filtering process.

Hence, the initial telephone interview is an occasion for clarification and qualification. Each party to the transaction wishes to know certain things about the other. The caller who is seriously seeking help generally wishes to learn something about the kind of human being that he or she has contacted. Human qualities as well as technical expertise are important. Is the professional approachable enough, strong enough, wise enough, experienced enough, kind enough to deal with us? These and related questions come through directly or can be inferred from what is said and how the caller says it. Perhaps the therapist has been highly recommended by another professional person or lavishly praised by a friend. The question remains in the mind of the caller, however, "But is this the person for me, for us?" The "bottom line" issue often appears to be whether the clinician is someone to whom the caller and their spouse feel that they can relate comfortably and confidently.

The first 4 minutes of face-to-face contact between clinician and client have been characterized as being exceedingly important for the course of subsequent interaction (Zunin & Zunin, 1972). Certainly, it seems that the impressions gained in the telephone interview determine the posture with which some clients subsequently enter a face-to-face interview. Strong impressions often are formed during the telephone contact. It is not uncommon for callers to decide that they wish to see someone else as a result of a turn-off" by the handling of their initial telephone call. The response to their initial call may have been made by a therapist, or by a secretary or receptionist. Similarly, clients sometimes report that they felt from the manner in which their request was handled that the clinician was caring enough or kind enough to be trusted and to be helpful.

The telephone interview is significant enough to warrant careful attention. I consider it essential to try to talk with prospective clients when both of us are free to talk. Arranging a callback at a time when the person can talk in privacy is preferable, for example, to attempting to deal with them when they are in the midst of a busy work or family situation. I wish to be in a position to listen to them and respond sensitively and sensibly to their request.

There are things that the clinician wishes to establish at the onset of contact. I wish to know whether they are looking in the right place and are making suitable requests. Does it seem appropriate for me to see them or to suggest other possibilities, including referral to another resource? If they have not spelled out their reasons for calling other than a general statement that they wish to make an appointment, it is helpful very early to ask, "Can you tell me something about the situation?"

As the complaints and issues are briefly described over the telephone, one attempts to listen carefully for tones of voice, attitudes, realistic and unrealistic expectations, and other clues as to the nature of the difficulties. How are the problems perceived, and what efforts have been made to deal with them?

If the information is not volunteered, it is appropriate to ask about contact with other professionals. "Have you or your [spouse] had any professional help?" This is a deliberately broad and vague query. If they ask what is meant, one can respond "individual, marital, family therapy, any kind of therapeutic assistance?" Attitudes toward previous therapy or attempts to secure help can be quite revealing about current expectations. Some understanding of the potential clients' other therapeutic endeavors may be essential to making a decision about whether to schedule an initial appointment with them. If one learns about other therapy during the first appointment, this information becomes part of determining whether to continue working with the couple. If clients simply mention that there has been contact with other professionals, it may be appropriate to ask, "Who did you see, if I may ask?" or to say something like "You are seeing someone individually now? Who is that, if I may ask?" An awareness and comprehension of the orientation and general approach of other therapists can provide a basis for understanding the clients' attitudes toward their contact with those professionals. Also, it is generally helpful in the first appointment to explore what the client(s) attempted to deal with in the other therapy and what they accomplished.

Careful examination of what may have transpired in previous therapeutic contacts can clear the path for a productive clinical endeavor. Clarifying feedback by the clinician, such as the following, may be helpful: "In other words, you feel pretty good about what you accomplished with _____, but don't feel that he or she would be right for you now." Or "From what you are telling me, and from what I understand of the professional person that you saw, it would seem that he was operating from an orientation that emphasizes individual psychotherapy. If so, what he did would make sense to him [e.g., refusing to see one of the partners] and would not be intended as a slight to you. I do understand that was not what you were looking for when you went to him for marital help."

One does not help the situation by getting into struggles with callers or clients over the accuracy of the ideas that they hold about therapy or therapists. It is sensible, however, to be knowledgeable about the bases for their ideas whenever possible. Clearing up misperceptions or sympathizing appropriately with clients about their previous abortive or unproductive attempts to get assistance can be healing as well as facilitative of their present efforts to launch a successful treatment effort.

Whether to schedule an appointment with persons who are in either individual or group treatment elsewhere is a knotty question. Some therapists simply decide as a matter of policy not to do so. Ongoing, long-term individual psychotherapy for one or both partners with other therapists certainly makes it difficult to conduct worthwhile marital therapy, but I tend to deal with each case on an individual basis. If an appointment is scheduled with persons who are in some kind of ongoing therapeutic relationship, the question of multiple therapists and multiple therapies gets straightforward exploration in the first face-to-face interview, particularly since reaching a firm understanding regarding expectations at this stage is exceedingly important. Among the points that I seek to make clear is that while I shall respect the individual therapy already in progress, there will be no sacrosant areas that "belong to" the individual therapy and cannot therefore be addressed in marital therapy.

Discerning attitudes on the part of both spouses about coming to therapy is another major concern of the clinician at the telephone stage. It generally seems to be worthwhile to ask, "Your [spouse] is willing to come in?" even if that has already been stated or implied. More information typically is forthcoming as a result of such a statement-query. If the caller has voluntarily emphasized that the spouse is willing and eager to come in, it may still be useful on occasion to say, "You've indicated rather strongly that your [spouse] wants to come in, but how do *you* feel about it?"

How the initial face-to-face appointment is to be structured is sometimes explained during the telephone contact. It is always important to let the potential client know that both spouses are expected to be present. Frequently, it is sensible to say something to the effect that assessment and some decision making are to occur—for example, "We'll take a look at the situation together and decide where we go from there."

If there are discernible questions or resistances on the part of the caller or the spouse, some attention may need to be given to dealing with them before attempts are made to schedule a face-to-face meeting: "Would you ask your [spouse] to call me if there are any questions? I would be glad to talk with [her or him]." On some occasions it may be appropriate to offer to call a frightened or otherwise reluctant spouse to clarify the nature and procedures of the proposed therapeutic endeavor. One does not wish, of course, to become the tool of a manipulative caller who is attempting to leverage the spouse into treatment through enlisting the professional as an ally. In all instances, it remains the prerogative of the reluctant spouse to decide whether he or she wishes to enter therapy.

Questions by the caller should not be facilely interpreted as resistance to therapy. Typically, it has been the wife who has called for an appointment and who has had more complaints, because women have tended to be more attuned to relationships and to be in the less powerful position in the marriage in relation to their husbands (Bernard, 1972; Goldner, 1985).

Clients as well as clinicians need to find out whether a workable therapeutic relationship can be established. Part of the qualifying of the clinician by the caller may consist of efforts to ascertain the kind of therapeutic approach taken by the therapist: "Do you do the kind of therapy that [whoever] does?" is not an uncommon question. The best response often is, "What are you looking for? What are you asking?" A question such as "Do you work like Dr. _____?" may reflect the caller's positive or negative feelings toward the kind of approach that he or she perceives the other clinician to take. Sometimes the perceptions are positive and based on some kind of media exposure to the work or orientation of the other professional, but just as often the question is an expression of dissatisfaction with previous treatment. A bit of probing may bring the response, "We saw him for a couple of months [or longer] and nothing happened. He just sat and listened and never said anything. He told us nothing." A return question may be in order. "Are you asking me whether I am active or not?" "Well, yeah. I don't want to go through that kind of experience again. It was a waste of time." A brief, accurate statement about how one reacts to and generally works with clients is appropriate in such situations.

CLINICAL ASSESSMENT AND INTERVENTION

The expectation that the professional will provide help establishes the parameters for what follows in the face-to-face interviews. To the extent that the professional agrees to help, a tentative "contract" is established. A major part of the contract calls for the therapist to make an assessment of the situation provided by the new clients and to do something about the problems that they present. Sometimes the priorities of the clients— who may desire immediate help—and the clinician—who may wish to go more slowly—are at opposite ends of the line.

Assessment and alliance formation are activities to be conducted simultaneously from the outset of the initial conjoint session. The therapist is concerned with assessing the couple's needs, including distinguishing between complaints and problems, and establishing a working alliance with them. The initial assessment includes evaluating both the marital subsystem (a relationship-interaction assessment) and the individuals (IP: an assessment of the Identified Patient(s), an individual "symptomatic" assessment), as well as assessing the spouses' motivations for therapy and change and the permanence of the relationship. Assessment and alliance maintenance also are ongoing aspects of therapy.

Face-to-face contact initiates a twofold process: An assessment/intervention process and a relating process go on simultaneously. The assessment features are, of course, undertaken for the purposes of ascertaining need and determining appropriate means of responding to the need; relating has to do with forming an alliance with the couple in order to work effectively and productively with them.

Assessment and intervention are thus inseparable in my approach to marital therapy. While making an assessment and drawing conclusions from the couple's descriptions and presentations of their problems and situations, the clinician makes the interventions he or she feels are appropriate. Some of these may be aimed at testing the hypotheses that the clinician has formed, while others may be intended to affect changes in the persons and in their marital system and interaction. Then the clinician responds to their responses with more assessment and consequent interventions. Repetitively, this process continues.

Clinical assessment is a recursive, repetitive process by which the clinician secures adequate understanding of clients for the purpose of making informed decisions and interventions. It also involves making diagnostic determinations so that clients can be categorized in terms of standard nosological categories (e.g., DSM-III categories for individuals when appropriate), but it is broader than such classifications. Diagnosis itself implies classification, coming as it does from a Greek word meaning "knowing between" or "determining between."

I am not concerned here with describing individual diagnostic work, assuming that the reader is acquainted with individual assessment or diagnostic procedures. The emphasis is on how the difficulties of the individual and the marital problems are related and also on how the strengths of the two systems are related.

There is no set of diagnostic categories for marital reactions comparable to those for individuals. There is no marital disease entity that can be described relatively succinctly, as the mental health field has struggled to produce for individual difficulties and disorders. Although no generally accepted taxonomy of marital relationships and problems has been established, all of those attempted may have some heuristic and pragmatic value for the clinician. Few of those described correlate with particular patterns of individual pathology, conversely, several kinds of individual symptomatology do point to marital discord or family disruption. Put another way, different kinds of individual symptomatology may signal marital discord, but not specify types of marital difficulty. There are several different behavioral-symptomatic ways in which one can react to marital/family system discord. A systemic approach allows the clinician to note that marital/family difficulties can show up in terms of individual problems and symptomatology. Individual symptomatology can contribute to systemic difficulties, but from a systemic point of view the individual's problems were not formed in isolation, from inside the individual, but from transactions in the developmental context. As has been repeatedly emphasized, this includes the family as a central part of the context.

Broadly speaking, I am concerned with assessing several dimensions of the marital relationship as they exist at the time the partners request help. Using a framework modeled after Berman and Lief's (1975) schema, I attempt to discover the boundaries of the marital relationship, the power dimension, and the intimacy/closeness dimension (Nichols & Everett, 1986). The boundaries pertain to what and who is included in the marriage. In brief, what and who are included in the client system with which I shall attempt to work? This question also deals with three interrelated factors besides inclusion: extrusion (What's being extruded from the marriage and assigned to the children or others?), intrusion (Who, what, what events or things are intruding into the marital relationship and in what ways?), and power (How do the partners deal with power in their relationship?). How do the partners tolerate or respond to the needs and desires of each other for closeness and intimate contact and relating? I have a particular interest at the point of the initial assessment in learning how the various dimensions have changed over time and how the alterations have affected the marital balance and interaction.

At the time of initial assessment and subsequently, I attempt to form an opinion as to how the partners are faring with respect to their commitment, caring, communication, and conflict/compromise abilities, as well as in their volunteering behavior. These heuristic guidelines are made operational as follows: commitment—the degree and kind of attachment and intention to stay involved with the spouse and/or the marriage; caring—the amount of kind of love, cherishing, and similar tender feelings that a mate has toward the marital partner; communication—the kind, quality, and range of communication that prevails between the spouses; conflict/compromise—the ability of the partners to acknowledge differences and to deal with them, including working out compromises in order to keep the marital relationship functional. Volunteering—an addition to the four "Cs" mentioned in Chapter 2—consists of behaviors offered by one partner on behalf of the other without the expectation of immediate reward or benefit. These concepts can be used both by the clinician and the clients as a kind of "rule of thumb" measure of the health or functionality of the marriage and marital relationship.

A significant question for me with regard to the caring of the partners is whether they are able to deal with each other on a mutual, reciprocal basis. Do they value the partner primarily as "a service station," as someone who can gratify their wishes or needs? Are they, in object-relations terms, functioning essentially at a need-gratification level, or are they operating at the level of object love or object constancy? Do they, in other words, value the spouse for herself or himself, rather than in terms of the needs that are being fulfilled at a given time (Nichols & Everett, 1986)?

One of the more pressing practical tasks for the clinician is determining the commitment of the mates to each other. Again, in pragmatic terms, it is helpful to describe clients as being preambivalent, ambivalent, or postambivalent in their commitment. Preambivalent persons have not seriously considered ending the marriage, while ambivalent persons regard the mate and the marriage with mixed feelings. Postambivalent-positive individuals have seriously struggled with whether or not to remain in the marriage and have decided to stay; postambivalent-negative persons have decided to get out of the marriage, although they may or may not have conveyed that decision to their spouse. Some common patterns presented to the clinician are both spouses preambivalent or both ambivalent, one ambivalent and the other preambivalent, and one ambivalent and the other postambivalent. Each of these patterns has implications for the clients' individual and joint commitment to therapy and for the therapist's work with the client system (Nichols & Everett, 1986). As noted earlier, what one faces in working with married persons is strongly affected by the voluntary nature of the marital tie.

Another way of broadly describing the content portion of assessment—that is, the information sought during the process—is as follows: how the partners are attached (in object relations terms and in terms of how committed to the marriage and the partner); individual symptomatology if any; relationship problems (e.g., role, expectations, communication, commitment); and the strengths of the individuals and of the marriage (general family strength, marital relationship skills, resources, general relationship satisfaction).

PROCEDURES

Procedures for performing marital assessment are limited in number and type: Verbal reports, observations of interaction, and standardized testing are all possibilities. This discussion will be focused primarily on both clients' self-reports and the therapist's observation of client interaction in particular since self-reports may be different when the partners are seen together than when they are interviewed separately.

Self-report and Therapist Observation

The partners typically are seen together, asked some questions, and given the opportunity to "tell their story" and react to the interventions of the clinician. The therapist observes the partners in interaction both with each other and in relation to herself or himself in the therapeutic situation. Information and impressions gained by the clinician are evaluated in terms of both the diagnostic categories that are used and the ecological/contextual information on the couple.

Assessment is thus concerned with the characteristics and behavior of each individual in the couple, with the characteristics and behaviors of the partners as an interactive unit (the marital dyad) and with the larger family contexts of both spouses. These family contexts consist not only of the settings out of which the partners developed but also of the current relationships and dynamics of their involvements with their respective families of origin. The material is integrated into as complete a mosaic as possible.

Both the words and nonverbal behaviors of the clients and the therapist's own reactions are an important part of the assessment procedures. To use a concept popularized in the therapeutic world by Sullivan (1954), the clinician is a participant observer. To me, this means that one uses both the "right brain" and the "left brain" capabilities; both intuition and rational cognitive operations are important instrumentalities for use in assessment.

What are the clinician's emotional and physical reactions to what is encountered in the interview situation? Feelings of anxiety, anger, puzzlement, general uneasiness, strangeness, or depersonalization, as well as muscular tension, rate of speech, and other reactions on the part of the clinician are useful guides in the assessment and diagnostic procedures. Additionally, what kinds of fantasies occur in response to the clients? What kinds of associations float up into awareness for the clinician?

Some of the therapist's emotional and physical reactions to what is encountered in the interview situation can be apprehended immediately and used as the basis for therapeutic interventions. Others may come into clearer focus subsequent to the session with the clients. Although the postsession evaluation and processing of reactions may be significant for the clinician to undertake after all contacts with clients, such retrospective work appears to be vitally important during the initial assessment/diagnostic stage. Careful attention to personal reactions and judicious "use of the self" at this stage can provide much helpful guidance in getting beyond the clients' complaints to a comprehension of their problems. Failure to heed such clues can lead to a premature closing off or ignoring of possibilities.

Interventions based on the therapist's use of self can be potent activators of further revelations by the marital partners. Appropriate revelations of the clinician's self-affective reactions that expose something of one's attitudes and nature often permit the clients to respond in kind, affectively revealing important things about themselves and their relationship. This may take the form of a statement such as "I can't help feeling a sense of sadness as you talk about the loss of _____." One may respond to a rather bland description of events with the reaction, "I think that would make me feel angry; it certainly would be understandable if it got you upset."

Standardized Testing

A large number of tests have been used by professional persons in attempts to assess marital interaction. Phillips (1973) described both paper-and-pencil tests (e.g., true–false, sentence completion) and others (e.g., Marital Roles Inventory) as being typically used with marital cases. Cromwell and associates (Cromwell, Olson, & Fournier, 1976) indicated that there are four major ways of assessing marital difficulties: one category is concerned primarily with assessing individual personality and affect; another involves assessing group structure with particular emphasis on examining discrepancies in role perceptions; the third consists of assessment of communicational interaction; and the fourth pertains to observation of the couple as they work on an analogue task.

Among the strongest claims made for predictive values in a test are those of Ravich (Ravich & Wyden, 1974) for the Ravich Interpersonal Game/Test, generally called "the train game." The game/test involves a pair of toy electric trains, track, a pair of switches, a barrier, and a computer. It takes approximately an hour to play. Ravich claims that the way the pair plays the game indicates exactly what goes on between them, how they solve conflicts, compete, cooperate, make decisions, submit, dominate, isolate themselves, or split apart. He further asserts that a computer printout available 15 minutes after the game is over will reveal as much as a therapist could discover in 6 to 12 months of treatment.

Most of the tests used with marital cases in fact appear to be of limited value to the clinician. Validity, reliability, and predictive strengths all seem to be restricted. The stronger tests available for assessment are those intended for individual personality assessment, though attempting to use individual tests in an effort to learn what the marriage and marital interaction are like certainly has drawbacks and deficits. The use of certain standardized observational situations has interest for the researcher, but generally does not offer the clinician the same things that would appear in less artificial settings and situations. Ravich's train game may have all of the strengths that he claims, but it has not been adopted in the field of marital therapy.

OTHER SOURCES OF INFORMATION

A considerable amount of information can be obtained from clients before they are seen by the clinician. Figure 2 illustrates one means of securing information. The Background Information Form (devised by the author and Gertrude Zemon-Gass from other forms) can be sent to clients by mail following the initial telephone contact and returned prior to the first appointment or brought to the meeting. Alternatively, clients can be requested to come in 10 to 15 minutes prior to the scheduled appointment in order to complete the form at that time. The clinician can examine the forms prior to the session or take a brief look at them during the interview and read them more carefully afterwards. Most of the information requested on the form is self-explanatory and does not require explication here. Careful attention to how the forms are completed often gives clues to important dynamics, including conflicts in the couple's relationship. Failure to complete parts or differences in how the partners respond may be indicative of possible conflict or concern: When the woman lists her husband's occupation as "manufacturer's representative" and he lists it as "executive," there is obviously a discrepancy in perception of his occupational position. Is she denigrating his position or is he exaggerating? (He was in reality the president of his own two-person company; conflicts over his occupational role were a major part of the couple's discord.) When a man records the "Date Married" as 12/31 of the present year instead of the appropriate year, it alerts the clinician to possible issues around getting married. (Here a couple of questions elicited the information that the couple had married on 12/31, some 14 years earlier as the wife's form indicated. She had been 3 months pregnant and 12/31 had been chosen because if they [overcame their ambivalence and] married before the end of that year they could get a joint tax deduction.)

The form also provides information that will enable the clinician to sketch quickly a preliminary genogram for each person. Questions may need to be asked about miscarriages, still-borns, matters such as relatives or others who were part of the family-of-origin household, and the parents' present role in the clients' lives. The form has been altered over the past 20 years in order to keep abreast of changes in marriage, divorce, remarriage, and the resulting marriage and family patterns showing up in clinical practice. Clients still may fail to list one of their three or four marriages on occasion, but such information can be obtained through questioning.

GOALS OF THE ASSESSMENT

What is the clinician looking for in the initial assessment phase? This question can be responded to in a variety of ways. Probably no two therapists would respond in exactly the same way. What follows, therefore, is an illustrative rather than an exhaustive treatment of the question.

Discerning the problems that accompany or underlie the complaints made by the distressed spouses is a major goal. For example, the wife may complain that her husband never pays attention to her, gives her no time. Probing may lead to the discovery that the couples' communication is poor and ineffective, that they have lost the ability to share satisfac-

**BACKGROUND INFORMATION
FORM**

Date _____

Name _____ Home Telephone _____

Home Address _____
(CITY AND ZIP CODE)

Business Address _____ Business Telephone _____

Height _____ Weight _____ Date and Place of Birth _____

Education _____

Occupation _____ Annual Income _____

Religious Affiliation _____ Childhood Religious Affiliation _____

Military Service (Date and Branch) _____

Name of Person Who Referred You _____

Previous Counseling or Psychotherapy (Dates and Names of Therapists)

_____

_____

_____

MEDICAL

Name of Physician _____ Last Medical Examination _____

What Medical Problems or Illness Do You Have? _____

_____

What Medication Are You Taking? _____

MARITAL

Mate's Age _____ Education _____ Religion _____

Mate's Occupation _____ Date Married _____

Children _____ Name _____ Sex _____ Age _____

_____ Sex _____ Age _____

_____ Sex _____ Age _____

_____ Sex _____ Age _____

_____ Sex _____ Age _____

-over-

FIGURE 2
Background Information Form.

Have There Been Previous Marriages? If So, Was Marriage Ended by Death or Divorce?_____

Were There Children by Previous Marriages? _____ Number_____ Sex_____ Age_____

PARENTS AND SIBLINGS

Brothers and Sisters (Include Any Deceased)

Age	Sex	Education	Marital Status	Occupation

Father   Birthplace_____   Education_____

Occupation_____   Religion _____

Present Age_____   If Deceased, When_____

Mother   Birthplace_____   Education_____

Occupation _____   Religion _____

Present Age _____   If Deceased, When_____

Was Either Parent Married More Than Once? Please Give Details_____

_____

_____

_____

FIGURE 2
(continued)

tions, and that they have developed at different rates and along different paths, so that as a result they are virtual strangers. Their individual expectations of the marriage and of the partner may be in significant conflict.

What are the psychological or psychiatric symptoms displayed by one or both partners? What are the sources and sustaining factors in the maintenance of their symptomatology? What are their strengths as well as their pathologies?

The clinician also wishes to discover the nature of the marital interaction and relationship. What kind of intimacy (caring/closeness) exists between the spouses? What kind of unity or commitment prevails between them? How have the interaction, the intimacy, the power relation, and the commitment and sense of unity changed over the course of the relationship? The nature and strength of the attachment is, in my judgment, the major factor to be assessed with the couple, being as it is at the core of understanding the couple and working therapeutically with them.

What is the history of the problem(s) and of the relationship itself? The approach taken here is one in which the clinician secures "enough" of the history of the problem and relationship to have a working sense of what has transpired and what it means. Additional details can be filled in later, as needed. History of the individual as individual is considered secondary during the initial assessment phase, except in the case of physical illness, substance abuse, or dangerousness (threat to self or others).

A quarter century ago Fry (1962) wrote about the marital context of an anxiety syndrome. That was one of the early conceptualizations of an "individual" symptom occurring in the setting of a marital relationship. Historically, psychodynamically oriented psychotherapists have viewed "individual" psychopathology as contributing to marital disturbances. Bergler's (1948) book, entitled *Divorce Won't Help*, in which he argued that unconscious individual conflicts led to a repetitive selection of inappropriate mates and continuation of the same kind of stereotyped conflicts, was one of the more extreme examples of the latter orientation. The point here is that the reverse is true, that marital difficulties often lead to individual symptoms.

One of the major tasks the clinician has with many marital cases is that of "deindividualizing" and "systematizing" the situation. This involves a form of recasting or reframing the clients' perceptions of what the difficulties are and how they can be changed. It may be necessary for the clinician to take a stand at the outset that balances off perceptions of individual pain and symptomatology with relationship involvement and responsibility. "Your individual problems certainly are a part of the marital difficulty as I understand things, but they don't necessarily cause it. At the same time, the marital problems have contributed to your individual difficulties and pain. The best way in my judgment to deal with both your individual pain and the marital problems is through working with your relationship."

Readiness for treatment is another major issue that the therapist needs to address during the initial face-to-face interview. Assessment of this factor actually starts with the opening telephone call, as noted above.

THE FIRST FACE-TO-FACE INTERVIEW

"Well, I know a little bit about you from our telephone conversation, but I think that I'll proceed as if I didn't and simply ask the pertinent questions. One, what brings you here, and what brings you in at this time instead of some other time, such as 6 months ago or perhaps 6 months from now? Second, what are you looking for? What do you want from me?"

These are typical opening statements and questions of the first face-to-face session with a marital couple. They come after initial pleasantries, perhaps some humor, and social chatter. How are the questions answered? Who responds? A long list of questions are in the mind of the clinician. The items on this internal "checklist" guide one's observations and interpretations of those observations.

The process of observation has gone on "live" at least from the point that the therapist walked into the reception area or waiting room and first saw the partners. Clues as to how things are going with them may be obtained from how they are sitting (e.g., apart, together); how they are dealing with each other (e.g., talking, reading magazines, ignoring each other); and from what is manifested in their body postures (e.g., tension, fear, depression, hostility). How do they respond to greetings? How do they seat themselves in the office or interviewing room? When social chatter and pleasantries are offered by the therapist, how do they respond? Are they glib, smooth, semihysterical, glum, reserved?

Returning to the matter of their responses to the therapist's opening questions, what is the nature of their "opening statement"? My questions as to why they are there and what they are looking for are directed right down the middle of the space between the two partners. Their opening statement is both verbal and interactive. What they say verbally and how they say it behaviorally are both important.

I try to listen to the couple's opening statement and observe them long enough to get a provisionary comprehension of how they interact, the nature of their significant dynamics, and their motivations for being at the interview. Simultaneously, I try to get a rudimentary grasp of the major presenting complaints and problems. While undertaking those cognitive-affective tasks, I am at the same time trying to develop a working relationship or therapeutic alliance with the couple system.

As the partners set forth their opening statement, one may let the process unfold without significant interference for anywhere from a few minutes to 20 or 30 minutes. If it is flowing so that I can learn what troubles them and where they are in their efforts to deal with their difficulties, my interruptions may consist primarily of facilitative questions.

If there is little movement, it becomes necessary to probe, guide, and encourage the opening up of complaints and problem statements by the partners.

The immediate goal is, of course, to get as clear an understanding as possible of the problems facing the couple. Once this has been accomplished or the process has become unproductive or too painful for the partners, it is time to make a change.

"I'd like to shift gears right now. Take me back to the beginning of your relationship. How did you meet? As best you know, what attracted you to the other person? How did your dating go? How did you decide to get married? How did things go when you were first married? How have things changed over the years?"

These or similar questions form a kind of "structured projective test." How the partners respond is, once again, helpful: Which questions they select as a basis for response, what they say about what attracted them to their future spouse? The reasons may appear profound or trite, the understanding serious or superficial. Answers to object-relations issues may be found as well in the responses of the partners: As they talk about their relationship and interaction, one picks up feeling tones and indications as to how they are attached and what they mean to one another.

Frequently, the clients begin to soften and relax somewhat as they move from current unhappiness to contemplation of days when things were different in their relationship. As this occurs it is sometimes helpful to reflect what is being seen: "Things weren't always as they are now. Where did they get off track, as best you can tell?" Such a move often introduces an element of balance and, occasionally, a ray of hope into the conflicted situation.

Sometimes it emerges that things were bad from the beginning. The clinician's task is to make a rapid assessment of what has happened. Were the partners in fact badly matched from the outset? Have they continued to be held together in a collusive arrangement in which their unhealthy needs furnish the glue? Were there misunderstandings in the "contract" between them that have inadvertently multiplied into difficulties down through the years? Are they in psychological corners that each of them would like to get out of if they could? Or are they strongly planted in positions that they feel they can alter only at the risk of serious damage to themselves?

Whatever the responses and stances of the partners, the role of the therapist at that point, in my judgment, is to make a clarifying statement, providing feedback to the clients on what they have revealed. If honesty is to prevail and clarity is to be obtained for the benefit of the partners, the therapist has to be straightforward in laying out what has been revealed in the disclosures by the marital dyad.

Clarifying statements can be made with firmness and with kindness at the same time. "Things have been difficult for you from the beginning." "It sounds like things went along reasonably well for you until _____." "It was hard during the first 4 or 5 years but you were able to work together and to cope with several painful situations rather well. Somehow, after your second child was born and you were transferred to Pittsburgh, things began to go sour. Is that how you remember it?"

Even at this stage of contact with the clients one not only begins to offer feedback but also tries to elicit commitment to a therapeutic process from them. This includes securing from the clients recognition and acknowledgement of the validity of what has transpired in their lives together. The therapist may need to be "naive" or reasonably provocative in order to help the clients recognize and acknowledge both for themselves and with the therapist what has occurred and how they feel about it—that is, to help them to clarify the situation for all parties.

An obstensibly naive or "help me out" approach often is helpful in getting clients to clarify where they are and to take a stand. "I'm not sure what you mean—would you help me understand?" "How do you mean?" "Do you mean _____?" Any one of a number of questions that call upon the clients to inform and correct the therapist and his or her perceptions may be useful.

Questions and probes may also be used in order to fill in missing information or to guide the flow of the interview. If the clients are supplying the desired information it may not be necessary to ask probing questions or to provide more than a minimal amount of structure. Some of the areas to be filled in depend on what has been raised in the presenting complaints and problems. If the complaints center around sexual problems, it would be more important to secure some sexual history in the interview than would be the case if there were no sexual complaints. Experienced marital therapists learn that it is not necessary to elicit large amounts of information routinely in order to do an adequate assessment, though for the relatively inexperienced it may be wise to use an approach that covers a wide range of possible problem areas.

If there has been no mention of extramarital involvement it is often worthwhile to inquire about that possibility. The straightforward query, "Has there been any extramarital involvement?" sometimes opens up one of the core problems that has not been spoken of up to that point. The question is purposely cast in broad and ambiguous terms. To ask if there have been any affairs sometimes causes couples to dismiss the question because they do not regard extramarital relationships that were brief or did not involve coital activity as "affairs."

A rather wide range of responses to the extramarital question may be forthcoming. "Well, yes. . . ." "Not on my part, I don't know about [spouse]." "No." Sometimes the spouses will look at one another and make a decision without words to tell the therapist about something that they had previously agreed not to disclose. "Uh, we had decided not to tell you anything about it because ["It's over." "We didn't think it had anything to do with our problems."], but, yes, . . ."

Careful attention to the body postures and nonverbal cues furnished by the clients when the question is asked often alerts the clinician to the probability of concealment. The verbal response may be negative, but the other behavioral reactions may not be congruent with that reply. When this is the case, often one of the clients will later telephone the therapist or bring out in a session the fact that there has in fact been extramarital involvement.

A final broadly based "fishnet" question by the therapist may elicit important information: "Before we stop, is there anything else that we haven't talked about that would be helpful to me in understanding you and your situation?" Here, again, it is important to attend to nonverbal cues as well as to what the clients say. As with the extramarital question, individual or couple secrets withheld earlier in the session may be forthcoming. Similarly, the postures and expressions of one or both partners may "telegraph" the fact that something is being withheld. This may be any one of several "secrets," including particularly information about a premarital pregnancy, an affair, incest, family violence, or some other matter that they individually or jointly were reluctant to mention.

RECOMMENDATIONS/NEXT STEPS

By the end of the first face-to-face session between therapist and clients, we both need to be in a position to decide where we are going with the therapeutic endeavor. Do we wish to continue? If so, what is the next step? Two things primarily determine the manner in which such decisions are made: (1) the nature of the problems presented and their appropriateness for marital therapy and (2) the motivations and readiness of the clients for therapy. "Are the difficulties such that I can help them with outpatient marital therapy?" "Do they wish to work with me?"

There are other questions for the therapist. Do I have a sound understanding not only of the complaints but also of the problems represented by the complaints? What is missing? How can that information and comprehension be obtained? If I do not have an adequate picture, I probably will say so to the clients. For example, I may say something along the life of, "We have reached the end of our time" (if it has not been possible to schedule on an open-ended basis with them), or "We have gone a long time and some things are not clear to me, so if possible, I would like to take another session with you in order to explore them before talking about where we go from here. How do you feel about that?"

More often, one gains enough of the picture to try to bring more closure within the first face-to-face session. At such times some feedback is in order. "You have sketched a situation to me as follows: _____. If I have understood you, that is the picture that you are presenting. Am I understanding you? If I am distorting any parts of it or leaving out anything important, please, correct me."

Following such correction or agreement by the clients that the picture described is essentially what they have presented, I typically present alternatives about proceeding. "There are several ways that we can go from here. You can stop and basically do nothing about the situation. You can see somebody else. We can schedule appointments and begin working on the things that trouble you. You can make a decision now if you are ready to do that. Or would you like to pull back, think about and discuss your reactions to this meeting, and then decide what you would like to do? What makes the most sense to you?"

There are a variety of ways to deal with ending the first face-to-face session and deciding how to proceed from that juncture. The particular course taken depends on the actions and statements of the clients, as interpreted by the therapist.

The therapist can take a traditional expert role. This results in setting forth a plan for the clients to follow. They can, of course, either accept or reject the plan. This could take any of several forms, such as the following: "I would recommend that you commit yourselves to working as hard as you can on solving the problems that we have looked at today for a minimum of eight sessions, and then we will examine things and decide whether or not to renew the contact." "Here is what I want you to do" [The clients are presented with a homework assignment or some kind of directive or plan devised by the therapist.]

Sometimes it may be worthwhile for an experienced therapist to predict for the clients what may be forthcoming if they enter treatment. The therapist may point out to them, for example, that dealing with some of the painful issues that they have presented will lead to some difficult times. "You have indicated that you have some stored up hurt and angry feelings. I think that it is predictable that opening them up and trying to get them resolved may cause some pain. That's part of why they sometimes have been avoided up to now. It seems that some of your communication failures really have been self-protective. If some of the difficult issues were never talked about or looked at directly, presumably you could avoid some of the pain of disagreement or disappointment. If you are ready to tackle them—and I think that they are manageable, or I wouldn't suggest this—we'll try to deal with them. It may not be easy all of the time, but we can try to get them out in workable doses."

It is also possible to extend the assessment process by asking the clients to do a homework assignment in which they write down their expectations of the marriage, their spouse, and themselves in the marriage. Occasionally, I will simply ask the partners to take some time alone and write down "in positive behavioral terms" (i.e., make specific, positive statements) what each expects from the marriage. After each has completed his or her list, they are encouraged to share them if they wish, but at any rate to bring them to the next session. When they are examined, I explain Sager's (1976) idea of conscious and verbalized, conscious but not verbalized, and out-of-awareness expectations, as well as how our expectations are regarded as a form of "contract." A simple illustration or two of how such "contracts" operate and the hurt, angry reactions that sometimes result when our assumed contract with the spouse is not met generally seem to make sense to clients. Generally, when this approach is used, it provides either a basis for opening communication and discussion or the recognition that the things they both desire are more similar than dissimilar.

One other thing that may be dealt with in the final part of the first face-to-face session consists of the clients' questions. They may range from whether they will be seen together, to what therapy is all about, to how long it will take. There may also be tacit questions. Not the least of the matters to be addressed is whether the clients feel that they can work with the therapist. If this question has not been answered in one form or another, the therapist may suggest, "I think that you need to decide how you feel about working with me. Am I the kind of human being with whom you feel comfortable enough to work? If not for any reason, I'll be glad to help you find someone else. I think that you have to decide that your yourself, along with the other decisions that you are making about therapy." Every effort is made to assist them to feel that such decisions are, indeed, appropriately theirs.

Clients may decide not to continue. The dropout rate for couples is high, 30 to 40% by the second appointment in standard clinics (Berman, 1987). This high rate, in my judgment, is probably a reflection of the unique motivational/structural picture that exists with couples. A family that presents for therapy consists of at least two generations and presumably some differences in authority and power. The marital partners present as peers who each have a choice as to whether they will work on the relationship and their problems, a choice that children, for instance, do not have in the same way or to the same degree.

Does the therapist ever decide as a result of the assessment not to work with a couple? Yes. In general, if the situation turns out to be markedly different than what was presented at the telephone level and is inappropriate for outpatient psychotherapy, if a relationship of trust cannot be established, or if any one of several other conditions exist that would negate a responsible treatment effort, it is appropriate to not continue with a case as therapist.

"RESISTANCE" AND ALLIANCE

The testing of the readiness of the therapist and client system for working together that begins with the initial contact continues in the subsequent sessions. Such testing by clients is often labeled resistance, a behavior that has a bad name in the history of psychotherapy. The psychoanalytic literature in particular has seemed to imply that resistance represents neurotic misbehavior (Napier, 1976). This viewpoint, according to Napier (1976), appears to be that a patient or client should be glad to have help in dealing with troublesome problems.

Pragmatically, resistance can be defined or described as all of the behaviors in the client system, therapist, and treatment setting that interact to prevent the therapeutic system from achieving therapeutic goals. Anderson and Stewart (1983) suggest that resistance is most likely to cause treatment failure or termination when resistances are found in all three of those parts of the therapeutic system and interact together.

A contemporary view—and one that I hold—is that much of what is customarily called resistance can be understood as a fear of change (Anderson & Stewart, 1983; Luther & Loev, 1981; Napier, 1976). There is no good reason why clients should not be apprehensive about opening themselves up to change. Resistance to change can be an indication of good judgment in some instances. As Anderson and Stewart (1983) note, if a couple is without a certain amount of resistance to change, chaos may result. Moreover, since risk is involved in change, not everybody can face the possibility of change comfortably and optimistically. Perhaps even the majority of persons cannot do so when the contemplated change involves basic sources of security and intimate relationships. The fear of loss and being in a worse position than presently occupied as a result of changing is a very human reaction.

Another part of the apprehension at the beginning of therapy pertains to making oneself vulnerable to a stranger—the therapist. Sometimes it is helpful to address the first appointment apprehension directly and openly. I may say something along the line of, "It is understandable that you are somewhat anxious about talking about the things that brought you here. It's not easy to talk about troubling things, especially with a stranger. Until a half-hour or so ago you had never even seen me. If you weren't somewhat apprehensive, we would have had to ask why." On occasion, a bit of humor may be added. For example, "If you weren't anxious we probably should check your pulse to make certain that you were still functioning." Some discussion of apprehensions within such a framework often reduces overt tensions and facilitates the building of a relationship of trust between therapist and clients.

Requests for individual sessions sometimes provide another clue that one of the partners wishes to talk about something that ostensibly is unknown to her or his mate. Such requests may be on occasion a maneuver to gain ground or favor with the therapist and thus to manipulate the therapy, though just as often the proposal for an individual session may be made by one spouse with the tacit or explicit concurrence of the other.

Therapists sometimes indicate that there are problems in conjoint therapy with clients trying to get them to take sides. Clients, they say, struggle to get the therapist to side with them or expect that the therapist will ally with their spouse against them. My own experience has been that this rarely occurs as a genuine problem once a case has been launched with a clear understanding of the ground rules. Perhaps the expectations and behaviors of the therapist have a significant impact on such alliance problems. I do not expect this to be a major problem and proceed accordingly. If there are overtures to bring me into alliance with either of the partners, I typically ignore them in the beginning; if they are strong or persist, I address them directly.

When such issues are faced overtly, we discuss what the expectations are. I explain that as far as I am aware, I do not have a need to help one of them over the other, but that I do have a stake in doing the best job that we can do together. Further, I may explain that one of them may get more time and attention at a given stage than the other, but that my experience indicates that such things usually even out in the course of therapy. If the struggle for attention, alliance, or "first place" with the clinician is strong and significant, this is examined as a relationship problem. It is not permitted to stand as an individual intrapsychic problem of one of the partners, but addressed with a direct question: "Is this how things usually go in your relationship?" "Is this unusual, or does this kind of concern come up at other times for the two of you?"

Client resistances can arise from either marital partner as an individual or from the mates as a couple. Luther and Loev (1981) have listed several individual and couple resistances. These include trying to ally with the therapist, failure to try to change with the excuse that the other mate will not change, concealing true feelings, shifting the blame to their spouse, and denying that progress is being made by their spouse. Joint resistances by the partners according to those authors include conscious collusion to withhold information and closing the marital boundaries against the therapist so as to terminate therapy prematurely.

Various approaches to dealing with client resistance either at the beginning or subsequently have been proposed. Luther and Loev (1981) describe the therapist's role as that of allying with the courageous part of each spouse against her or his fear of change. Management of marital resistance also include the establishment of trust and the manifestation of positive regard, genuineness, and empathy by the therapist. They suggest that exploration with the clients can lead to identifying the cause, progress, and impact of the resistances on the therapy. Further, they indicate that the development of a dynamic understanding of specific issues can result in changes in client perceptions, feelings, and behavior.

The most thorough treatment of resistance in family therapy generally has been provided by Anderson and Stewart (1983), most of which can be applied to marital therapy. They describe approaches that can be used by therapists to deal with resistances at the beginning and throughout the course of therapy.

I use a variety of approaches to dealing with client resistance, ranging from ignoring resistance behaviors, to reframing and relabeling, to dealing directly with them. Some of these approaches were mentioned in Chapter 4 and earlier in this chapter. Another simple but often effective approach to dealing with resistance to change involves linking it to the normal reactions of human beings. This "normalizing" approach works with other aspects of therapy as well as in dealing with resistance to change; here it may take the form of pointing out the difficulties and meanings of resistive behavior somewhat as follows: "What's happening here is very much like what people tend to do very often when change occurs. If we have been wanting something to happen for a long time, we may not believe it when it finally begins to happen. We'll test it out and perhaps even deny that it's happening. What seems to be going on is that we want it so badly that we're afraid that it may not last, so we don't want to let our hopes get too high and risk getting disappointed." Whatever the approach used, the recognition that change produces anxiety at all stages of treatment and that its appearance is normal and understandable is a very important part of therapy.

During the assessment phase, as noted, I have a goal of beginning to establish a working or therapeutic alliance with the couple or client system and the therapist system (see Pinsof & Catherall, 1986). Simply put, the therapeutic alliance consists of the cooperative attitudes and behaviors that we are able to muster and use for the purpose of working together in a therapeutic endeavor. The therapeutic alliance, as Pinsof and Catherall (1986) have indicated, involves an alliance between two systems and includes all of the people who are involved in the treatment process.

The aim in working toward a therapeutic alliance is to produce an outcome in which cooperation between therapist and client system prevails. Have the clients joined with the therapist in assuming responsibility for what occurs in treatment? Are both spouses able to perceive the therapist as being nonjudgmental and impartial in the therapy? Are both clients willing and able to work with the therapist in order to achieve what they want? Is the therapist able to bring about a situation in which all three have an adequate amount of trust, and the clients do not experience either an insufficiently or an overly gratifying relationship?

The relationship between clients and therapist continues to be significant throughout the course of therapy. As the therapist "passes" various tests during the early course of therapy (Kantor & Kuperman, 1985), the partners are ready to expose the deeper and more sensitive issues that trouble them. This process of testing before trusting is repeated throughout treatment.

CHANGE

> How do I love thee?
> Let me count the ways.
> How do we change?
> Can we count the ways?

That's one way of noting that change in human beings and in therapy follows many paths. There was a time in which many therapists thought that significant change occurred only as a result of obtaining insight, but then it was demonstrated by others that insight often followed behavioral change, and eventually systemic thinking entered the picture. Change came to be understood as being circular and as involving feedback and interplay among various parts of the system. Change occurs in marital couples as a result of learning new skills, adding cognitions, altering perceptions, responding to changes or various stimuli on the part of others, developing insight, releasing stifling and constrictive emotions, confiding in others and socializing painful experiences and emotions, clarifying communications, exercising one's will, lowering anxiety, resolving grief, identifying with others and their patterns, and in a variety of other ways. Change is affective, cognitive, and conative in nature, as well as active and behavioral in form.

Beavers (1977) has indicated that there are four ways to change the behavior of other persons: coercion, empathic sharing, persuasion, and problem solving with them. A therapist may use all of those in one form or another in order to assist other persons in making changes. The particular mix of approaches depends on both the clients and the therapist. No therapy and no therapist holds a corner on ways to facilitate change. Fortunately, there do not seem to be any human emotional problems that can be changed by only one method. This makes it more possible—and in my opinion desirable—to use an integrative approach to marital therapy.

Chapter Six

The Treatment Process

This chapter is concerned with a broad description of the kind of integrative approach that I take to working with marital couples in conjoint therapy. It is an illustrative rather than a complete coverage of one kind of integrative approach to marital therapy.

The method is one in which an assumption of "least pathology" is made (cf. Pinsof, 1983). That is, it is not assumed automatically that underlying pathology must be treated in order to secure change. Therapeutic interventions are made initially on the basis of straightforward efforts to secure change. If blocks develop, the clinician then has to alter course. If working with the couple's communication and straightforward problem solving is effective, for example, the therapy may consist essentially of such efforts. If alteration of collusive processes requires more intensive work, therapy moves to that phase; if family-of-origin work is indicated, that will be done in one of several ways.

Not all clinicians will approach cases in the same ways that are outlined in this chapter. Other therapists will need to adapt therapeutic concepts and use therapeutic techniques according to their own orientations, personality styles, and comfort levels. Over a number of years I have tried to deal with marital problems through several different therapeutic approaches. Consecutive, concurrent, and collaborative treatment of spouses all provided some positive results. Collaborative treatment was employed with several different collaborating therapists and was effective in some instances, but it also was the most difficult approach to use. Over time, it became evident that what we were doing was treating the spouses separately and individually; when I did all of the treatment myself and used concurrent marital therapy, I was doing essentially the same thing. Finally, conjoint therapy augmented occasionally by individual sessions became my interviewing and treatment modality of choice for marital cases.

Two important findings from such experiences were: (1) the partners and their relationship looked different and responded differently when they were interviewed together than when they were seen separately; and (2) the therapeutic interventions were much more focused and their power much greater when the partners were seen together. Outcome research by Gurman and others (e.g., Gurman, 1973, 1978; Gurman & Kniskern, 1978a, 1978b, 1981) eventually confirmed my own observations that conjoint marital therapy was effective and efficacious.

Clinical experience with a variety of cases over a long period of time also led to increased effort to integrate systems, psychodynamic, and learning theory (behavioral) orientations. My early commitment to technical flexibility also grew as a result of additional experience. Seeing clients in a variety of diverse settings and under different circumstances should cause all of us to continue to challenge the ways we were taught to do therapy.

The spacing of appointments provides an example: There appears to be nothing magical about seeing clients once a week or once a month, or at whatever interval a therapist may have assumed to be optimal. Depending both on the needs of the case and the circumstances, a therapist may see clients with great frequency within a short time period or at widely scattered intervals.

At certain points, particularly during crises when situational factors are impinging negatively on clients' lives and their anxiety is running high, it may be important and appropriate to see couples more than once a week, though if I do this, it is usually only for a short time. Occasionally one is called on to work with couples in a compressed time period, such as when the exigiencies of time and availability permit a couple to be seen only during a 10-day period. In such instances, decisions have to be made about seeing them daily or several times a week in a concerted therapeutic endeavor. Working with marital partners under such circumstances seems to be somewhat analogous to using compact versus extended periods of time for educational purposes. One can impart a considerable amount of information in a concentrated course, but there is not the same kind of opportunity for the absorption, reflection, and integration that exists in an extended term such as a semester pattern. To the extent that therapeutic work involves learning, distributed learning (therapy) may be more effective for many kinds of problems than massed learning (therapy).

All schedules of interviewing have their use. My preference is for once-weekly sessions or, at times, appointments once every 2 weeks. I especially find it helpful with some cases to shift to a twice-monthly pattern when the emphasis has moved to helping clients effect new patterns in their daily living. That is, when a phase has been reached in which the partners are out of crisis and "hard digging" and painful work are behind them, and they are trying to gain experience in effecting new patterns that they both agree are desirable, more responsibility is put on the couple to deal with their changes outside of therapy. If crises or blocks develop, the frequency of appointments can be increased temporarily.

Marital therapy can be divided somewhat arbitrarily into categories of short-term, medium length, and long-term treatment. I apply the designation short-term to treatment that lasts for fewer than 20 sessions; medium length is defined as lasting approximately 6 months to a year; a year or longer is considered long-term marital therapy. Most marital therapy appears to last for 6 months or less. This tends to be true in the experience of colleagues as well as in my own practice.

STAGES OF TREATMENT

Marital therapy can also be divided into three major stages, early, middle, and final (termination). Again, these are somewhat arbitrary distinctions. Use of the term "stage" refers to the fact that there is a period of time between the initial session or first few sessions and the final interviews or termination stage. The stage of therapy should not be confused with phases of treatment. As Wynne (1983) has pointed out, one can take a phase-oriented approach to therapy in which treatment is directed toward the problem that is most salient at any given point. As one major problem is resolved to whatever degree possible, treatment moves on to the next problem, so that therapy is modified in order to deal with the emerging salient problems. Some major problems that are successfully mitigated may move off center stage temporarily and return later as a result of subsequent developments in the marital interaction.

Phase, as the term is used here, thus refers to both problems in the couple's relationships and lives and in their working with the clinician in the therapeutic endeavor. For example, Napier (1987) has described a "process" stage in couples' therapy in which the partners are assisted to bring their struggles into the therapist's office. There they are helped to take the initiative to identify their difficulties, and to begin to strive for change. When they are able to do this effectively, they cease to blame their partner and begin to recognize that the problems involve both of them. When this has occurred, they have entered into what Napier (1987) calls a "bilaterial phase" of treatment, in which blaming patterns have been dropped in favor of a two-way exchange of complaints and pleas for change in the therapeutic sessions. My term for a treatment phase in which responsibility for both the problems and change is shared by the marital partners is a "joint responsibility" phase. In my experience, the partners do not necessarily remain in a posture of sharing the responsibility for the problems and for change, but there is sometimes a shift back to postures of blaming and assignment of responsibility to the other spouse when new difficulties are uncovered in the process of treatment.

The use of the term "stage" does not imply, therefore, that events occur in a strictly linear fashion or that therapy proceeds in a predictable and progressive clear-cut manner. Many of the things that happen early in treatment have to be reworked subsequently. Always the process is recursive. Nevertheless, there is often a sense in which the accomplishment of certain early tasks opens the way for other events and problems. The framework described below is intended to serve as an heuristic guideline.

THE EARLY STAGE

During the initial interview or sessions with the couple I am usually concerned with several explicit tasks and goals. One of the first pertains to securing an initial assessment of the needs, problems, strengths, and motivations of the marital partners. At this stage, clarifying the motivation of the partners regarding working together and commitment to striving for change does not necessarily mean that I am concerned with probing deeply into their innermost thoughts and feelings, but that I observe their behaviors and verbalizations concerning the marriage, themselves, and therapy. Are their behaviors and their statements congruent? What is the thrust of their motivation as revealed to my observations and assessment? It may or may not be necessary to confront directly the question of their motivation and readiness for therapy or to probe deeply into their feelings and motivations.

Another part of this first task pertains to elucidating the expectations of the partners for the marriage and for therapy. Sometimes exploration of expectations concerning the marriage, the partner, and one's own role requires a considerable amount of time and focus during the early sessions (Sager, 1976). In some instances, it is important not only to examine the implicit "contract" between the mates but also to give explicit attention to the kind of "contract" or "bargain" they are willing and able to make with the therapist. The couple may wish to have only short-term intervention around a specific, limited issue, for example, in which case effective treatment of a brief, problem-focused nature can be used, as de Shazer (1982, 1985) and others have demonstrated.

Expectations regarding treatment also involve the goals sought respectively by clients and therapist. I consider it important to try to secure a reasonable degree of congruence between my goals for therapy and those of the clients. At the very least, all three of us need to understand any marked discrepancies between what they are seeking and what I am trying to help them accomplish in therapy, ascertaining whether there is sufficient compatibility between what I can offer and what they seek to make therapeutic work viable.

Establishing congruence or compatibility between our goals as therapists and those of our clients frequently requires that we work directly and explicitly with them on clarifying what they want from treatment. It is not always possible to help them to agree between themselves that they want the same things from therapy. Fortunately, it is possible in some instances to use treatment approaches that allow us to seek the simultaneous attainment of ostensibly discrepant goals (Feldman, 1976). In other instances it may be useful and appropriate to point out to a couple that "it is necessary to deal with *x*-issue before we can get to *y*-issue. We can get there, but in my judgment this is the best way to proceed in order to get what you want" (Nichols & Everett, 1986, p. 220).

The task of clarifying and establishing goals may go on continually throughout the course of treatment, since what happens at one point determines the possibilities for additional therapeutic work. Treatment goals also may be either general or specific. As an example, Lewin (1948) pointed out long ago that conflict and emotional outbreaks in a marriage are significantly affected by the general level of tension in the marriage. Additionally, he noted four outstanding causes of tension: (1) the extent to which certain basic needs of individuals such as security or sex are being met; (2) the amount of space available for the free movement of the person; (3) a lack of freedom to leave the situation; and (4) the extent to which the goals of the spouses contradict each other and the general readiness of each spouse to consider their mate's point of view. The goal of therapy thus could be to change any one or more of these four specific causes or to reduce the general tension in the marriage. Any of these causes could be operationalized in terms of specifying changes that could be realized through behavioral interventions.

With a bit of adaptation, a point made elsewhere (Nichols & Everett, 1986) with regard to family therapy goals also applies here. That is, the formulation of therapeutic goals involves several levels: the immediate goals of the couple regarding the presenting complaint/problem, potential longer range goals of the couple pertaining to larger and permanent changes, the therapist's immediate goals for symptom relief, the therapist's overall outcome goals, and the various subordinate goals of the therapist. For therapy that lasts past a brief, problem-centered intervention point, it is the task of the therapist to clarify and revise the goals of treatment continually.

A second task of the beginning stage involves establishing a beginning therapeutic alliance with the marital partners. This implies, as noted, the attainment of a workable degree of commitment and cooperation so that we can work together productively on their problems. The way in which the therapist relates to the client system is a major factor in the formation and maintenance of a therapeutic alliance. It also appears to many therapists to be an essential part of doing effective therapeutic work. Feldman (1976) found that the writings of a wide variety of family therapists emphasized empathy, respect, concern, and genuineness in the clinician's "manner of relating" to clients. These are the same qualities that Rogers (1957) and others considered essential for individual and group therapists.

Among the family therapists stressing the importance of empathy ("feeling with" another and communicating an understanding) are Ackerman (1966), Liberman (1970), Minuchin (1974), and Paul (1967). Showing respect, concern, and genuineness are emphasized by Ackerman (1966) and Satir (1967), among others. Skynner (1969) has spelled out ways in which a clinician can and in his opinion should be a real person in the marital therapy session. One can manifest a wide range of feelings and serve as both a model and a catalyst for the couple. He suggests that by being a real, clearly identifiable person the therapist can discourage the formation of transference to herself or himself and thus keep transference reactions within the client system. My own experience essentially supports Skynner's position.

Perhaps the greatest test of the therapist's skill in this regard is found in the challenge to relate to the client system as a system while helping each partner to feel individually one's empathy, respect, concern, and genuineness. This is done within the confines of the individual therapist's own personality and therapeutic orientation. There are no universal techniques for manifesting these qualities.

A third goal and task of the therapist during the early phase is con-

cerned with providing immediate help for the clients. Most persons expect and deserve some assistance in coping with the tensions associated
with their problems. This does not mean that one should always expect
to help clients find an immediate solution that will bring them relief.
Although on occasion it is possible to help the partners to resolve a relationship issue or a crisis in a short time, in my experience, this is comparatively rare with complex cases. All cases, however, need attention to
the tensions that emanate from the problems themselves, even if immediate amelioration of causal factors is not possible. Coping with the tensions can take several forms. Occasionally, the simple actions of listening
to what the partners have to say and providing hope lowers enervating
tension (Beavers & Kaslow, 1981).

A simple example of this third task and goal may be found in the
therapist's explanatory-interpretative work: The therapist may describe
to a couple typical reactions to loss. As this is done, the therapist points
out, "Knowing this and understanding what is happening to you does
not necessarily lessen the pain. It may, however, make it possible for
you to deal with the process more effectively and not to get so anxious
that you make the situation more difficult than it already is." This goal
and task can be described as that of helping the partners to "settle down"
from the distress and conflict that brought them to the therapist.

A corollary to "settling down" is "settling into" treatment, which is
closely associated with establishing a therapeutic alliance. Clients need
to establish, as noted, a trusting, cooperative relationship with the therapist, secure adequate and appropriate hope that things can be changed
in a positive manner, and learn how to work in therapy.

"Settling in" has to do with finding the limits and beginning to work
in therapy. One of the first things that couples generally do when they
are seen in conjoint therapy is to seek to find the boundaries of permissible behavior, for example. Getting into treatment often permits the
mates to release hostility and anger that were previously held back or
partially restrained and seldom fully released. Having a third party present often may encourage them to engage in an emotional sparring match
in the fashion of two boxers who feel each other out and then begin to
throw punches, secure in the knowledge that a referee is present. Each
may be seeking to get the referee to be her or his advocate, ally, or
protector, but there usually is a more complex set of issues involved:
This sparring can be a metaphorical playing out of the marital experience, in which the partners are exploring the possibilities either of getting closer to each other emotionally or of getting out of the relationship.

The sheer ignorance of many persons about what therapy involves and what they are expected to do is easily underestimated or overlooked by therapists. My fantasy is that every therapist would periodically take herself or himself through a therapeutic assessment process. The goal would not be simply to learn something about oneself; equally or perhaps more important would be what the therapist might learn about the reactions of clients to entering treatment. Even when one is aware of what is expected of clients in therapy, it is possible to forget easily the emotional impact of seeking help. Such emotional reactions may dull one's abilities to learn and function effectively. Clients often need to be taught what is required of them in order to make the therapeutic process effective and useful to them.

The activity level of the therapist is high during the first stage: Not only is there a need to relate effectively to the client system but also to be active in structuring treatment. Whether the therapeutic contacts are going to be brief or extended, the therapist needs to take charge, establish the working conditions between therapist and client system, and deal as effectively as possible with client resistances. This can be done with adequate respect for the needs and wishes of clients.

THE MIDDLE STAGE

The middle stage of treatment is where most of the therapeutic work is accomplished. Several issues and phases of treatment fall within this stage. The therapeutic tasks in this stage vary, of course, according to the problems manifested by the couple and to their ability to use different kinds of help. Depending on whether the problems presented to the therapist involve chronic or acute difficulties, the symptomatology, and the developmental stage of the marriage, a greater or lesser degree of work may be needed in order to establish a workable complementarity between the partners.

Rebalancing efforts during this stage are aimed at dealing with the marital relationship both internally and in relation to other family systems. Family-of-origin sessions, for example, are conducted during the middle stage, if they are used as part of the treatment. The term "rebalancing" as used here does not refer to establishing a homeostatic balance, but to what systems theorists have called a "dynamic steady state." The marriage is understood here as needing help in order to function in a state of dynamic tension, a state that will allow it to change continually and to adapt successfully to altering circumstances and needs.

Two general issues—dependency and direct/indirect therapeutic approaches—require some attention before we move on to look at more specific types of interventions and therapeutic emphases used during this stage.

Dependency

Dependency is a major issue during the middle stage of my approach to marital therapy. The role of the therapist with clients, like that of parents with children, is to allow adequate dependency while working oneself out of a job as soon as it is appropriate to get the clients out on their own. Therapy thus involves patterns in which early client reliance on the therapist is replaced by client reliance on the marital system. This pattern is repeated many times in some cases as the clients move from one area to another in their thinking, feeling, and experiencing. Such a shifting of reliance occurs repeatedly, both with different issues and in a general movement from reliance on the therapist to dependence on self and the marital system.

Four different parts to this process can be described, listed here separately in a step-like framework. In reality these parts are not so easily separated and delineated because of the circular and overlapping nature of the change process. The first step involves winning the trust of the couple so that they can begin to expose their needs and vulnerabilities in the therapy hour in appropriate ways. As they do so, they are helped to explore the emerging issues and to begin taking actions to effect changes in their interactions inside the sessions. Clients usually reach the point of being able to assume shared responsibility for their interaction and for change as they take on these tasks. When the partners come to experience some success in these endeavors and increase their trust and hopefulness, it becomes possible to move toward the second step.

The next part usually consists of suggestions and encouragement by the therapist to the couple to expand what they are doing in the sessions outside of the therapy hours. The clinician may say, for example, "Talking about [a given topic] has worked pretty well here. Do you think that you could deal with it in somewhat the same way at home?" Such suggestions and such encouragement needs to be accompanied by careful attention to the apprehensions of the partners and to the difficulties they may face in implementing the behaviors outside of therapy. Suggestions can be made to put time limits on such talks and directions for providing for "time outs" if either spouse becomes upset or disturbed by the interaction. When attempts are made by the clients there needs also to be follow-up in which support is given for the difficulties encountered, and "celebration" (Zuk, 1986) or appropriate affirmation provided for whatever gains they have been able to make.

The third part involves suggestions or directives by the therapist that the clients explore selected areas that have not been dealt with in therapy sessions. Without the presence of the therapist or the experience of dealing with those selected areas or issues in treatment, the clients are encouraged to "spread their wings" a bit and to begin exploring the designated "new ground." Once again, this part would include preparation of the couple by the therapist and follow-up in subsequent treatment hours.

The fourth part of the movement from reliance on the therapist and from the protection of the therapeutic session is reached when the clients begin to initiate actions and explorations on their own, without either the personal presence or the suggestions/directions of the therapist. Many couples will move to this stage in some areas without any prompting on the part of the therapist. By this time, when the marital partners have become able to expose their needs and vulnerabilities and deal with issues surrounding most of the significant parts of their relationship, they typically are feeling ready to terminate therapy.

Direct and Indirect Treatment Approaches

Integrative marital therapy is intended to be both a growth process and an experience that facilitates future growth and development on the part of clients. The approach described here is based on the idea that where possible clients should be both helped to understand what is occurring and enlisted in a process that will help them to continue learning how to function after they have left therapy. Direct and straightforward approaches to clients and their problems are thus taken wherever possible.

Most of the interventions described this far are essentially direct in nature: The discussion of shifting dependency during treatment, for example, focuses primarily on direct approaches. Along with exploration and uncovering of feelings, ideas, and behaviors and the elucidation of patterns, attempts are made in such an approach to engage the couple in expanding their knowledge, skills, and areas of productive functioning. Such efforts are aimed at providing clients with the opportunity to become aware of what is occurring at the time, to learn how to use the developing skills and knowledge to gain additional understanding of their behaviors and transactions, and to apply this experience to do further problem solving. The experience–information–skill combination that they gain is frequently helpful to them in other areas as well as in what they specifically are dealing with in therapy.

In an elucidating, direct approach the clients are helped insofar as is possible to become acquainted with ways of gaining information and experience, rather than just with the relevant information or experience itself. This approach involves an active feedback and sharing system between the therapist and the client system. Exploration, education, persuasion, and what I have termed elsewhere (Nichols & Everett, 1986) "midwiving the relationship" (providing an active kind of bridging and facilitating help between the two spouses in an atmosphere of firmness, warmth, and support) all are part of an essentially direct approach in which the ultimate focus is on dealing with the couple's problems and improving the relationship or helping them to end it mercifully if they decide to terminate the marriage.

Indirect approaches, by contrast, do not involve an effort to enlist the couple so straightforwardly in the change process. Rather, the therapist is likely to make efforts to affect the marital system without providing the partners with the kinds of information and feedback to which I have referred. Paradoxical interventions and strategies are among the major kinds of indirect methods typically used. These range from the use of metaphors to self-contradictory messages and instructions that are apparently inconsistent with the aims of therapy. For example, Haley (1976) has referred to joining one spouse against the other, taking that mate's side no matter what the issue. Ostensibly, the alliance is on a permanent basis, even though the therapist may intend to change later. The purpose of the action is to destabilize a marriage in order to change it, though Haley (1976) cautioned that such techniques should not be used except by skilled therapists.

Indirect approaches become the approach of choice when a direct approach appears inappropriate or impractical because of time constraints or because of the clients' inability to tolerate, handle emotionally, or otherwise respond effectively to a direct approach. Some clinicians such as Madanes (1984) believe that therapists generally do not have enough power with clients to use direct approaches and, hence, need to influence them indirectly.

My approach, outlined above, is much closer to that of Papp (1980), who has said that experience indicates that it is neither necessary nor desirable to use paradoxical approaches all the time. Paradoxical endeavors—interventions that bring about the opposite of what they seemingly are intended to accomplish through the clients defying therapeutic directives/instructions or following them to the point of absurdity and then recoiling—are reserved for situations that do not respond to direct interventions.

Combinations of direct and indirect approaches can be used, because both approaches are aimed at producing change in couples from their present dysfunctional state or patterns of functioning. Perturbations of the marital system can be used to provide additional information as the system reacts to the interferences and disturbances generated by the therapist. Elucidation of current patterns and the efforts of the partners to regain an old state of functioning can result from such interferences, for example. That elucidation can lead to conscious and rational decisions and efforts to make changes in the system.

An example from an individual case provides an illustration of how both direct (in terms of psychodynamic work) and indirect (paradoxical directives) approaches can be used together. The client was a young woman who had been plagued with obesity and problems of overeating for half of her 28 years and had tried everything from diets and hypnosis to Overeaters Anonymous and several different therapists without success. After carefully exploring her problem with her and determining that she was an "angry" overeater and a "sneak" eater, the therapist provided her with a directive that went essentially as follows:

"What you are doing certainly is painful for you. You don't enjoy sneaking food in your automobile or hiding in the basement when you binge so that your husband won't know about your eating. What I want you to do is to eat only at times and places where it is pleasurable and enjoyable for you.

"You get home from work several hours before your husband does. When you get home and wish to eat, set up the nicest arrangement that you can, so that it is pleasurable for you. Put a good tablecloth on your dining room table, get out your best china and silver, and whatever you wish to eat. Take your time, sit down, and enjoy.

"We're not going to be concerned about what you eat or how much, but we do want it to be pleasurable for you. Why don't you keep a record for the next week in which you put down what you do eat? That way we'll be able to know something more about whether you are only eating when it is pleasurable, and if you are not, we'll try to make some changes so that you are."

Within 2 days the binges stopped. During the next therapy session the client recalled a traumatic situation when she had been a junior in high school. Her mother had promised her that if she lost weight she would have more friends, be popular, and be attractive to boys. The client had lost 30 pounds or so, but the grand and glorious things promised by her mother had not occurred. The long repressed anger with her mother that emerged was worked through in the next few sessions and the client was coached in dealing with her mother concerning some previously unresolved issues between them.

Direct approaches had not worked. This was a case in which we could say that the "attempted solution is the problem" (Watzlawick *et al.*, 1974, p. 57); that is, prohibitions from adolescence against overeating and the client's attempts to avoid doing so had led to a situation in which the intense struggles over eating at all were worse than the original problem of being overweight. The approach used with her followed the steps for change delineated by Watzlawick and associates (1974). The problem was clearly defined in concrete terms (the client was not enjoying eating), the previous attempts at solution were investigated, the concrete change that was to be achieved was clearly defined (i.e., from unpleasurable eating to enjoyable eating), and a plan to produce the change was formulated and implemented. The reframing of the problem from overeating to unpleasurable eating lifted things out of a "symptom" context, and the client was shown that she was trusted.

This person did not resume her overeating except for one brief period in which she was "testing out some things with my parents." Eventually she lost 80 pounds and made some life-style changes to accommodate her new "think thin" approach. At a checkup time 2 years later she had maintained her new weight and had not resumed the overeating.

Indirect treatment techniques with couples work best for me when they are combined with direct approaches. Frequently there is a need and desire on the part of the partners to talk about what has occurred, and they especially may wish to deal with feelings and behaviors that are released by the changes that occur as a result of the indirect intervention. This happens in two ways. One pattern involves a release of previously stored up feelings in much the same fashion that the young woman with the eating problems opened up the previously forgotten incident and issues with her mother; the other has to do with "breaking new ground" or moving into new patterns of behaving and relating by the partners.

Activity Level of the Therapist

During the middle stage of treatment my activity level varies. Much of the time I am quite active, whereas at others I may sit for several minutes without speaking or otherwise intervening while the partners conduct a dialogue. If in my judgment the flow and process of the session are going well and progress is being made by the clients, I will be much more of an observer than a participant. Deciding when to intervene and when to let the process continue without interruption is a matter of art rather than science.

Giving the clients opportunity to take the initiative at the beginning of the session is a regular feature of each appointment after the initial assessment phase. I simply ask, "Where would you like to start?" or some variation of that question. This does several things: It permits the clients to begin the session however they wish; it requires them to take some responsibility for deciding who will start, how he or she will start, and with what; and it allows me to observe the interaction of the partners and to get a quick introduction to where things are in their current interaction and relationship.

The partners are free to open up with trivial matters or significant issues. When one spouse opens with a trivial or "smoke-screening" issue the other frequently issues a challenge and moves the session to something that is more pertinent and important. On occasion, particularly when the partners appear to be colluding to keep things on a superficial level, I intervene to shed light on what is happening and to change the course of the session. The intervention may take the form of a question (e.g., "Is this really that much of a concern?" "Is this what you came in to deal with today?") or of a statement (e.g., "It seems to me that it is difficult for you to get started. Can we move to something else?" "I wonder if there is anything that you feel is difficult to deal with that's being avoided." "It seems to me that what we were dealing with last time was not finished and that we need to return to it.").

Giving the clients the opportunity to open the session thus does not mean that they necessarily set the agenda and direct the entire course of the appointment. The therapist can and should take responsibility for directing the course of a session whenever things do not seem to her or him to be moving productively. This includes not only when clients deflect attention as described above but also when clients are at an impasse, when harmful verbal battles are underway, and when other situations prevail that are not contributing to therapeutic progress.

Clients frequently engage in a kind of back-and-forth behavior in which first one and then the other will state her or his case verbally and symbolically. The therapeutic task is to manage this process whenever possible so that it assumes a dialectic form, eventually reaching synthesis or some kind of resolution instead of remaining incomplete and at an impasse. The simple observation, "In my experience with couples, the amount of time used generally levels out during the course of therapy.

One person may talk more at one point and the other another, but it typically evens out" and some attention to providing adequate opportunity for both to be involved has worked well for me in dealing with the equal time issue.

Clients also engage in similar "center stage" behavior when one of them needs to take up most of the therapeutic time for one or perhaps even two sessions, sometimes dealing primarily with personal, individual concerns. Such activity by the client appears frequently to be a necessary prelude to moving on to something else. When this seems to be the case, I permit it to occur and try to help both partners see what is happening and so deal with the meaning being expressed by the behavior.

Communication

An early task in the middle stage typically involves helping to improve communication between the spouses. It is a commonplace and accurate observation that most couples requesting marital help have problems with communication. Sometimes the communication is blocked with regard to certain problem areas, such as when the partners become too emotional, too upset to talk about certain matters. In these cases the task is relatively simple, being somewhat analogous to clearing out barriers in a stream and permitting water to flow freely. More often, the partners not only are blocked and constricted with regard to particular areas and issues but also do not possess good skills for engaging generally in clear and effective communication. Dealing with these two types of communication problems can be broadly described as "removing the barriers" (for specific areas) and "building good channels" (for the general flow of communication).

My concern is to begin facilitating communication within the therapeutic sessions and to extend it outward to the world in which the spouses live. The modeling by the clinician of how to be straightforward and clear in one's statements and referents; how to use "I" statements; how to avoid speaking for the other, attributing motivations or feelings to the other; and listening reflectively all are important to learning and communicational change on the part of clients. I wish to observe them trying to communicate and problem solve in my presence. Such behaviors provide "prime data" in that the clinician can observe directly and make immediate interventions.

In this live teaching and experiencing I am at least as concerned with the attitudes that clients display as with the skills they acquire and manifest. Sometimes they can acquire greater understanding and tolerance as a result of the therapist intervention in and interpretation of such communication in therapeutic sessions. It also is important to pay attention to how clients feel about what is happening with themselves, in their marriage, and in their therapy. These experiential elements are not easily described, but both client and therapist attempts to articulate such elements are equally important to the therapeutic process.

There is no need to describe here in detail the communications approach to therapy developed during the 1950s both by the Palo Alto group associated with Gregory Bateson and at the Mental Research Institute. Briefly, one of the central ideas is that all behavior involves acts of communication. Changing the communication patterns that maintain the problem behavior is the aim of treatment based on such a communications approach (L'Abate & McHenry, 1983).

It has become an article of faith in the family therapy field that improvement of communication skills helps marital partners. Part of this belief is based on outcome research (Gurman, 1973, 1978; Gurman & Kniskern, 1978a, 1978b; Gurman *et al.*, 1986; Todd & Stanton, 1983), and part on some direct empirical research into such efforts (L'Abate & McHenry, 1983). General observation indicates that couples do show some changes as a result of participating in skill-training programs.

If marital difficulties were based totally or essentially on poor communication skills, the chances are that improving such skills would solve most marital problems and provide the partners with satisfaction. Marital discord, however, arises from many factors other than communication. Communication difficulties, as implied above, may be both a result of marital discord and a contributor to it; and there are cases in which communication is clear and discord rampant. The semanticist S. I. Hayakawi once declared, "Communication is no panacea." He pointed out that persons (or nations) can communicate clearly and disagree profoundly.

Couples often need to be helped to recognize and deal with the fact that we sometimes are afraid of communicating. Selecting a communicational interchange, the clinician may point out that the messages being conveyed are unclear. Working patiently with what is being said, it may be possible to elucidate the fact that sometimes we don't communicate clearly in order to make certain that we *don't* understand each other.

The therapist may ask, for example, "What do you suppose would happen if your messages were clear? For instance, if you told your husband clearly what you meant and what you wanted with regard to [help with the children, going on a trip, lovemaking, or whatever specific issue was involved], what do you think would happen?" Or, "What do you suppose keeps you from letting your wife know clearly how you feel about going over to her sister's house every Friday night?"

The responses to such probing typically discloses that there is some fear that disagreements will surface, that a quarrel may ensue, or that "It won't do any good, anyway" to make one's wishes known clearly. Often there is a fear of pain or disappointment, so that coaching may be helpful in getting the partners to expose their feelings and risk this disappointment or pain. On occasion, there is a rather dramatic change in the session: The partner who is the recipient of the clarified message may respond positively, letting the reluctant mate know that the wish will be granted without undue struggle.

Starting therapy by focusing on the couple's communication is often one of the safest ways to begin working with them, since communication is acknowledged to be a joint endeavor and as such generally does not carry some of the connotations of blame that are associated with other parts of marital interaction. Somehow, it seems morally neutral to say "We just don't communicate." Communication difficulties are widespread, "everybody" has them.

Starting with communication problems, which often are mentioned as a complaint or concern by the couple in early sessions, also provides a pathway to other relationship difficulties. Some of these are not easy to manage but may be important to securing change. Exploring communication deficits may disclose not only fearfulness but also a lack of trust between the partners, for example. As this occurs, blaming and conflict can be expected to emerge; object relations issues often become the focus of the treatment out of such exploration.

Working with a hot and hostile interchange that erupted between Mr. and Mrs. Davis during the fourth appointment with them led to the following developments, which provide an example of this progression. The husband had misinformed his wife that he had painters coming as a ploy to get her to order draperies and other redecorating materials. The wife had exploded with anger about his behavior, and he had begun to backtrack, defending himself.

Therapist: What do you suppose would have happened if you had told her directly what you wanted?

Husband: Procrastination. Nothing would happen. She wouldn't do anything.

Wife: That's what makes me mad—your manipulation!

Therapist: His telling you something in order to get you to react the way he wants you to?

Wife: Yes. His manipulating me, instead of telling me like I have a brain and like I'm a responsible adult. I think I've proved that. I headed a department of 20 people in one of the largest stores in [the metropolitan area].

Therapist: You would like for him to deal with you directly, instead of indirectly.

Wife: (*Smiling*) You're being charitable by calling it indirect, but, yes, I would.

Therapist: (*To husband*) You fear that nothing would happen, that she would procrastinate as she used to do when you were first married?

Husband: I don't understand women! I don't know what she would do.

[The broader implications of this statement were noted without comment and mentally filed by the therapist for future reference.]

Therapist: When you don't communicate, it's easy to continue thinking that the other person will behave as they did when they were 22 or 25, when things actually have changed. (*To wife*) You've said that you don't procrastinate like you did when you were first married.

Wife: No, I don't. I react when he tries to manipulate me. Sometimes he sets me up in other ways. [She related a couple of anecdotes in which her husband had not given her adequate information for her to make an informed response.] When he tells me what's going on, I can see his point, and I can agree with him sometimes.

The therapist labeled such situations as "gaps in information," events in which the wife was operating "in a vacuum," and began to explore that phenomenon along with the other instances of "indirectness." The therapist obtained from the husband an acknowledgement that the wife did make some appropriate responses when she was provided with adequate information. What is described here are essentially the same things that Minuchin and Fishman (1981) call reframing and enactment (i.e., family members interacting with each other in the therapist's presence).

Therapist: One other thing appears to be evident. That is, the two of you have not worked out effective ways of making joint decisions. You can make some good individual decisions, as we have seen, but around a lot of things that involve both of you, there doesn't seem to be much "jointness." Decisions are made unilaterally. One of you tends to make the decision alone. What keeps you from developing ways of making decisions together, do you suppose?

Husband: That's easy. My mother made all of the decisions. She dominated my father. He gave her his paycheck and she gave him $25 a week spending money and a sack lunch. That's not going to happen to me. I'm not going to have that.

Wife: That's right. She really did, but I keep telling you that I'm not your mother.

Therapist: Where's your evidence that your wife tries to dominate you? On the contrary, we have a lot of indications that what she wishes to do is to be able to lean on you, to rely on you.

Husband: (Pause) That's true. She really doesn't try to dominate me, never has.

Therapist: Well, it's not hard to understand your wish not to be treated like your father. But there's something rather ironic happening. You haven't wished to repeat your parents' marital pattern and be in the position your father was in, but you are repeating some features of the pattern. You aren't being treated like your father, but you are repeating your mother's behaviors and making unilateral decisions like she did.

Husband: Oh, my God! I am! *(Pause)* You're right. I had never thought of it, but that's exactly what I do.

Therapist: I think so. Unfortunately, your attempt to avoid being treated like father, your attempt to avoid pain, isn't working very well. [The therapist cited some illustrations of how the patterns were malfunctional.] Do you suppose that the pain that you might get from being direct with your wife would be any greater than the difficulties of the last 15 years?

Wife: Good lord, no!

Husband: Probably not, it's gotten bad.

The session ended with the husband's statement, "We've got a lot to think about" and the therapist's response, "I want you to do more than think," which was accompanied by some guidance for homework assignments in terms of communication tasks.

This illustrates one of many ways in which object-relations issues and family of origin materials appear in therapeutic sessions. The therapist decided to keep the focus essentially on the present and the relating of the spouses, while acknowledging the ties between the man's developmental past and his present marital behaviors. The way was opened, however, to return to family of origin issues in the sessions that followed.

The kinds of tasks described here are typically repeated several times during the course of therapy, due to the necessity for changing the beliefs and behaviors of the marital partners slowly and gradually. Although some of the changes mentioned here pertain to how clients work within therapy sessions, a major focus is on helping the partners to work on changing outside the therapy as well as during appointments.

Encouragement and assistance of clients involves what I have called a "Pollyanna" approach. This pertains to attempts to establish "no-lose" situations by assigning clients small tasks that have a low potential for failure. Whenever clients are given a task to perform outside the sessions, the clinician recognizes and rewards their effort, whether or not they are successful in their attempts to make behavioral changes, since such is not the issue. The clinician's purpose here is to acknowledge their efforts and not permit them to denigrate their attempt to work on change:

Therapist: How did it go? What were you able to do with the things that we talked about you doing this week?

Client: Not much. We tried to talk 10 minutes a day, but we didn't do it but one day and maybe one more. We just couldn't seem to get time or get around to it most of the time.

Therapist: Okay, you're saying that it worked all right one day and to some extent on another. You tried. Both of you tried? Right? You didn't bat a thousand, but you made a start. That's not bad. We'll come back to this later today and see what keeps you from doing what you agree that you want to do, but that's not bad at all. Both of you tried at the same time, and that's a real advance over what has been happening with you for most of the last several years.

Another important aspect of communicational difficulties and complaints has to do with communication as a form of relating. The complaint "We don't communicate" is sometimes a euphemistic way of saying "We don't relate in satisfactory ways." A bit of digging in some instances discloses that one of the spouses feels that he or she is being rejected by the other. The person feels that they are not being confirmed by the spouse.

Confirming responses (Seiberg, 1985) include those behaviors that enable an individual to feel that they are being recognized, that they are relating to others, that their communication efforts are being recognized, and that they are being accepted by the other. Dialogue occurs when both parties to the communicative effort are putting forth confirming responses and each is feeling that he or she is confirmed. There are several different forms of confirming responses, including recognition, acknowledgement, and endorsement. The therapist has the task of helping clients to put forth confirming responses, starting with such simple things as helping one spouse to recognize that it is important to look their mate in the eyes and to acknowledge that the other has said something.

Conflict/Compromise

Working with the couple's conflicts and disagreements typically occurs concurrently with helping them with their communication abilities. The therapist generally does not function as a one-time mediator who helps the couple to solve a given problem and then moves on. Rather, the task is to help them make the emotional shifts that are necessary in order to effect compromises as well as to learn the kinds of problem-solving skills that are essential to functioning in the marital relationship.

Many vehicles are available for intervening in conflict/compromise situations. One that frequently serves multiple therapeutic purposes simultaneously is the "personal time conceptualization" approach. At an appropriate time I will attach to some of the desires or complaints voiced by one or both of the clients and say something along the lines of the following:

"I divide our personal, nonwork time into three kinds of time: private, parallel, and interactive. Private time is the time that we wish to have to do something by ourselves, read, go to the hardware store, meditate, whatever. We don't have to respond to or deal with anybody else. Parallel time is time in which we are in the vicinity of someone else but don't interact with him or her very much. One of you may be reading and the other may be watching television. You may be working on separate tasks fairly close to each other, just basically sharing the space and environment. Interactive time is time in which there is a fairly high degree of interaction, in which you are talking, arguing, making love, whatever, just so long as you are basically in interaction with each other. Most of us seem to need various amounts of each of these kinds of personal time. We may need more of one kind at one stage of our life than at others. It varies."

From that introduction we typically move on to look at the couple's needs and desires for the various kinds of personal time. We also examine the ways in which they attempt to "decompress" or "gear down" from their workday. What kinds of patterns or "rituals," if any, do they use for decompressing. How much time do they need for decompressing? How can they get it? How can the spouses help one another to get some decompression time?

Mr. and Mrs. Ray, a dual-career couple whose children had left home, renegotiated their personal time during the evenings as part of restructuring their somewhat delapidated relationship. Mrs. Ray had complained bitterly about her husband's practice of bringing work home with him, as well as of spending a considerable amount of time on the telephone on business matters during the evening. Paraphrasing a well-known comedian, she declared, "I get no attention. You've got yourself shut up in the study or a telephone stuck to your ear."

When we began to examine the needs and desires of the partners, Mrs. Ray softened considerably. As we established the fact that she got home first and had plenty of decompression time before her husband arrived, she began to see the situation in a slightly different light. Giving him some time to gear down began to make sense and seemed equitable to her. Mr. Ray seemed relieved, as well as pleased at the possibility of having time and opportunity to change his clothes and read the newspaper or putter in his workshop for 20 or 30 minutes before being expected to interact to any significant degree with his wife. They also worked out an understanding and agreement for mutual responsibility for preparing or furnishing dinner. Following Mr. Ray's decompression time, they agreed to spend half an hour or perhaps less talking about their respective days or anything else they felt a need to share. Mrs. Ray subsequently indicated that she could fare adequately with only 15 minutes of interactive time, so long as it was "real quality time":

Mrs. Ray: If we have that, that's okay. In fact, we can spend most of the evening in parallel time. I have preparations to make for the next day. I don't need to spend the entire evening with George. It's all right with me for him to go in the study and work if he needs to, just so long as we get that [interactive] time and some more interactive time before we go to sleep. In fact, [to her husband, laughingly] things might go much better in the area of sex if we can be together and apart like we're talking about.

Behavioral marital therapists have been the most explicit of the marital therapists in describing how much skills can be developed. Problem solving can be broken down into steps of selecting and stating a problem, listing possible alternative solutions, and agreeing on a final solution (Lester, Beckham, & Baucom, 1980). This process can be taught in therapy sessions where the therapist takes an active teaching, guiding, facilitating role, and can be modified from the ways in which a strict behaviorist may teach it. The clinician can give attention to the body postures and various emotional reactions of the partners, for example, and interpret them. I sometimes use a "reversal technique" when I am trying to help partners negotiate a settlement on a particular issue. Each partner is simply asked to state the things to be gained from or the importance of following the course advocated by the other mate, and then to do the same thing with their own proposal. The issues brought out are discussed as calmly as possible and each partner is supported and reinforced at several points during the discussion.

Clients often soften during this process and make progress toward "getting to yes" (Fisher & Ury, 1981) in their negotiations. This is especially likely to happen if emergent patterns are described and examined where practical and efforts made to defuse hot issues before change is requested. Attitudes can often be significantly altered and misperceptions corrected; dealing with the emotional reactions of the clients to the problem-solving process may be vitally important, in my judgment.

Helping a couple to accept and consolidate an advance that has been made in their relationship often requires a considerable amount of active work on the part of the therapist. The power relationship in Mr. and Mrs. Wood's 25-year marriage provides an example of this situation. Their relationship had been such that the wife felt coerced by her husband; she complained that he had been much more assertive than she, adding, "We do what he wants to do, and he doesn't do what he doesn't want to do."

In therapy sessions the therapist struggled to stay on the path of outlining and underlining the fact that the wife alone knew what she thought and felt. He attempted to make it clear to both partners by citing examples from their interactions that it was "not productive to try to read or label the thoughts and feelings of the other." Mrs. Woods, however, repeatedly reverted to the past, talking about how things "used to be" and how her husband failed to meet her needs:

Therapist: Yes, things were that way in the past. Both of you basically agree on how things went until very recently. [This statement was the forerunner of a confrontive and shaping response.] Your husband has finally gotten your message and does wish to hear you. He's making some positive responses to your needs and wishes [as illustrated by several examples from both the therapy sessions and the clients' reports of their outside interaction]. Agreed?

Wife: Yes, he is.

Therapist: Correct. He's listening to you, and he gives indications that he is concerned about how you feel. That faces you with a new task. When he makes a change, it calls for a response from you. You have both the freedom and, I think, the responsibility of responding to his positive actions if you wish to affirm and consolidate the changes that he has made.

Interactively, it was evident that the couple tended to see things in "either/or" terms. This was corroborated when Mr. Woods said, "I think I'm open to hearing what she has to say when she tells me something should be corrected, rather than criticizing me and telling me what I did wrong in the past." He went on to cite an incident from the previous night in which his wife said to him, "The next time you're going to [get the roof of their house cleaned], let me know, and I'd like to say something." He indicated that his response had been "Fine," meaning that he regarded the statement by his wife as a positive contribution and not merely negative criticism.

At that point in the session, Mrs. Woods acknowledged that she had heard him as meaning that he was open to her request, but quickly launched into a kind of "Yes, but" response. She began to talk about him "dropping the load off" on her. From there she segued into a litany of complaints about how "You always dump the household responsibilities on me and the children."

The therapist interrupted to point out that two things seemed to be emerging. One was Mrs. Woods' general reluctance to take a stance because of fear that her husband might retaliate against her. The retaliation as she described it would be essentially passive. The husband was not depicted as actively pursuing her to express his displeasure if she took a stance on a matter but as withdrawing. The second emergent issue was that the partners did not seem to have adequate methods for dealing with things together, handling matters unilaterally or not at all. The two issues—Mrs. Woods reluctance to take a stand until after something had been done and then responding critically, and their lack of cooperative patterns—were pulled together as a joint concern and marked out as a focus for that and subsequent sessions.

With the Woods, slowly, painstakingly, efforts were made to help them learn how to explore their feelings and expectations and to begin risking change. Parts of the process were repetitive, even as movement occurred from one phase to another. Changes disclosed more barriers to change.

Mrs. Woods stubbornly maintained that she had "been the only one to complain" and that, as a consequence, she had the right to expect her husband to make all of the moves toward changing their marriage. Her feelings were summarized in the statement "He would change if he cared." By this time she was acknowledging that her expectations were that her husband should make all the moves toward restoration of communication and expression of affection. Efforts by her husband to help her see that he had also been dissatisfied and that his withdrawal and silence had been expressions of his own unhappiness were essentially futile. Invaribly, she returned to making her point that she had been the only one complaining and because of that her husband had to make the first moves. Efforts by the therapist to reach her underlying emotions such as the hurt and fear that lay beneath her anger were similarly unsuccessful. Consequently, the therapist shifted to another line of approach.

Out of Mrs. Woods' complaints in the sessions the therapist ferreted an acknowledgment that she desired her husband to talk with her when he came home at night. His times of arriving home were variable because of business engagements that appeared to be legitimate in nature. Probing her feelings elicited protestations that Mrs. Woods did "not mind the fact that he is out or the things that keep him out." "What bothers me," she said, is "the fact that when he comes in he does not talk with me and sometimes goes almost straight to bed without talking with me."

"You're usually lying on the sofa watching television when I come in, and I don't know whether or not you want to be disturbed," replied her husband.

Efforts to suggest that Mrs. Woods give her husband some kind of indication or signal that he is not interrupting and that she is available to talk, such as shutting off the television or going into the kitchen if he stopped there when he came into the house were not successful. She responded that her husband read the newspaper when he came in and that "he can't be reached when he is reading the paper." It also emerged that in the past when she would get up in the morning and go into the kitchen, she felt that her husband did not need her. "He would eat a bowl of cold cereal, read the paper, and not talk with me." At this time she was remaining in bed until 8:00 A.M. or later, and there was no way that her husband could say anything to her before he left even if he tried, because she was too sleepy. She made it clear that she did not plan to change her patterns.

The therapist suggested a *quid pro quo* contingency contract in which Mr. Woods would have an opportunity for some "decompression time" and then share some time with his wife when he came in at night. She would permit him to read the evening newspaper while she finished her television program and he would then give her his undivided attention for 10 minutes. The 10-minute period was the amount requested by Mrs. Wood. The contract was fashioned in the context of other efforts to find ways for the pair to get some productive time together and to help Mrs. Woods take advantage of the realistic possibilities that she had to get out of the home for social/recreational purposes during the week.

Why did such a contract work in this instance, when efforts to make behavioral and paradoxical interventions by previous therapists had been futile? It is difficult to know precisely, but the therapist's conclusion that the amount of time given to confrontive-supportive work evidently was the key factor seems to have some validity. The recognition of Mrs. Woods' "lack of confidence" as being related in part to a life-long pattern of reliance on others to step forward and do things was part of the picture. The recognition that Mr. Woods' slowness in differentiating from his family of origin had helped to establish patterns of disappointment and conflict earlier in their marriage was another factor. Working with the couple to deal with their marital life-cycle tasks associated with the departure of the children from home was still another part of helping them get to a point that they could change, as most likely was the fact that the "productive" time sought for them was structured in such ways that initially there were limits on their possibilities for intimacy. Not only were time limits set, such as in the 10-minute "undivided attention" periods, but also activities such as golf, tennis, and shopping gave them the opportunity to be together with something to serve as a buffer between them.

Possessing the bare skills of negotiation or communicational facility does not in itself solve marital problems. The assumption that improving understanding, empathy, and effective communication skills will relieve marital discord has been questioned by L'Abate and McHenry (1983) as a unilateral and perhaps overly simplistic approach. A couple that I once knew who had extensive training in communication and sensitization to feelings made this point tragically: Their skills and strongest efforts to be reasonable and understanding did not prevent one of the mates from committing suicide when feelings around the other's extramarital affair could not be tolerated.

One problem with skill training alone that shows up in therapeutic cases is that partners acquire skills without dealing with the affective issues in their relationship. Bare skills are somewhat like bare technology—that is, neutral and potentially harmful or helpful. When skill training is paired with therapeutic work that deals with the affective and related important aspects of a couple's relationship, the result certainly can be a great help to the partners.

It is of course not always the case that the couple will respond positively to such therapeutic interventions. Where blocks emerge in the process of negotiation and change efforts, the clinician needs to note the nature of the blockage. Are the blocks due to fear, misperception, entanglements in object relations that deter change?

The clinical judgment may be made in some cases that it is desirable to take a detour before making further attempts to solve the immediate problems of the couple. This may involve interventions such as family-of-origin sessions for each spouse and their original family, examination of expectations and renegotiation of important parts of their "couple contract" (Sager, 1976), significant alteration of their collusive relationship, or other actions. Once some of the emergent issues have been dealt with satisfactorily (e.g., anger exposed and worked through or misperceptions significantly modified), the task of compromising may become more possible and sometimes markedly easier.

What is needed to moderate or remove the block? Some clinicians will choose to use indirect treatment approaches and devise additional paradoxical interventions in an effort to get around a block, while others will seek to address the emotions (Greenberg & Johnson, 1986) of the clients or practical problems. Still others may think it important to examine the object relations that prevail between the partners.

Object Relations

Object-relations theory provides a perspective in which what are generally considered pathological traits in individuals actually have a healthy restorative or reparative aspect (Stewart, Peters, Marsh, & Peters, 1975). As Dicks (1963) has pointed out, some marriages in which the partners each represent one half of a total personality continue in force because staying in the relationship is the way the spouses seek to grow and attain personal integration. The answer to the common question of "Why do they stay in the relationship?" often is "Because that's probably the best pattern of healthy striving that they have been able to establish up to this time. That's how they have tried to handle their intimacy, power, and related needs."

Some cases will in my judgment show only limited progress without alteration of the object-relations attachments between the spouses. Projective identification and collusion may emerge as important clinical issues as a result of initial presentations by the clients or through subsequent events in treatment. They may also have shown up as relationship problems after the marriage has been underway for an extended period of time or existed as evident problems from the outset of the relationship.

The Davis couple mentioned above in a discussion concerning communication provides an example of the emergence of such problems after several years of marriage. Their early relationship embodied a collusive process somewhat as follows: Mrs. Davis valued family life highly and sought a "safe harbor" relationship; she did not seek power in the marriage. Mr. Davis assumed power readily, viewing his wife as someone who would take over and dominate him completely if he did not take a strong, controlling stance. He viewed all women that way. His fear of getting close to women was reflected in the transitory nature of a series of clandestine extramarital affairs and in his steering clear of intensive emotional involvement with his wife. Mrs. Davis colluded also in not pushing him for more emotional closeness, viewing him as "somewhat timid." At another level, Mr. Davis' actions regarding women were supported by his need to fulfill a "macho" stereotype with his male friends.

The needs and dynamics of the partners began to shift as they moved into their middle and later thirties. By that time Mrs. Davis had become more confident as a result of her experiences in the work world and more dissatisfied with the lack of intimacy and poor quality of family life that she experienced with her husband, a dissatisfaction in part due to the fact that things had not developed as she had expected when they had children. Her own needs and essentially unconscious wishes to experience vicariously "good fathering" through her husband's treatment of their children were not fulfilled.

The marital relationship began to encounter serious problems when Mrs. Davis no longer colluded in ways that permitted the partners to remain distant, beginning to ask that her husband spend more time at home and give attention to the family. Although there was considerable evidence that her requests were mild and that she literally begged him for what she desired for herself and the children, Mr. Davis continued to misperceive her as potentially dominating. Because these misperceptions met certain denied needs of Mr. Davis, he was strongly motivated to continue them, regardless of his wife's behaviors or verbalizations (Mannino & Greenspan, 1976). The process of projective identification in which he projected his inner psychic contents onto his wife, perceived her responses in terms of his projections, and reintrojected the responses as reality continued to operate.

Therapeutic operations with the couple involved attempts to correct the misperceptions stemming from the projections by pointing out parts of reality that were being ignored or missed in the transactions. As this proceeded, it was possible to note such things as, "It's clear that there are distortions and omissions in how you regard the other's actions and motivations," and to illustrate these misperceptions. Each partner could then have the experience of being supported appropriately in their quest for understanding as well as of being confronted with reality reinforcement where they were misperceiving. Such gradual "midwiving" of the relationship began to put them in a position of being able both to get in touch with their spouse in more realistic terms and to get in touch with their own thoughts, feelings, and needs more adequately.

This work was accompanied by efforts to raise the possibility that the sources of the misperceptions could be discovered and altered. This involved working with Mr. Davis' perceptions of females based on his experiences with his mother and Mrs. Davis' perceptions of significant other persons stemming from her early and continuing experiences in her family of origin. Attention was also given to the models of relationships that each had internalized as those models affected their expectations of marriage.

The rather direct confrontational approach described here is not indicated for all couples. There must be sufficient personality (selfhood) strength and flexibility for the clients to tolerate such directness, even when it is embedded in a context of strong supportiveness. The fact that Mr. Davis had undergone personal psychotherapy with another clinician prior to entering marital therapy made the movement more possible and faster than it would have been otherwise, because he had experienced treatment that was both warmly supportive and appropriately representational of reality. Thus, some of the necessary steps of developing positive feelings about the self and learning that it was possible to face sources of pain had already been taken.

All of this work was done gradually and with careful attention to the fears of the clients about getting in touch with the split-off parts of themselves. As Wachtel and Wachtel (1986) have recently pointed out, one of the most significant ways to reduce anxiety is via exposure to what has been fearfully avoided. I have found a number of simple analogies and metaphors useful in encouraging clients to open up and deal with fearful topics. One would be the comparison to being fearful of a dark basement and quite uncomfortable while trying to find the light switch, but finding that there was nothing present when the light was turned on that could not be comprehended and managed. The point is not that there is nothing to fear, because there sometimes is, but that the possible risk needs to be put into the proper perspective (Wachtel & Wachtel, 1986).

Such techniques can aid in getting clients to the point that they can talk about previously feared matters. Such endeavors by the clients may require not only support from the therapist but also education and skill development that allows them to communicate more clearly, compromise more effectively, and generally deal better with their marriage and lives. The next step is to prepare them to face the sources of their old fears and apprehensions where possible and to learn for themselves where and in what ways they can modify the situation both in their marriage and with their family of origin.

Family-of-Origin Issue

There are several different approaches to dealing with family-of-origin issues. The therapist can, for example, coach the husband in the presence of his wife on how to go home and address unresolved differentiation issues with his family of origin (Bowen, 1978). The therapist can work with an adult client to help him or her resolve authority issues so that their parents become "former parents" (Williamson, 1981, 1982). Parents and other family members can be brought into therapy sessions to work on family-of-origin matters directly, as Framo (1981) advocates. It should be noted here that there are differences between unresolved issues from the past and present relationship difficulties with one's family. To recognize, for example, that "I behave like my mother" or react to strong males "as if they were my father" and need to change the contributory thoughts and feelings is not the same thing as recognizing a need to alter the contemporary relationship and interaction with one's parent.

Some issues stemming from clients' backgrounds can be handled directly with the spouses without involvement of members of their respective families of origin. Exploration of the family of origin of one spouse in the presence of the other is frequently helpful in exposing issues and bringing them into the therapeutic arena for change efforts. I often construct a genogram of the husband's family, for example, and have the wife fill in information and make comments following the initial disclosures by the husband. The process is then reversed and the wife's family of origin explored with input from the husband. Not only the total process but also the specific observations of the spouse regarding her or his in-laws and spouse generally prove to be helpful in therapy. The caveat that such shared exploration is risky and unwise when the partners manifest indications that they are vindictive and vengeful needs to be noted. In short, shared exploration is not indicated with all couples.

Exploring a couples' marital history in relation to their families of origin also proves useful in some instances. The Lakes furnish an example. Exploration of "money" and associated meanings led to the reworking of issues that had plagued the couple from the time of their engagement onward.

Mention of the actions of Mr. Lake's mother during the first 15 years or so of their marriage surfaced several times in sessions. Until she had become terminally ill, she had given them money and other gifts continually, while at the same time voicing the question repeatedly, "When are [Mrs. Lake's parents] going to do something for the children?" Mrs. Lake's family had been landed and powerful, and had emphasized hard work, "early to bed, early to rise," and similar virtues. Mr. Lake's father, the son of a blue-collar worker, was a newly rich physician who had amassed a considerable amount of money through his own shrewdness and sometimes questionable financial dealings.

Several things emerged in a session to elucidate patterns of living for the Lakes. Mrs. Lake related an incident in which a statement had been made during the couple's engagement by a friend of her future husband's family about his "good fortune in marrying into money." Her family not only felt that everybody had to earn their money, as they had done over several generations, but also that anybody marrying into the family might be trying to "get something for nothing." They had viewed Dr. Lake as a "corner cutter," and viewed his son similarly. Neither his pattern of going to work in an accounting firm at 9 or 10 A.M. nor his extensive golfing with clients were understood or accepted by her parents and extended family; they did not "play" until after the work had been completed. Persons coming into the family had to "stand up for themselves" and be self-protective, and anybody who could not do so, such as an alcoholic in-law, was likely to be ostracized. The revelatory session also included statements by Mrs. Lake on how she had protected her husband from her family, which information genuinely surprised her husband.

Mr. Lake readily acknowledged being intimidated by Mrs. Lake's family, and the agreement by the partners that making money was one major way of proving that one could "make it" in her family opened the way for a significant piece of insight regarding this. He had been attempting to give money (or possessions that were quite expensive) to her in order to prove his worth and his love. The impact of his mother's money and giving emphases in shaping his early and continuing drive to give to his wife became dramatically clear to both partners.

Other pieces of awareness enabled Mr. Lake to cease some of his own corner-cutting activities and some of his flouting of rules and authority. This flouting of rules at his "hard work ethic" company not only allowed him to show her family symbolically that he could do things his way but also proved to Mr. Lake that he could do as well as his father in corner cutting.

The immediate gains for the marriage were joint discoveries by the partners that old behaviors could be discontinued. Mrs. Lake found that she did not have to protect her husband any longer from her family, and Mr. Lake learned that he did not have to try so hard to present his wife with money. This latter discovery was underlined particularly when Mrs. Lake encouraged her husband to drop out of a profitable but somewhat questionable sideline business, saying, "We don't need the money that badly—you provide more than adequately without it."

Family-of-origin issues emerge in therapeutic sessions in a variety of ways, as shown in the examples of the Davis couple, the Woods couple, and the Lakes. A fourth couple, the Birds, brought family-of-origin matters into the therapeutic sessions in still another way. While Mr. Bird noted that his wife was behaving in ways that were similar to how her father acted, Mrs. Bird reactively pointed out that her husband was acting in a manner that paralled her mother's actions. Each of these situations called for an examination by the therapist of the issues involved in the marital relationship.

Brief Summary of the Middle Stage

This stage of therapy with marital couples is one in which the activity level of the therapist is variable and in which several issues are addressed. There is a continued structuring of treatment in which clients are expected to both "settle down" from their initial anxiety and to "settle into" an ongoing therapeutic relationship. The methods of treatment may be either direct or indirect, depending on which method seems more effective for dealing with the difficulties faced by the clients. The therapist is concerned with such difficulties and with the ways in which the partners are handling the developmental marital tasks appropriate to where they are located in the marital life cycle.

The integrative approach sketched here is one in which the therapist typically starts with a relatively neutral area such as the couple's communication. This generally leads to the issue of how the marital partners deal with their differences and thus to asking the following types of questions:

1. What are the acute and chronic problems between the husband and wife? What kinds of symptomatology exist in either the husband or wife or in both?

2. What kinds of skills need to be developed in the partners so that they can communicate, negotiate, and problem solve? What kinds of alteration of attitudes, perceptions, and misperceptions are required? What kinds of exploration of expectations are needed in order to help them clarify their relationship and make the changes that will lead to a viable marital relationship?

3. What are the blocks to communication and problem solving? What kinds of reeducation are needed? What kinds of object-relations issues prevail? What unresolved issues from their respective families or origin remain and how do they affect the marital/individual functioning of the persons with whom we are working? What is needed in order to make the pertinent changes for each partner individually and for their marital interaction?

THE TERMINATION STAGE

Ending marital therapy in a formal sense can take anywhere from one or two to several appointments. From my perspective, the ideal way to end treatment is for the therapist and the clients to decide independently that it is time to terminate the therapy and then to determine cooperatively the pattern to be followed. This holds true both in cases in which the partners have dealt with their difficulties as effectively as possible and in instances in which an apparently insoluble therapeutic impasse prevails. The least desirable pattern is one in which one or both partners drops out of treatment without examining with the therapist their reasons for doing so.

Planned termination may occur in one or two sessions if the clients are ready to stop treatment, while other instances may involve a pattern of gradual termination in which appointments will be spaced out at wide intervals (e.g., once a month) for a few sessions. A third pattern involves termination with a "check-up" session scheduled after a period of 1 to 3 months, usually arranged with the proviso that the clients can decide to call and cancel the scheduled appointment if they do not feel that they need the checkup session. A fourth pattern involves termination with the understanding that the couple can call back and arrange to come in again at any time they elect to do so.

Criteria for Termination

What are the bases for deciding that marital therapy should be terminated? When therapy is ended on a planned basis, several factors enter into the decision to terminate. One of these is the determination that the presenting problems—the issues that brought the couple into treatment—have been resolved as completely as possible; the symptomatology that was present has been altered or has disappeared. Another is the decision that additional problems that arose during the course of therapy have been dealt with as adequately as possible at the time.

There also are, as noted, certain specified criteria or rule-of-thumb bases for assessing the functioning of the marital relationship that can be used in conjunction with the presenting problem and symptomatology guidelines in deciding whether it is appropriate to terminate. These are the components of commitment, caring, communication, conflict/compromise, and volunteering. The relevant considerations are the following (Nichols & Everett, 1986): How much and what kind of commitment and caring are present? How does the communication function? How do the mates handle conflict? To what extent and in what ways are they able to compromise? How and in what ways do they "volunteer" (i.e., offer to do things for the spouse and in general function in the marital relationship?

Chapter Seven

Sexual Problems

Marital sexual problems either are presented to the clinician as part of the initial complaints or subsequently emerge when other issues have been addressed during the course of therapy. Whether couples seek therapy explicitly because of sexual complaints or the problems surface after treatment has begun, the majority of marital partners contacting marital therapists seem to experience sexual difficulty.

MARITAL SEXUAL PROBLEMS

The incidence of sexual difficulties among couples seeking marital therapy has been reported by some clinicians to run as high as 75 to 80% (Greene, 1970; Sager, 1974). Regardless of whether current proportions are at that high level, it still is true that dealing with sexual problems is a significant issue for today's marital therapists. Important clinical questions arise regarding the determination of the meaning and role of the dysfunctions in the marriage and need to decide what kind of treatment is required.

CLASSIFICATION OF MARITAL SEXUAL DYSFUNCTION

Marital sexual dysfunctions can be variously classified and treated in different ways, some by the new brief sex therapy and others through long-term, more intensive therapy. Sexual difficulties do not necessarily automatically signal the presence of deep and severe pathology, as psychoanalytic theory has held, nor necessarily imply that the marital relationship is severely disturbed.

Kaplan's Triphasic Classification

Kaplan (1974, 1979) has classified sexual dysfunction in terms of a triphasic model. Each of the three phases—desire, excitement, and orgasm—is importantly related to the sexual anxiety that Kaplan sees as affecting the physiological responses of the persons in their sexual behavior. The rule-of-thumb approach from clinical observation is that the more intense and severe the anxiety, the earlier in the sequence of desire–excitement–orgasm it emerges. Desire-phase problems emerge, for example, when the anxiety is severe, the sexual phase thus being affected very early on in the arousal process. The mere thought or anticipation of possible sexual experience may be sufficient to arouse anxiety and thus to dampen or eradicate sexual desire. Less severe and intense anxiety arises later in an individual, after the person has become physically aroused. Other individuals experience normal sexual responses until very late in sexual activity when their anxiety, milder than the anxieties that affect desire and excitement phases, emerges to interfere with their orgasm.

Described differently, desire-phase disorders involve more serious intrapsychic and/or marital disorders than either excitement- or orgasm-phase dysfunctions. Excitement-phase disorders fall midway between desire- and orgasm-phase difficulties and include such problems as impotence, which is associated with moderate degrees of underlying anxiety, while orgasm-phase disorders reflect the milder and more manageable underlying problems.

Kaplan (1979) also pointed out that the immediate causes of various sexual dysfunctions tend to be fairly specific, whereas the deeper causes are not specific. The specificity of the immediate causes makes it possible for the therapist to assign structured sexual tasks to a couple in an effort to modify these causes, while the deeper causes require psychodynamic techniques that are similar for all forms of dysfunction, according to Kaplan (1979). Problems associated with mild and transient concerns such as a passing fear of rejection, uncomplicated performance anxieties, and overconcern for the partner can be dealt with by means of brief sex therapy. Such mild underlying causes tend to be recognized consciously by the clients, unlike deeply rooted causes such as sexual conflict based in childhood injury and harmful residual effects or hostile and neurotic relationships between the partners, which are not considered treatable by the specific interventions of brief therapy but require more general and intensive therapeutic work.

Other Classifications

Most of Kaplan's classification was used in the DSM-III (American Psychiatric Association, 1980). The sexual response cycle there is divided into appetitive, excitement, orgasm, and resolution phases. Diagnostic criteria are given for all phases. The DSM-III classification also includes under psychosexual dysfunctions involuntary vaginismus (involuntary spasms of the muscles of the vagina that interfere with sexual intercourse), functional dyspareunia (recurrent, persistent genital pain), and atypically psychosexual dysfunction.

A somewhat broader and more clinically useful classification has been made by Schover and associates (Schover, Friedman, Weiler, Heiman, & LoPiccolo, 1982). They separate sexual dysfunction into six axes: desire, arousal, orgasm, coital pain, satisfaction with current frequency of sex, and qualifying information. Complaints about frequency of sexual activity are among the more common sexual issues presented in my clinical practice. These complaints may pertain directly and primarily to dissatisfaction with the frequency of lovemaking (e.g., "We almost *never* have sex," "He wants to go to bed three times a day") or may point to problems in other areas such as lack of desire or a wish to avoid physically painful coital activity. The "qualifying information" axis refers to homosexuality, sexual deviation, sadomasochistic practices, past or present psychopathology, the use of alcohol and nonprescription drugs, extramarital affairs, spouse abuse, physical/medical conditions, and the use of medication, any of which may affect the marital sexual relationship.

ASSESSMENT

Some conditions, as noted above, are amenable to the new brief sex therapy approach, whereas others require long-term, intensive psychotherapeutic work. While there are no firm and inflexible guidelines, there are some general pointers to help the clinician in deciding whether to refer to case for specific sex therapy or to treat the problems within the context of ongoing marital or individual psychotherapy.

Brief Sex Therapy

This relatively new part of the clinical scene is focused solely on overcoming the specified sexual dysfunction; it is not intended as a therapeutic approach for coping with other parts of marital dysfunction. Brief sex therapy involves sexual conditioning, deconditioning, and other learning; the assignment of specific tasks to the couple; and the therapist's use of the couple's responses. The immediate goals are to open communication, secure reactions from the couple to the interventions, and develop specific kinds of cooperation between the partners. In addition to Kaplan's (1979) indications that brief sex therapy is helpful primarily with orgasm dysfunctions and with some of the midrange excitement problems, there are other limitations to its use. Sager (1974) has strongly emphasized the necessity that the couple be able to meet certain requirements for cooperation in order for brief sex therapy to be workable. The most important of these are the ability to shelve hostility and fighting for a few weeks while the therapy is conducted, to accept one another as sexual partners, and for each to be desirous of helping herself or himself and the other partner. Inability to achieve such a level of cooperation is seen as a contraindication for brief sex therapy, since severe marital discord and basic hostility prevent spouses from cooperating in brief, rapid treatment of the dysfunction (Kaplan, 1979; Sager, 1974).

Sexual Problem History

Whenever a sexual complaint is a significant part of the initial presenting complaint, some history of the problem should be taken. Mrs. Creeks's initial statement of the difficulties at the telephone level was, in part, as follows: "We don't communicate effectively, especially about money. Money, I guess that's it. And our sex life is practically nonexistent." Such a statement is a clear indication, of course, that attention should be given to exploration of the couple's sexual difficulties.

Exploring the sexual complaint and the joint sexual history of the couple may or may not lead to the clinical decision that a complete sexual history for each spouse is indicated. The amount of information needed in order to determine the nature and extent of the dysfunction and the kind of treatment required is the amount of information that the clinician needs. The experienced clinician does not need to secure information for the sake of amassing information.

If sexual complaints are not voiced during the initial assessment phase, the clinician should inquire about sexual issues. "What about sexual difficulties?" is an appropriate question and one more useful than a query that permits a simple "Yes," "No," or "It's all right" response. If the answers of the spouses indicate that there are no sexual problems, especially after a follow-up question or two, my general procedure is to drop the matter, at least for the time being. Experience indicates that in many marriages sexual problems are not a significant issue, and that in others sexual problems either improve as the general marital relationship improves or are brought into treatment subsequently if the partners feel that they are a concern after some other things have been handled. If the latter is the case, it is important to attempt to determine what are the general psychological conditions and adjustment of the spouses and what impact those conditions have on the sexual relationship and functioning.

Examination of the current sexual relationship involves explicit questions about complaints. What exactly are the problems? Are you satisfied with the frequency of intercourse? With the lovemaking itself? If not, in what ways? At what point or points do you have difficulties? When getting aroused? With maintaining an erection? With pain? With following through to orgasm? Specific inquiries regarding timing, place of lovemaking, actions leading up to sexual intimacy, actions of the partner both outside and inside the bedroom may be useful. These and a large number of questions regarding feelings about functioning and the functioning itself can be used by the therapist. Careful attention to the verbal and nonverbal responses of the partners provides the therapist with further leads as to specific areas on which to focus. This should be heading toward an elucidation of the dysfunction: inhibited sexual desire, problems with erection or ejaculation, vaginismus, dispareunia, orgasmic functions, or other sexual difficulties.

As with all clinical problems it is important to gain some understanding of the onset and subsequent course of the sexual dysfunction. How was the early sexual relationship and functioning? Did the couple have a good sexual relationship and then lose it? If so, at what stage or point did the difficulties begin to develop? When did the sexual relationship cease to develop positively, become less satisfying, less functional? What was happening immediately prior to the time it began to go "off the track"? What kinds of things in the partners' relational history may underlie the current dysfunction? If the relationship was good and changed, what kinds of things occurred in their lives and relationship immediately prior to the onset of the difficulty? What happened inside the marriage and what external things such as job changes, geographical relocations, or other forms of potentially stressful events can be found? Careful attention to where the partners are in terms of coping with the tasks of the marital, family, and individual life cycles is indicated. If according to the partners the relationship was never good, the clinician should be prepared to explore the expectations of the spouses, their individual sexual histories, and the interactive history of their general relationship.

The joint exploration should also be concerned with obtaining information about factors possibly contributing to the dysfunction. If information has not already been secured on such matters as alcohol and drug use and physical problems such as diabetes mellitus, cardiovascular disease, multiple sclerosis, renal disease, and stroke, among others (Hammond, 1984), inquiries should be made about such matters. Reports from physicians may be helpful in some instances in evaluating the possible physical contributions of disease and medication on sexual functioning. What kinds of instructions have been given the person by their physician? What kinds of understandings or misunderstandings about sexual activity have resulted from such physician instructions?

Inquiry should also be made into what kinds of expectations the partners hold about sexual relating and sexual experience in order to determine whether the expectations appear to be realistic. Current expectations are often related not simply to how oneself and one's spouse behave specifically in sexual activity but concern general assumptions about sexual relating and hence sexual dysfunction that can be associated with significant discrepancies in sex-role conditioning and expectations. The wife or husband may not be doing what the other feels or thinks "should" be done, inside or outside the bedroom. This kind of condition is particularly prevalent today with couples who are in transition from the traditional sex-role patterns of their respective families of origin toward something different. Bedroom and extrabedroom expectations may change for a woman who has gone to work outside the home and expects to be treated more equally than when her husband was the sole breadwinner, for example. Men in such positions often do not change their expectations—despite their verbalizations concerning equality—and continue to expect to enjoy the same feelings of prestige and be in control of the same areas they have always controlled in the marriage. Struggles over equality and control may originate in the bedroom, may start outside and move into the sexual relationship, or, what is more likely, may arise simultaneously in both areas. Therapeutic work on sex-role conflicts is ancillary to dealing with the sexual dysfunction but may make significant contributions to the amelioration of sexual difficulties. Feldman (1986) has described therapeutic theory, assessment, and techniques for dealing with sex-role conflicts as involving behavioral, cognitive, and emotional aspects. These include identifying and changing—through behavioral, cognitive, and psychodynamic treatment—the behavioral, cognitive, and emotional effects of sex-role conditioning for each partner and how these form part of the marital discord.

The clinician also seeks to determine the kinds of ignorance about anatomical or functional sexual matters that exist, as well as the kinds of things in the couple's current relational experience that may be contributing to or causing their sexual dysfunction.

Triggering devices for the beginning of the difficulty may have been simply that—triggering devices. Once dysfunction has started, it may continue long after the original precipitating cause has disappeared from the scene. Either a form of inertia or a combination of emotional scar tissue from the original disruption in their sexual relating and anxiety about functioning sexually with the partner and possibly experiencing failure or rejection may combine to keep spouses from trying to remedy the situation.

Careful attention also is needed in looking at the previous efforts the partners have made to change things. What attempts have they made on their own? What kinds of help have they sought from reading, from attending meetings or classes, from friends or family members, or from contacting other professionals? What have been the outcomes of their attempts to help themselves or to secure assistance from others? What kinds of expectations do they have regarding the help that the clinician can provide?

Individual Sexual History

By the time the clinician has completed such exploration of the couple's sexual problem(s), if it has not been possible to develop some sound hypotheses and possible explanations for the difficulties, it becomes important to consider undertaking exploration with each partner individually. Unlike family-of-origin exploration, which generally is done most productively in the presence of the person's marital partner, in my judgment, a sexual history is most effectively and appropriately conducted without the presence of the spouse. There are some areas that typically will not be or perhaps should not be discussed with the spouse present at this point in the therapeutic contact (e.g., perhaps masturbatory history, incestual activities, negative reactions to the spouse's hygenic practices, sexual relations with other persons besides the spouse). Some of these issues may be carried into conjoint sessions at a later time if they significantly affect the spouse and the current relationship and the clinical judgment is that they can best be worked on in conjoint sessions.

There are a number of ways to secure sexual histories. My preference is to look for both events and attitudes in the background of the individual and to treat things in as much of a normalizing fashion as possible. The individual life cycle forms the framework. Questions such as the following are included: "Going back as far as you can remember, how did your parents handle your developing curiosity about human bodies?" "How did you learn about male–female differences?" "How was nudity handled in your home?" As these and similiar questions are raised, there is exploration and discussion of the attitudes and events that are recalled, which includes a search for the client's understanding at the time these childhood events and experiences were encountered as well as for her or his subsequent comprehension.

Questions are raised about developing curiosity and about the exploration of one's own body and exploration with other children. I ask about incidents of "playing doctor" or "show and tell." Again, attention is given to feelings, to how these situations were responded to by adults in cases where the adults became aware, and residual reactions and questions on the part of the individual. It is not uncommon to have clients talk about childhood questions and residual feelings for the first time when they are dealing with a clinician.

Using the life-cycle and developmental framework, the therapist should also ask about normal developmental issues such as the onset of menstruation for girls, their preparation for beginning their menses, and their feelings and questions. The changes of puberty and where they ranked in relation to their peers, particularly if they matured early or late,and the questions and experiences they had during adolescence flow naturally in a sexual history.

"When did your masturbation begin?" is a straightforward question that elicits a variety of responses: "When I was about _____." "I'm not certain, but. . . ." "I didn't; I never did." Some educational work may help clients to recognize that the pleasant experiences they secured by rocking back and forth on their stomach on the bed or by rubbing up against a chair leg when they were preschoolers or elementary-age children were masturbatory activities. Generally this explanation also helps to some degree in putting human sexuality into a normal developmental framework. During adolescence and subsequently when masturbation was clearly recognized as masturbation, the matter of feelings about such activities and the use of fantasy deserve exploration. Once again, education and information about the normality of such experiences may be helpful to clients.

Exploration of adolescent–youth experiences and experimentation also requires careful attention to events and feelings, and sometimes offers the opportunity to educate and alleviate ignorance and residual feelings of shame and guilt. "What about sexual experimentation?" "Any homosexual or same sex activity?" These questions or variants tailored to the personality of the client are an essential part of the sexual history. Especially important, again, is the need to spend as much time as the situation seems to warrant dealing with any residual feelings from such activities. This does not imply that all clients have carry-over problems from their developmental experiences,because this certainly is not the case. Rather, it is to point out that where sexual history exploration elicits indications of unresolved issues, the clinician both is wise and has an ethical responsibility to try to help the client deal with what has been uncovered and not to simply gather information.

"Your first sexual intercourse came when?" is a question that often is answered by the client in responding to other questions or in discussing other matters. Follow-up queries pertain to the individual's reactions to early coital experiences: Were they pleasant, painful, bland, disappointing? One of the clinician's concerns is to secure an understanding of the meaning of coital activity and general lovemaking through the individual's active sexual history. If there have been multiple partners, what were the relationships like? What role did sex play in the relationships? Did mutuality exist, or were the relationships one-sided, exploitative? How do those relationships compare with the current marital relationship and interaction?

Areas for examination that may emerge spontaneously or sometimes may need to be inquired about involve sexual abuse, incest, and other matters that are typically hedged about with feelings of shame or guilt. One major question in instances of sexual abuse or incest is whether force was used so that the individual was hurt and experienced physical pain. Again, the client's understanding of what occurred and her or his feelings—particularly feelings of helplessness or exploitation—are important to examine, as are feelings of confusion because parts of the experiences were stimulating or enjoyable. Anger toward the other person in abuse or incest situations and toward parents who failed to protect them may be a residual part of such experiences with some clients. When an individual talks about sex play with a pet—not an exceptionally rare situation—the reactions are more likely to involve feelings of guilt or shame about admitting the involvement or about "using" the pet. Occasionally there are questions about whether they were "perverted" because of the sexual experiences with the pet. Again, the opportunity for educating, interpreting, supporting, and appropriately normalizing the experiences can be helpful to the marital therapy.

The dual purpose of the assessment phase here, as in other parts of marital therapy, is to gather information in order to plan for treatment and to make interventions as the assessment process is conducted. One major clinical goal in taking histories, either of the couple's sexual problem(s) or of their individual sexual development and experiences, is to discern the nature of their present difficulties and to link the difficulties with the immediate antecedents of the dysfunction and with the underlying causes and contributing factors. Another is to intervene and modify or to begin a modification process from the beginning of the exploration.

TREATMENT

Once the assessment of the difficulties has been completed, the task becomes that of deciding whether the sexual dysfunction should become the immediate focus of treatment and whether brief sex therapy or long-term treatment is indicated. My own practice, for whatever reasons, has attracted comparatively few couples whose needs were specifically suited to brief sex therapy. Most have other significant problems and do not regard their sexual dysfunction as primary. On the other hand, over the past 10 to 15 years there have been a noticeable number of cases appearing in which the partners had undergone brief sex therapy prior to seeking marital therapy as such. These clients have presented a mixed picture: Some have felt that they were helped with their sexual problem but found that they still had major marital/personal difficulties, while others did not think that their sexual dysfunction had improved. My approach to most of such clients has been, "Well, you have tried focusing solely on the sexual difficulties. That did some [or no] good, but there are still some problems in your marriage and in your lives. Let's start with your general relationship and any difficulties you have there and get to the sexual problems as that seems appropriate." With clients who do wish to focus specifically on the sexual problem at that time, the clinical work generally starts wherever it is they wish to start. Such an approach tends not only to defuse anxiety about sexual dysfunction but also to place it in a suitable context.

A similar approach to that described here is taken by some other clinicians. Heiman (1986), for example, divides treatment goals into two phases. The first phase focuses on forming an understanding with the couple of the function that the current sexual problem fulfills in their relationship. This involves an acknowledgment that the difficulty probably has a positive function and that each of the partners has made a positive contribution by their efforts to stay in the relationship while adapting to the sexual dysfunction. The goals of the second phase focus more on intervention. As Heiman (1986) notes, some couples may decide with the therapist to try to deal with the specific dysfunction, while others may chose to work on their general relationship and then deal with the sexual issues.

The same kind of integrative therapeutic approach described earlier in this book also applies to sexual problem cases: One can start with the more apparent, more readily available issues and make interventions there without assuming the necessity of working with deeper, underlying issues, moving beyond the more readily accessible materials as it becomes necessary. This is essentially consistent with what Kaplan (1979) has described for working in psychosexual therapy as such. She has indicated that the first goal is to modify the immediate causes of the sexual symptoms, since as one works to modify the symptoms, underlying resistances emerge and are handled to the degree necessary in order to effect change in the sexual dysfunction.

A simple illustration of one treatment approach to excitement/orgasm-phase difficulties is provided by work with Mr. and Mrs. Lane. Dealing with their sexual relating was taken on after work had been done with other issues, including helping them to settle down and settle into therapy and to begin reestablishing mutual trust. Mrs. Lane was the chaser and Mr. Lane the pursued in their emotional and sexual relationship. As treatment began to focus in on what was occurring in their sexual relationship, it became apparent that things seemed to proceed smoothly enough until they got close to actually engaging in sex play and coital activity. Sometimes a loss of erection occurred, sometimes premature ejaculation, sometimes they did succeed in completing intercourse but it was seldom satisfactory for either of them.

Each partner was asked to monitor their thoughts and feelings during certain points as they started into foreplay and intercourse. "What do you think and what do you feel _____?" This was accompanied by the statement: "From what you have said, things appear to be all right so long as you feel comfortable. If you start to feel uncomfortable, monitor your feelings and thoughts and try to get a firm grasp on what is happening with your thoughts and feelings so that we can try to understand where the blocks are."

This turned out to be an issue primarily for Mr. Lane, the partner who pulled out of the sexual cycle, his wife's reactions being essentially in response to what happened with him. Mr. Lane noted that as he started to get physically close and begin foreplay—or if his wife began foreplay—he got "anxious." The therapist and couple explored this situation and determined that there seemed to be nothing in the immediate circumstances that either partner could find that could reasonably be expected to cause an anxious reaction. Although in many instances there are unnoted factors in the immediate situation that produce anxiety, dealing with the present system alone did not appear to be an adequate way to deal with the dysfunction in this case.

"Can you remember other times that you felt similarly?" Mr. Lane was asked. After some efforts at recall, he remembered feeling similarly at age 15 or 16 when he had been rejected by his first girlfriend, a rejection that had become associated in his mind with their petting/sexual activity. His pain at losing her when she dropped him for somebody else had been deep and difficult to handle. Other losses in his family had contributed to his being upset, Mr. Lane related, and it had been a long time before he "could take a chance on getting close to another female." Things had gone well in the early stages with his wife, who had been warm and passionate and had been the initiator in their courtship, the sexual relationship ranging from "all right" to "pretty good" until after the birth of their child.

As the couple explored the situation with the therapist, Mrs. Lane was able to express some of her bewilderment and resentment at her husband's emotional and sexual withdrawal from her. Consequently, she began to soften somewhat and to lose some of the unacknowledged tension that had developed in her approach to her husband. Mr. Lane worked through some of his residual feelings of rejection fears, and a contract was worked out with the couple whereby Mr. Lane was given the task of approaching his wife for foreplay with the understanding that she not only would not reject him but would respond with a mild to moderate lustful reaction. Mrs. Lane agreed enthusiastically. The partners were then given the additional task of reversing the roles on alternate nights. With this alternating pattern and some assistance in learning to talk about what was pleasurable, the Lanes soon reported a disappearance of the dysfunction. At follow-up, they were still doing well and had added another child to their family without difficulty. Mr. Lane had become an active parent as well as an attentive and ardent husband.

Could this same result have been achieved by a straightforward behavioral approach, without the exploration of the source of the husband's anxiety? Perhaps so. The approach used here, which occurred in the context of ongoing marital therapy, took only a brief time in the larger therapeutic framework and was effective. It was also related to other issues affecting the couple, such as Mr. Lane's relationship with his young son, and matters that would not be dealt with in symptomatically focused brief sex therapy.

Not all cases fall neatly into one category of dysfunction, although some can be treated by the same approach even though they involve a mixture of complaints and dysfunction. Two sets of interesting "intimacy" issues frequently appear in marital cases in connection with sexual complaints. (Different cases with similar complaints may have different etiologies.) One set is found in couples who can get physically close but not intimate in an emotional sense; the other involves partners who claim to be—and appear to be—emotionally close without experiencing physical intimacy. The former situation—physical closeness and contact including sexual intercourse—certainly can be achieved without the attainment of an emotional closeness by the partners. Couples occasionally describe themselves as "going through the motions" or as being like "automatons, robots" in their sexual relationship and coital activity.

The Roses provide an example of this kind of relating. Mrs. Rose referred to their sexual relationship as "action that is devoid of meaning and feeling." At the same time, she acknowledged that there were significant parts of herself, of her thinking, feeling, and desires, that she had never revealed to her husband.

Mrs. Rose: Yes, that is characteristic of the way I deal with other people, especially about sex. I hold back. I've held back from Ben even though we've been married 3 years and had intercourse for 2 to 3 years before that. It's ironic, I suppose, that we regard ourselves as liberal and as being honest with each other. And we are honest with each other on most things. But in spite of all of that, I've never been able to tell him what I really like sexually, and I've never been able to let go as I feel like doing.

Mr. Rose: (encourages his wife to talk about what she was afraid to talk about) For God's sake, things couldn't be any deadlier and worse than they are now. I promise you I'll try to understand.

Mrs. Rose: Ben, I'm not sure that you will understand. I am afraid. I'm afraid that you'll think I'm vile and nasty if I tell you what I really want and what I really feel like doing when we have sex. I'm not sure that you can take it.

Her fear of his disapproval and rejection was strong, approximately as strong as her husband's anger at his perception of her "rejecting" him by obviously holding back in their physical intimacy and by not telling him what was the matter.

With some supportive probing for specificity about her desires and her concerns, Mrs. Rose related in rather earthy terms that were quite different from her usual sophisticated speech how she would like to be free to "scream, to totally let go and let out whatever fucking words come out without worrying about it." She talked also about her desire for oral sex, both cunnilingus and fellatio, "and whatever else comes naturally and spontaneously and doesn't hurt us," adding, "Now, I've told you!"

Mr. Rose: Yes, you have. And I'm not sure how to respond. I think that I can handle the yelling, if you want to do that. And swearing doesn't bother me. I've gotten used to all kinds of four-letter words from everybody, including little old grandmothers at work.

Mrs. Rose: But what about the rest of it?

Mr. Rose: I don't know, Janie. I used to think oral sex was "far out" when we first met, and I made a pretty strong statement about that, and probably other things, too. I've changed some. I think that I'm willing to at least be open to the possibilities. I don't think that you can ask me to promise any more at this point.

Mrs. Rose: Okay, look, I don't know how much yelling or swearing or whatever else I may actually do. But I want to be free to not worry about what I do. I don't want to have to worry about being embarrassed and having to be uptight every time we get in bed.

The therapist gave support and encouragement to the idea that it was all right for both of them to be "enthusiastic" and "earthy" in sexual relating. The partners eventually reached the point in subsequent discussion where either of them could "wear earplugs" if either were bothered by the language or gusto of the other. Letting go and giving were closely related in the couple's attempts to find both physical and emotional intimacy.

Partners that complain of being emotionally close but not physically intimate are likely to require help in dealing with desire-phase dysfunction in a significant proportion of such cases in my clinical experience. The Priests, who had come from extremely conservative backgrounds and who had been married for 15 years, claimed to have a high degree of respect and liking for each other, but had a spasmodic, tentative, and unsatisfactory sexual relationship. "Not much goes on" was Mr. Priest's description. "We avoid going to bed at the same time or one of us picks an argument, so that I think we never have to get together [sexually]," declared Mrs. Priest.

Several individual sessions were spent with each partner. Mr. Priest had struggled with masturbation and guilt about his "self-abuse" throughout late adolescence, through his years at a religiously conservative college, and well into marriage. Psychoeducational work, including the assignment of reading on normal sexual behaviors and discussion of the reading with the therapist, began to free him from some of the misinformation that had exacerbated his internal conflicts and debilitating guilt feelings.

Mrs. Priest's background included some traumatic experiences involving a father who had torn his clothes off and forced his wife into sexual intercourse on several occasions. A considerable amount of exploration, interpretation, and working through of previously repressed conflicts that emerged in dreams and dredged up memories was done with Mrs. Priest, including giving support for the feelings about the traumatic scenes she had witnessed as a child. Not only working with her about her fears but also about her feelings of shame and embarrassment about her parents and family of origin was an important part of the therapy. After she was able to talk about her mother's negative views about sex and men—including the recognition on her part that the parental relationship had been pathological and that her deceased father had been psychotic at times—Mrs. Priest began to find it possible to look anew at her own marriage. As she contrasted the parental relationship with her marriage, she began to see her husband as "really kind and gentle."

Imagery was used with the couple in conjoint sessions. They were asked to look around their bedroom in their imagination and to see who was present. What images did they see? Who are the "people" there? Predictably in this case, Mrs. Priest's parents were both present, her mother being a stronger image than her father, and Mr. Priest's strongly authoritarian father was part of the cast of characters "peopling" their bedroom. Slowly, the partners were able to make some progress in following the therapist's suggestion that they "sweep the ghosts out of the bedroom."

CHANGE OR NO CHANGE?

Clinicians need to keep in mind the possibility that clients do not always wish to make the changes that they have said they wish to make. Once they get past their initial ambivalence about treatment and change, they may still wish things to be different from the way they are at the present but not actually want what they have said they do. When evasiveness begins to appear each time efforts are made to secure change or make moves that presumably will bring about the requested result, a therapist will be reminded that a different agenda than the official one is operating with the clients. One or both may actually prefer divorce or a maintenance of the current situation, but feel that they should or must request the stated change. As Heiman (1986) also has pointed out, clients have a right not to change.

The therapist also needs to be alert to the possibility that he or she may be coercing clients into changing in the directions that the therapist deems appropriate. Accusing the clients of being "engaged in a power struggle," or of being "neurotically invested in behaving in an infantile fashion," or of being "uncooperative" or "untreatable" because they do not respond favorably to the clinician's interventions, interpretations, or behavioral change programs is unfair and occurs all too often. Heiman (1986) has described the lack of change as affording the opportunity for the clinician to examine what this means with regard to how the problems have been defined between the partners and between the partners and the therapist. Once again, helping the clients to share in the understanding of what the problematic behaviors and the resistance to change mean has, from my perspective as well as that of others (e.g., Heiman, 1986), some value for the therapeutic endeavor.

SEXUAL ABUSE

Sexual abuse as used here refers to sexual exploitation of one of the marital partners during their childhood or adolescent years. Either partner could have been the victim, of course, although clinical experience indicates that females are more likely than males to report having been sexually abused as children. Most of the abusers of young females (and young males as well, for that matter) are likely to have been males, a result in my opinion of the continuing male dominance and sexism in our society.

DEFINITION AND MEANING

Sexual abuse is specifically defined here as the use of a child by an adult or other much older person for their own sexual gratification (Finkelhor, 1985). Sexual abuse of children differs from physical abuse of the young in at least six ways, according to a prominent researcher (Finkelhor, 1985): (1) most sexual abusers of children are male, whereas men and women physically abuse children in almost equal proportions; (2) physical abuse primarily occurs inside the family, but sexual abuse takes place both inside and outside the family; (3) there typically is little physical injury and trauma in cases of sexual abuse; (4) sexual abusers generally enjoy what they are doing; (5) the criminal justice system has long been heavily involved with cases of sexual abuse but only recently has entered into the arena of physical abuse of children; and (6) recent research has disclosed that sexual abuse is more of a middle-class phenomenon than physical abuse.

What are the issues stemming from being sexually abused in childhood for persons seen in marital therapy? Two major problems are likely to be found. Adult partners may be blocked in their efforts to carry out parenting tasks as a result of being sexually abused as children, and in some instances may experience difficulties in relating and performing sexually with their mate. It should be clearly understood that not all sexual abuse leads to adult problems. My own clinical experience indicates that some persons weather childhood sexual exploitation very well and are not harmed in a long-range sense.

ASSESSMENT AND TREATMENT

How I proceed with the exploration of sexual abuse during the developmental years is guided by the manner in which the material is presented during the initial assessment phase or subsequently during treatment. How is the information first introduced? What are the affective accompaniments to the disclosure of the information? Can the individual talk about it fairly freely or is he or she obviously pained and reluctant to discuss the matter?

Important questions for the clinician are whether the person has been harmed and her or his adult functioning seriously affected as a result of being sexually abused during the developmental years. What kinds of residual effects persist? Does the spouse know about these experiences? Does the spouse wish to know or need to know?

The spouse who is aware of her or his partner's history of abuse often thinks that her or his mate was harmed by childhood experiences and that current problems in the marriage stem from the childhood events. This may or may not be the case. If possible I like to explore the situation with both spouses present in order to put to rest as much as possible any lingering questions and apprehensions on the part of the nonabused spouse. If there are indications from the abused spouse that residual harmful effects exist, I consider it desirable to explore the situation with that person alone and then to address relevant portions of the material in a conjoint session. As with so many issues in marital therapy, decisions on how to proceed need to be made on an individual case basis.

Residual results sometimes include feelings of shame, guilt, fear, confusion, and anger. As has been mentioned, the anger may be directed both toward the family friend or other person who was the abuser and toward the parent or parents who did not protect the youngster. "They knew what was going on. They had to know! Every time this couple would come over to our house to play cards, "Uncle" Ernie would try to catch me alone. He'd go down the hall to the bathroom, which was past my room and come in my room and fondle me. I didn't have a lock on my door. My parents had to know! I tried to tell my mother, but she brushed it off and stopped me before I could say anything other than that I didn't like "Uncle" Ernie. She told me that he was a nice man and good friend of hers and Dad's. I couldn't say anything else. She wouldn't listen."

Support and help in dealing with the pent-up anger and other feelings sometimes brings about significant changes in the abused person. In the case cited above the young woman was able to become free enough to resolve her ambivalent feelings about having children as a result of what was dealt with concerning her reactions to her childhood sexual abuse. Bringing in a sibling who also has been sexually abused by the same person can be an exceedingly useful therapeutic procedure. Helping the two siblings to talk about what happened to them and their feelings about it enables them to unwrap the experience from its cloak of mystery and secrecy and to take some active steps in coping with what has been confined internally. On some occasions they decide to deal with the situation with their parents and to bring the long-held family secret into the open in their family of origin. Others have decided that working with the therapist and sometimes also with their siblings and/or their spouses was adequate, that they did not need to address matters with their parents. The goal in all instances is to remove or moderate as well as possible any remaining blocks in the continuing personal and marital development of the formerly abused person.

INCEST

Much of what has been said about sexual abuse applies to cases involving incest as well, although there are some differences between the two categories of behavior.

DEFINITION

Incest in the strictest terms refers to sexual activity between biologically related persons, usually between parent and child or between siblings. The recent development of large numbers of stepfamilies, however, has presented us with a situation in which sexual involvement between a stepparent and a child is not uncommon. Psychologically at least, this constitutes incest for some persons, because incest, unlike sexual abuse generally, occurs by definition within the limits of family relationships. It can involve age peers instead of consisting solely of the exploitation of a child for the gratification of an adult or much older person. Incestual relationships reflect family problems predating the development of inappropriate sexual actions between family members, including marital problems, role reversals between parents and children, and various kinds of multiple stresses. Thus, incestual actions and relationships typically develop slowly (Rosenzweig, 1985).

There are similarities as well between childhood sexual abuse and incest. The incestuously involved child may try to let a parent or other family member know what is occurring, sometimes long before the situation is recognized in the family. Some children are unable to alert others because of fear or a lack of openness to their story, and consequently, bear their secret in silence into adulthood (Rosenzweig, 1985).

PRESENTATION AND TREATMENT

Incest presents in two broad ways in connection with marital therapy cases. One is in terms of incestuous behavior on the part of one of the partners, most often the husband, with a child or children of the couple. Such cases require that the clinician notify appropriate legal authorities such as child protection officials. The child or the parent may be removed from the home by legal action, and therapy may be ordered by the court for the abusing parent, the victim, and perhaps others. The treatment becomes something other than marital therapy or at least broader in scope than marital treatment. Individual, sibling subsystem, and total family therapy sessions may be used in addition to marital sessions (Barrett, Sykes, & Byrnes, 1986). Such powerful approaches as "the apology session" (Trepper, 1985) also may be employed. The characteristics and treatment needs of incest families have been outlined by Sgroi (1982) in terms of abuse of power, fear of authority, isolation, denial, poor communication patterns, lack of empathy, inadequate controls and limit setting, blurred boundaries, extreme emotional deprivation, and neediness, and magical expectations regarding the solution of their problems.

The focus in this section, however, is on the other broad form of presentation, incestuous behaviors by one of the partners in their family of origin. The relative impacts of these two different situations tend to be quite dissimilar, usually requiring different therapeutic work. Clinically, I deal with such cases in much the same way that I approach cases of sexual abuse generally, except that I am even more sensitive to the possible effects of exposure and disclosure on both the victim and their spouse. Depending on such factors as whether the spouse is already aware of the abuse (either generally or in terms of particulars), his or her possible reactions, and the needs of the victim, individual sessions may be used.

Children often encapsulate traumatic events and dissociate themselves from them mentally and emotionally. Damage to their sense of self, sense of body image and awareness, sexual arousal and inhibitory abilities, sense of personal power, and other parts of their personality and development (Browne & Finkelhor, 1984) may occur and be carried over to adulthood. I am especially concerned with how the incestuous action was responded to at the time it occurred. If the secret was disclosed, when did it become known to the family? Was it overtly acknowledged and treated as a problem or was it ignored and handled as if it were of no consequence? If considered a problem, was it regarded as a family problem or as an individual problem and the client blamed or scapegoated?

The general tendency of clinicians to overlook sibling incestuous activity has been noted by Bank and Kahn (1982), who have distinguished it from sex play between siblings. They also have named seven "crucial factors" that must be involved in any attempt to understand this complex phenomenon: (1) the source and means of obtaining information about the incest; (2) the ages and developmental stages of both siblings when incest began; (3) the length and frequency of the activity; (4) the general context—the family's ethnic, religious, cultural, economic, social, and geographical features and attitudes toward sex; (5) family system and psychological influences on the siblings; (6) the behaviors and motivation involved; and (7) both the long-term and short-term effects of the incestuous activity (Bank & Kahn, 1982, pp. 166–167). Their evidence from a small sample has led them to conclude that the long-term negative effects of sibling incest during the developmental years are more profound with women than with men. The women's functioning in terms of ability to trust, self-concept and identity, sex, marriage, and work may be negatively affected (Bank & Kahn, 1982).

Three case illustrations from parent–child incestuous activity provide examples of different outcomes and different ways in which individuals have responded to their experiences.

Reared by a single-parent mother after his father deserted them, Mr. Madison was seduced by his mother in late childhood. He was her bedmate periodically for several years, the mother controlling the nature and extent of the sexual activity. This ended during his early teenage years when his mother established a mistress relationship with an older man. Information is somewhat scanty, some coming from Mr. Madison's sister's disclosures to his wife and some from brief and somewhat cryptic references by Mr. Madison to his wife during the early years of their relationship. Although problems with intimacy and infidelity (on his part) were perennial, Mr. Madison steadfastly refused to talk with either his wife or a therapist about his childhood relationship with his mother. His sporadic contacts with an individual therapist always focused on work tensions.

Mrs. Lightly's reaction was quite different. She went to therapy originally with her husband around a variety of marital problems. It was clear immediately to the clinician that the partners were engaged in a spiralling dance of hostility in which she was "paying him back" for his years of dominance. There were signs, however, that she was internally in conflict about something that had not been mentioned and that her control over her emotions and behaviors were being severely tested. Both partners reported instances in the preceeding weeks in which the controls had slipped and she had done "crazy" things. She was becoming increasingly frightened.

In an individual interview, in response to both firmness and a considerable amount of gentleness on the part of the therapist, Mrs. Lightly revealed the "secret": sexual intercourse with her father for nearly a year during her high school days when her mother had been in a mental hospital. In intrapsychic terms both repression and suppression were failing and the memories and feelings of guilt, anger, and self-disgust were threatening to overwhelm her. Several factors were contributing to the weakening of Mrs. Lightly's controls, including reactions to her own daughter's attainment of the same age that she had been when the incest occurred and reactions to attaining essentially the same age her mother had been at that time.

After some preparatory work by the therapist Mrs. Lightly decided with obvious relief to go into a psychiatric unit in a hospital where she could "be taken care of around the clock, medicated as needed, and [could] 'let it blow'." Taking a 2-week vacation, she let the threatening episode occur in the hospital, got some supportive psychotherapeutic help there, went back to her job as a secretary with a large business, and continued psychotherapy following the hospitalization. Eventually she and her husband divorced for reasons essentially unrelated to the incest and its residues. Information some 10 to 12 years later was that she had happily remarried and that she had done from all reports "an excellent job" of parenting with all three of her daughters.

Incest appeared as an issue in the Miles case in still another and more typical manner. Mr. Miles was convinced that his wife's sexual activity with her father when she was in grade school was affecting their marital relationship. She indicated that their marital sexual relationship had been good for many years and said that there were other reasons for her withdrawal and distance at times, including Mr. Miles' abnormally strong desires for nurturance, reassurance, and physical/sexual contact. "You want me to be an emotional service station and your mother," she protested to him.

Evidently there had been some severely disturbed behavior on the part of her parents, both of whom were hospitalized on more than one occasion. During a period of approximately 3 years her father had sexually fondled her, she related. It had started with "tickling" behavior and "teasing." She denied that she had experienced orgasm during that period and said that she did not think that her father had ever ejaculated. It stopped because she "told him to stop. I threatened to tell my grandfather, who literally would have killed him if he had had intercourse with me."

Additional therapeutic work was done with the material produced by Mrs. Miles. She accepted the fact that her father had been severely disturbed and began to acknowledge the "hurt and angry" feelings toward her mother that were still creating a barrier between them. With some coaching she was able to talk with her mother about the barrier between them as a result of the unresolved feelings and to make some changes. Another major outcome of her disclosures was her husband's responsive *quid pro quo* in which he became much more open to examining his own contributions to the marital intimacy/sexual problems.

Residual effects of sibling incestuous behaviors can be reopened in sibling sessions with considerably less risk and greater opportunity to effect needed change and clearing up of old issues than those with parents. This seems to be true in part because of the peer nature of the relationship between adult siblings. The goal in my judgment in working with such materials is insofar as is possible to remove the results of the incestuous behavior as a live issue from the life of the affected partner and from the marriage.

Women's support groups may be helpful for sexually abused females, just as they sometimes aid in cases of physical abuse. The group support and the person's awareness that others have undergone similar experiences and that they are not alone, awful, or different appear to be especially helpful. Not only are the sense of isolation and shame or guilt reduced but also the debilitating feelings of helplessness and vulnerability may be lowered.

MEDICATION AND SEXUAL RESPONSE

Drugs are a consideration in marital therapy in two ways, aside from any role they may play in substance abuse. Prescription drugs may be provided to men and women either as an adjunct to therapy or for other reasons not directly related to the therapy for the marital difficulties. The effects of the medication, therefore, may be viewed directly in terms of its effects on the ills and problems of the affected individual. Furthermore, drugs often need to be considered in terms of their side-effects on the person and their indirect effects on the marital interaction and relationship.

Several examples of ways in which prescriptive medication may be used as an adjunct to psychotherapeutic treatment can be found. Greene and colleagues (Greene, Lee, & Lustig, 1973, 1975), whose work was mentioned earlier, have described the use of lithium carbonate in the treatment of 100 cases in which at least one spouse had a primary affective disorder (manic-depressive illness). Use of the drug helped the affected spouse to function and made the marital system manageable. Several management approaches were used, including "transient structured distance," a planned and structured separation of the spouses during certain critical stages in their relating and dealing with each other. Beavers (1985) has described a case in which medication was used with a couple plagued with physical illness. In all instances it appears helpful not only for the therapist but also for both spouses to understand the effects of the medication on the person and on the marital/sexual interaction.

The *Physician's Desk Reference*, published annually, gives some guidance regarding not only the composition, dosages, indications, and contraindications of medications but also regarding the possible side-effects of the chemicals. Any therapist whose clients are taking medication has the responsibility to be cognizant of the purposes and effects of the substances.

Kaplan (1979, pp. 203–211) has provided a helpful table on the effects of drugs on the person's sexual response. She breaks down the effects of the various chemicals on sexual desire, sexual excitement, and sexual orgasm phases of sexual response. The drugs are classified as those that act on the brain, hormones, antihypertensives, anticholigernic, "aphrodisiacs," neurotoxic agents, and miscellaneous drugs. Some of the tranquilizing drugs and antidepressants tend to decrease sexual desire, for example. Kaplan (1979) indicates that the antianxiety drugs (i.e., Valium, Librium, Troxene, Meprobamate) in high doses may diminish sexual desire. Antidepressants (e.g., tryclics) may delay orgasm in some females or (Lithium Carbonate) may reduce urgency or desire (pp. 203–205).

Kaplan has also constructed a table showing the effects of illness on sexual response, which is helpful in understanding the effects of certain illness and classes of illnesses on the libido, excitement, and orgasm phases of sexual response (pp. 212–219).

As noted above, there are usually multiple causes for sexual dysfunction. Medication may be contributory, but not necessarily totally determinative of the dysfunctional sexual outcome.

Chapter Eight

Special Issues

Several issues, especially as they relate to conjoint marital therapy, are treated briefly in this chapter. They are extramarital affairs, marital violence (spouse abuse), and alcohol problems.

EXTRAMARITAL AFFAIRS

Extramarital affairs are an issue in many marital therapy cases. How they appear in the case has some important implications for their role in the life of the couple and for the work of the therapist: When they are an explicit issue in the therapy (i.e., when the affair is acknowledged by both spouses), they are a different factor than when they are not acknowledged as an issue by the partners. Extramarital affairs have different impacts when they are brought into the open during therapy as compared to before treatment begins.

THE PRESENTING COMPLAINT

The extramarital affair of one or both partners seldom appears in my clinical experience as the sole or major presenting complaint, though when it does appear as such the affair typically has brought about a crisis. The upsets thus evoked vary in terms of several dimensions, including the manner in which the crisis was precipitated and its severity. Did the partner tell her or his spouse about the extramarital involvement or was the news gained from someone else? Has the spouse been publically embarrassed? A one-partner affair (i.e., an affair with one other person) typically produces different reverberations and upsets in the marriage than multiple-partner affairs, or the latest in a string of extramarital liaisons. Casual, one-night stands generally result in different reactions than a strong attachment to one other person outside the marriage. Revelations of a first-time affair often cause more acute reactions than learning that "once again" a spouse has been extramaritally involved. Reactions in the latter case may be more subdued in the sense that there often is less surprise and more of a resigned reaction.

The creation of a crisis faces the clinician with the task of doing crisis intervention work to help the partners "settle down" in order to enter treatment. Dealing with the upset and especially getting the more disturbed partner settled down sufficiently to begin working on the problems may take some individual as well as conjoint sessions. Telephone calls may be expected as one or both of the spouses attempt to handle their anxiety, anger, hurt, and confusion.

DISCOVERY/ACKNOWLEDGMENT DURING THERAPY

Sometimes the fact that there has been one or more affairs becomes an issue in therapy after treatment for other matters has been launched. One mate may discover subsequent to entering treatment with the spouse that the other either is or has been engaged in an affair, an event that also creates a crisis in most instances. Again, there are some differences in impact between first-time affairs and repeated affairs, especially when the previously involved spouse has promised, "It won't happen again; there's nothing going on." The therapist sometimes witnesses directly such differential responses as the first shock of one partner learning that the original "naive" trust between the mates has been broken and the sick disappointment of a spouse at discovering that he or she has been "betrayed again." Discovery of extramarital involvement after treatment is underway sometimes leads one partner to feel that there has been additional "hypocrisy" on the part of the spouse who has revealed the information. This spouse is perceived as being insincere in entering marital therapy without revealing the affair, a feeling that is especially pronounced when the affair is continuing.

This is a crucial time in therapy. Can the crisis be handled? What are the wishes and intentions of the spouse with regard to therapy? With regard to their marriage? Has the involved spouse entered therapy primarily in order to find a place to "drop the mate" safely in the hands of a therapist in order to be able to leave the marriage without guilt or undue difficulty? The fact that the discovery occurs within the context of an ongoing therapeutic relationship generally gives the clinician some advantages to the extent that a therapeutic relationship has been achieved with the marital partners.

AFFAIRS AS "SECRETS" IN TREATMENT

Affairs appear as secrets in therapy in two major ways. On some occasions, the fact of an affair or affairs is known to both mates prior to entry into treatment and is initially concealed from the therapist. Sometimes, after they have come to trust the clinician, the spouses will decide that it is safe to let the therapist in on the secret, that "perhaps it does have something to do with our problems." More often, the secret is held by one mate, who may ask the therapist for a separate appointment or telephone for the purpose of informing the clinician about the affair. Parenthetically, my clinical and supervisory experiences support the idea that a client will reveal information about an affair when he or she is ready to do so, regardless of the modality of interviewing used by the therapist. Hence, using individual interviews at the initial assessment stage may or may not elicit the secret of affairs.

Major issues arise when one of the marital partners in treatment seeks to involve the therapist in a conspiracy to share a secret and to keep the shared information from the other spouse. Among the questions arising are the following: What are the therapist's "ground rules" with clients regarding secrets? What are the ethical issues of holding the secret? What are the possible legal implications of holding the secret? The legal question in particular is difficult to answer, certainly there is the possibility of being sued by a disgruntled client. Legal advice should be sought if there is any question about potential legal liability or complications from withholding information regarding one spouse's extramarital involvements from the other mate while treating the couple.

Whether the therapist should deal with such issues on a case by case basis or hold to a policy of accepting no confidential disclosures from clients at all is a question that has to be answered and dealt with by the individual therapist. I have chosen to deal with this kind of issue on a case by case basis. At the outset, if there is an attempt by one spouse to reveal information to me without the other knowing about it, I make it clear that I shall use my own judgment about holding it in confidence, giving the person the choice as to whether or not to reveal the information to me. The issues of trust and conspiracy thus come to the fore early and quickly in the contacts with clients who raise such issues.

There are differences between a situation in which a client discloses to the therapist that he or she was formerly in an affair and one in which there is an ongoing extramarital relationship. When the extramarital involvement is a thing of the past, should the "unknowing" spouse be told? Even if one assumes that the "unknowing" spouse always knows about extramarital involvement at some level, what is to be gained by confronting them with information about a nonexistent situation? Similarly, what damage may be done to the spouse by learning about an affair of the past?

Being informed by one of the marital partners that she or he is currently engaged in an extramarital relationship and asked to keep that information from the spouse is quite another matter, in my judgment. I consider it unethical and at best inequitable to continue to treat a couple while agreeing with one of the partners to withhold information about a current affair from the other for more than a brief period of time. Both dynamically and ethically affairs belong to the marital couple, not to the therapist and one individual. The question for me becomes the manner in which either the affair will be terminated and full attention devoted to the marital therapy—the spouse being informed and given a chance to respond to the situation—or conjoint treatment will be terminated. This statement is made with the full awareness that at some level, conscious or unconscious, both spouses may be aware of the existence of present or past extramarital affairs, and that a collusive arrangement between spouses may exist. Certainly, a current affair belongs to the marital partners as something they have the joint responsibility of dealing with, whatever the details.

WHAT AN AFFAIR DOES

The Breaching of Marital Boundaries

Descriptively, entering into an extramarital affair breaches the boundaries around the marital couple and relationship. This is the case even when there is tacit or explicit agreement to triangulate another individual into a two-party relationship. There are some situations in which the boundaries are breeched by overt agreement without the production of marital upset or crisis.

During a period from approximately 1969 to 1973 there was a highly visible emphasis on "open marriage." As popularly interpreted, this meant that both partners in such marriages were free to engage in personal relationships including sexual activities with persons other than the mate so long as both spouses were agreeable to an "open marriage" contract.

This concept faded from the scene rather rapidly, evidently because few couples could or wished to follow such a pattern for any significant period of time. For those who are engaged in such relationships at this time, much of what is being said here possibly does not hold true.

Does such activity as "swinging," in which the partners openly and consensually engage in mateswapping for sex constitute a breeching of the marital boundaries? Evidently not, where such activity is genuinely desired by both partners. Observation and some research have indicated that often the male marital partner is the encourager and instigator of swinging. Where the clinician tends to be called on for help is in the instances in which one or both spouses are not happy with the arrangements. The concern in this chapter is thus with extramarital involvement that causes problems in the marriage requiring professional help.

"It's not the sex! Screw the sex! It's the fact that [he or she] has a relationship with somebody else." Such is a common declaration by a hurt, angry spouse, who may add something along the line of, "If it were just a one-night stand, or even an occasional meeting, I wouldn't mind so much. But the fact that things that belong between us are being shared with somebody else hurts."

The Breaking of Marital Trust

For most relationships extramarital affairs constitute a violation of trust, because there is an agreement and expectation between the spouses that neither will be involved in relationships that take precedence over the spousal relationship. This trust violation frequently is the most significant aspect of what occurs: It is not necessarily what the partner does with someone else, but the fact that he or she is deceiving the spouse that produces the greatest amounts of anger and damage to the marital relationship.

"It's the lying!"

"I had asked her (him) if there was somebody else, several times. And the answer was always 'no.' *(Turning to the spouse)* You lied to me. It's being made a fool of. I believed you when you said that you had to work late. I believed you when you said there was nothing going on. And then I found that you're having an affair with my best friend. I blame her (him) more than you. And that's almost a bigger loss. I lost my friend."

That statement can be reported with the gender of the speaker used interchangeably because it has been given in my office in those exact words or close approximations by both females and males many times over the years. Generally there is more than a modicum of genuine feeling behind all of such declarations.

The lying and deceit take a particularly virulent form when a spouse engages in "gaslighting." Following the theme of the 1940s movie by that title, gaslighting, as used by Zemon-Gass and Nichols (1988), is the deliberate attempt to mislead a spouse, to convince the spouse that he or she is imagining things, that he or she is "crazy," that nothing is going on, when there is a factual basis for the "imagining."

Retaliatory-Restorative Impulses

A distraught young man sat across from me.

"I have imagined ways to get back at her. Ways to poison her. Push her off the roof. Take her out in the lake and drown her. I imagine what it would be like if she died in an automobile accident. I know it won't happen. And I know I wouldn't do any of the things that crossed my mind. They're all against the way that I see myself. But it helps me deal with my anger. Some of it gets out and it doesn't simply stay inside and burn me up."

Retaliatory-restorative feelings and impulses are a common outcome of learning about an affair. Such thoughts—of getting back at a partner who has offended—and of doing something to restore one's sense of damaged self-esteem are to be expected when there is a sense of betrayal. Acting on such impulses, as the young man indicated, is something else altogether.

Occasionally, a client will indicate that he or she has engaged in a one-night stand (e.g., at a convention) or a brief fling that "meant nothing emotionally." The recognized and acknowledged purpose was to get back at a spouse and/or to deal with their own sense of victimzation/impotence. Often the spouse does not know and will never know that the event or events occurred. Sometimes the major outcome appears to be an affirmation, or occasionally the establishment, of one's sense of being attractive, desirable, and able to function independently. For some persons the instigation of a reactive affair enables them to feel that they can once again relate to their spouse on an equal basis.

Variable Outcomes

Whatever extramarital relationships may do for the individuals involved—and there is certainly clinical evidence that some men and women who are in a bad marriage may be helped personally by being in a loving, esteem building extramarital relationship—they do cause pain and do change the nature and history of the marriage. Obviously, what the affair or external relationship means to the spouse who participates in it is often different from what it means to the other spouse. Sometimes when the nonparticipating mate learns that the affair does not signify the partner's desire to get out of the marriage, the way is opened for difficult but fruitful attempts to reestablish a viable, satisfactory marital relationship for both spouses. Conversely, as is well known, affairs sometimes lead to or signify the end of a marriage.

Sometimes the effects of an affair upon persons are such that a separation is required in order to permit one of the partners to decide whether or not they wish to continue the marriage. This may occur because of a felt need for "more space" or because resentments have built up to the point that one spouse feels that they need to divorce the other, or for any one or more of a combination of reasons. The Cables provide an example.

During the early stages of their relationship and marriage Mr. Cable was the leader of the couple, his wife being very uncertain and unsure of herself. After marriage he supported her desires to work and eventually helped her to move from being a secretary to going to college and working toward a teaching degree. At the same time that those events were occurring, Mr. Cable's behaviors in social situations were causing problems for both his wife and others: His angry outbursts and need to dominate and to be always in control caused negative reactions from his spouse as well as from friends and acquaintances.

Interestingly enough, aside from those situations and from an affectional-sexual relationship that was less than satisfying for Mrs. Cable, she perceived the marriage as "fine." The partners had many interests in common and could be "great friends" if those two negatives were excised, she declared. In retrospect, there was evidence that Mr. Cable had tried over the years to put tight controls on his wife in order to keep her from becoming too independent and perhaps leaving him, even as he was encouraging her to secure her teaching degree. He controlled the only family automobile, indicating that he needed it in his job as a salesman, and effectively limited her coming and going, thus making it possible for him to know where she was virtually all of the time. Mrs. Cable eventually acted on her emotional-sexual dissatisfaction by entering into a nonsexual but close relationship with a male teaching colleague. Mr. Cable was aware of the closeness, but did not do very much in a direct manner about his jealous reactions to his wife's friendship with the other man.

Eventually, Mrs. Cable began to make some drastic changes. A summer affair with an instructor at the university where she took some continuing education courses provided the catalyst. Within a few months she announced her plans to get a divorce from her husband, moved out of their house into an apartment, purchased her own automobile, and entered into individual psychotherapy. As she worked in therapy, she spent a considerable amount of time crying. The devastated husband, who was unaware of the summer affair, went into treatment with another therapist in reaction to his wife's actions and began telling her that he could and would make the changes she wished him to make. The summer paramour made it clear that he was not a marriage candidate. Although that development was not totally unexpected, it caused some depressive reactions on Mrs. Cable's part.

From that point onward, Mrs. Cable began to work on her exploration of herself and her feelings about her marriage. She talked about her husband and his attempts to make the changes she had requested, namely, to grow up emotionally, to stop trying to limit and control her, to cease being jealous, and to stop getting angry and berating her. She also talked about how she thought they could work out a satisfactory relationship if they could improve their sexual relationship. Subsequently, the Cables entered into marital therapy and began working to resolve their difficulties and differences.

WHAT AFFAIRS MEAN

What an extramarital affair or relationship means to the individuals participating in it varies among persons, of course. Some of the common meanings presented by clients fall into the categories that follow.

An attempt to heat up a cooled off marriage. This meaning of an affair is stated in a variety of ways by clients. Sometimes, a partner who has been extramaritally involved will say something like, "Things had gotten commonplace. I was bored. And I think that I was angry. I don't want the marriage to end, but I don't want it to be like it was. The person I was involved with really doesn't mean anything to me." Whitaker (1971) had mentioned this motivation and meaning for some participants in affairs. There is no desire or intent to leave the marriage, but at some level of awareness—frequently a conscious one—the involved party wishes her or his spouse to know that the affair has occurred. The intent is for the spouse to receive a message regarding the dissatisfaction and to respond by becoming interested and passionately reinvolved in the marital relationship.

An "eat my cake and have it too" activity. Some individuals make it clear that they experience little or no personal discomfort or conflict over being married and engaged in extramarital affairs. Occasionally, one will say, "I just like to have it both ways," while some refer to their outside activities as "sport fucking" or recreational sex. The spouse is sometimes expected to be tolerant and forgiving if he or she learns about the extramarital behaviors. This kind of situation is difficult to deal with clinically when the uninvolved spouse is overtly aware and verbally unhappy with the way things are going but is unwilling or unable to take actions that will bring about significant change. Complaints may be voiced, but the accompanying inactivity and passivity signal that he or she is not going to do anything to alter the situation. Not all cases involve a collusion between the spouses to maintain a triangulated situation. In some instances the practical limitations on the reactions of the unhappy and often frightened partner keep them frozen in the situation. A considerable amount of support from therapists and others may be required in order to help them to take steps to make changes.

A testing of the waters outside of the marriage. Individuals who are conflicted about the marriage sometimes begin to explore alternatives, uncertain about whether they wish to stay or to leave. Unhappy with the marriage and apprehensive about whether it would be any better outside, they experiment with another relationship or with a series of affairs. For a long period of time they may be uncertain as to whether they wish to remain married or to change their marital status (i.e., leave in order to pursue a single life, another marriage, or another specific relationship).

An attempt to "make my marriage tolerable." Some individuals do not wish and/or intend to get out of their marriage—for any one or more of a number of practical, religious, or emotional reasons—but do not feel that the marital relationship will ever be fulfilling. "I can't get out, but I couldn't stand it, if all I could get [emotionally and/or sexually] was what I get from my [spouse]" is a common statement from persons expressing this reason for engaging in extramarital relationships. Either a series of affairs or a single long-term relationship may be used in this "supplementation" pattern. Sometimes this pattern appears to be essentially restorative in nature and retaliatory in only a minor sense at best. The spouse may or may not be directly informed about the outside activities: A woman whose husband had been impotent for 10 years indicated in therapy that "I have had a few flings, and I have told you [her husband] about most of them, as you know, because I couldn't lie to you."

A bridge out of the marriage. Consciously or without being aware of what they are doing during the early stages, some unhappy married persons use their affair as a "bridge" out of the marriage, that is, they provide themselves with a relationship so that if they leave the marriage, they will not be alone. Such "bridge" relationships may or may not last once the individual has been out of the marriage for a few months. Clinical observation indicates that many such relationships do not last once the "freed" formerly married person has become secure on her or his own, the bridge having served its purpose and the freed person having recognized that they do not wish to continue with their lover.

Therapists have provided still other explanations of what extramarital affairs mean to the participants. Williamson (1984), drawing upon Whitaker (Warkentin & Whitaker, 1967; Whitaker, 1971), has given several reasons and explanations for extramarital affairs. Along with the fear of growing old, the yearning for romance, and fundamental defects in the psychosexual development of individuals, he has also used Whitaker's term "amateur psychotherapy" as means of explaining some extramarital affairs. In the "amateur psychotherapy" terms, an affair represents an attempt to enmesh a third party in the dynamics of a conflicted and distressed marriage. This is most likely to be the pattern when the marital partners have a "therapeutic" marriage or a fused relationship: that is, a relationship that is contracted in an effort to provide healing for the spouses or a relationship that holds the partners together in such a fashion that neither is able to move without the other. A third party is required in both instances in order to bring about change in order to alter what has become an intolerable situation. Consequently, the decision to engage in an affair is viewed by Williamson as a collusive decision of the married partners, which is held as applying to the situation whether the decision is explicit or implicit, conscious or unconscious, or actively made or simply permitted to occur.

The valid point is also made by Williamson (1984) that the extramarital affair is not fully understandable at this time and that it should be regarded as being very complex in nature. Attempts to make categorical statements about the meaning of extramarital affairs result in oversimplification since affairs may and often do have very different meanings for all three parties, or multiple meanings to one or more of the participants. Not all of them are the product of collusion between the spouses and a joint triangulation endeavor. Careful study and assessment of the meaning and function that they serve requires the understanding that they are complex and not always predictable in nature.

SOME TREATMENT ISSUES

Whenever an extramarital affair—active, just-concluded, or periodic/ chronic—emerges as a relevant treatment issue in marital therapy, it needs to be dealt with in contextual terms. Such affairs cannot be handled effectively if they are regarded as individual matters or as isolated entities that have nothing to do with the ongoing marital relationship. Generally, information about an affair is brought to therapy because it does pose a relevant therapeutic and relationship issue. Such affairs need to be regarded and understood as affecting both husband and wife, and so should be addressed by both spouses in the therapy sessions. The relevant affair is "their" affair, a complex matter that requires the best efforts of both in order to deal with the situation productively. Making these points effectively and engaging both spouses in an examination process is an important first step toward dealing with affairs. Getting past blaming—either the blaming of the "victimizer" or the "victim"—is an essential part of this process.

Such observations as the following may be in order: "Both of you are affected by what is [or has been] going on. We need to understand as best we can the meaning of the things that are happening. It certainly seems possible and even likely from what we have looked at that you have some shared responsibility for what has occurred in your marriage that led to the current unhappiness. This is not to blame either of you, and it is not to whitewash the actions of [the spouse engaging in an affair]. You were unhappy and dissatisfied with the marriage. Your response of getting involved outside the marriage was one way of responding. There were other ways of responding. The significant thing here, besides the pain that both of you are experiencing, probably is that you were dissatisfied with the marriage and sought to bring about change. There may have been other and perhaps more direct and effective ways, but you have brought the issues to the forefront."

This kind of approach by the therapist has the dual purposes of assisting both spouses to share responsibility for working toward change and of recasting/reframing the behaviors into a framework of striving for change from an unsatisfactory situation. The change that is sought may turn out to be either a resolution of difficulties within the marriage so that the partners can deal with each other in satisfying ways in the future, or a recognition that they do not and are not going to meet each other's needs adequately and a termination of the marriage. The goal of treatment with a couple with a currently involved spouse is, according to Williamson (1984), to help them resolve their intensely ambivalent feelings about each other so that they can continue the marriage or to help them get out of the marriage if they cannot resolve the ambivalence.

Restoration of communication and deepening of understanding of the current meaning or meanings of the affair behavior are also exceedingly important. What are the causes and what are the functions, the purposes being served, as best the therapist and the couple can ascertain? This may include determining what the partners know and what they wish to know about the affair, as well as its meaning. This does not imply that all of the details of the affair and the interaction with the third party need to be revealed and aired, but that the partners become able to talk about their feelings. On occasion there may be a need for the noninvolved spouse to get answers to one or two questions in order to put something to rest. For example, Mrs. Merchant had been upset, anxious, and threatened for 3 years over her husband's extramarital involvement. The affair was over; it had been brief, but she could not bring closure on it. With some guidance and encouragement Mr. Merchant answered a couple of questions that had caused his wife to spend sleepless nights and agitated days, and thereby changed his wife's reactions and helped her get back to normal functioning.

Restoration of communication includes dealing with what is known and acknowledged by both spouses, what is (was) the meaning of the affair to the marital partners and their marriage, and a damage control assessment (i.e., how extensive the damage is to the marriage and the partners). It also involves the recognition that the issue of trust will always be present between the partners, regardless of the understanding of the meaning of the extramarital involvement. As noted above, once the boundaries of the relationship have been breeched and the commitment between the partners abrogated, there can never again be a blind or naive trust between the mates. Many persons have indicated feelings similar to the statement "Never again can I not be concerned when [he or she] is late, and I can never again not worry about whether [he or she] is where [he or she] said [he or she] would be and doing what [he or she] is supposed to be doing. I try not to worry or to get paranoid or hysterical, but it's hard. I try, but I can't not get shaky." A task of the therapist with such issues is to help the spouses recognize that simple, naive trust is not to be expected, and to assist them to learning how to take steps to prevent the unnecessary arousal of fear and suspicion, as well as how to cope with fears once they do arise.

An additional part of the process of reestablishing communication and understanding between the partners consists of helping them to bury what needs to be buried. Can the spouse be forgiven? That means, can each spouse forgive the other? Can each spouse forgive herself or himself? Has the blame issue—self-blame or blame of the other—been settled? How have the mates sought to bridge the damaged relationship?

What steps have been taken and what progress has been made in effecting reconciliation? Provided the spouses have indicated that they wish to make their relationship work, what steps have been taken to make it work?

Ending the live affair appropriately often means that it should not be abruptly terminated. As Williamson (1984) has pointed out, it may be important to recognize with the couple that they are not ready for change, and thus that the affair should not be given up until the couple are ready to change. On some occasions it may be possible and helpful to bring the third party into the therapy sessions with the couple in order to examine the triangle of husband, wife, and third party. Whether this is done in actual practice or through conceptualization, it provides opportunity for the partners to examine the meaning of the triangle and to begin reworking their feelings regarding the third party and each other. Readiness for change, once again, is a significant issue in marital therapy.

MARITAL VIOLENCE

If extramarital affairs are an issue in marital therapy, violence should be no less a concern. Family violence has "come out of the closet" in the last 2 decades: During the 1960s attention was focused on child abuse; the 1970s brought awareness of spouse abuse; and physical abuse of the elderly, sometimes referred to as "granny bashing," entered into professional (and to some extent, public) awareness in the 1980s. The emphasis in this section is on spouse abuse, the physical maltreatment of husband or wife by their mate. Primary attention will be given to wife abuse, since that is the form of spouse abuse that most often appears as an issue in marital therapy. Women are violent about as often as men in the family but a great deal of their aggression against their husbands is self-defensive or retaliatory (Straus & Gelles, 1986), and men generally do the most physical damage.

What is violence? What is abuse? Following the major researchers in the field of family violence, "normal" violence is an act intended or perceived to cause physical pain or injury to another person. Violence is considered abusive when an act has a high potential for injuring the victim (Straus, Gelles, & Steinmetz, 1980).

Spouse abuse is the third most common form of family violence, ranking behind sibling violence and child abuse, according to the best available research. The first study based on a national probability sample in 1975 found that approximately one out of every 26 American women was beaten by her husband every year (Straus *et al.*, 1980). A decade later a second such study disclosed a 27% decrease in wife-beating (Straus & Gelles, 1986). Spouse abuse occurs at all income levels, although it is not randomly distributed among the population. Younger couples are the most violent. Spouse abuse is higher among lower-income families and in situations in which there is unemployment and economic stress, although middle-class violence is common, and therapists should be alert to its potential presence. Conflict over children is the form of husband–wife disagreement most likely to lead to physical violence (Straus *et al.*, 1980).

Straus and associates (Straus *et al.*, 1980; Straus & Gelles, 1986) in both of their national studies found abuse of the spouse by both men and women to be common. Certain characteristics emerged as important for violence by one spouse and not by the other. Those important for violence by husband but not wives included the husband being dominant in family decisions, the wife being a full-time housewife, and the wife being worried about economic security. For the women, characteristics that were important for violence for them but not for their husbands included growing up in a family in which their mother hit their father, receiving physical punishment after age 13, and employment (of the woman) outside the home as a manual laborer (Straus *et al.*, 1980, pp. 206–207).

ERASING THE MYTHS

Professionals have often been misled by popular myths concerning family and spousal violence: These myths include the ideas that battered women are "masochistic," that they actually like and enjoy being beaten, that battered women are "crazy," that the batterers are "psychopathic personalities" who are violent in all their relationships, and similar erroneous assumptions (Walker, 1979). Research conducted by Straus and others supports the conclusion that none of these ideas has general validity. Straus (1977) concluded that 90% or more of the violence that occurs in American families stems not from individual psychopathology but from the nature of the family and the larger society. In short, the American family appears to be a violent social group in which the older, larger, and stronger use physical force against the younger, smaller, and weaker. The society has been historically and is now one in which violence is widely condoned as a method for solving problems, according to Straus. Individuals who abuse do not fit into neat clinical classifications because they are not psychologically different from most of the population (Gelles, 1985).

Rather than resulting from aberrant individual behavior, marital violence is generally part of a cycle of family violence carried on over three or more generations. Those who abuse their spouses (and their children) frequently witnessed abuse and were abused as children. Most individuals who engage in aggressive behaviors against other family members learned to use violence in the same ways they learned other things in their family of origin. As Straus has pointed out repeatedly in his research reports, spanking, whipping, and slapping teach children a connection between love and violence, thus building into them the notion that violence is an appropriate way to respond to stress or to solve problems. The ability to put limits on the amount and kind of violent and aggressive behaviors one uses is not so well learned as is the lesson that it is all right to hit those that you love and feel that you need to control.

All of the foregoing—including social norms condoning the use of force and the "sacredness of the family" as a private group—contributes to a situation in which, according to noted researcher Richard J. Gelles (1985), people abuse other family members because they can. This certainly appears to hold true in terms of male dominance and sexism (e.g., wife beating is much more common when the husband has the power in the home, according to Straus *et al.*, 1980), as well as in relation to parents abusing children. Recent reports from results of using legal restraint such as the arrest of abusing males has supported the idea that making it socially unacceptable and costly to abuse family members does lead to a reduction in certain types of family violence, which fact lends credence to Gelles' conclusion that people abuse because they can.

RECAPITULATION: TREATMENT ASSUMPTIONS

An extended study of the research compiled by the Family Violence Research Program at the University of New Hampshire under the direction of Murray A. Straus, a review of the work of other researchers and concerned social groups, and a testing of many of the ideas in clinical practice has led me to an approach to treating family violence, including spouse abuse, that is based on the assumptions and conclusions delineated below (Nichols, 1986b).

Violence in the family is common and falls into predictable patterns. Therefore, violence can reasonably be expected to occur in a significant number of cases that present for marital therapy, although it is more likely to be found in some types of marriages than in others. Abuse is more likely to appear in families in lower economic levels, where there is serious unemployment and economic deprivation, and where the family is patriarchically organized, isolated, and has few social network supports (Finkelhor, 1983). Abuse also tends to be more common when the wife makes more money than the husband (Stock, 1985).

Social causes rather than individual psychological factors account for the majority of family violence. Some of the support for this conclusion has already been given. Additionally, Straus (1977) has suggested that as violence in the societal system increases, so does violence in the family system; and conversely. There is, in other words, a systemic, positive feedback relationship between the values and behaviors in the two systems, family and society. Consequently, the clinician should not automatically conclude that abusers are "sick" because they are physically violent with their spouse. The circular reasoning that "He (or she) is sick because somebody would have to be sick to batter his (or her) spouse that way" is erroneous and unhelpful. The therapist who deems the abusive behavior of a husband psychopathological in its origin may be as bewildered in attempting to understand and deal with the client as the client is in understanding the therapist who is labeling him "sick" when he is in his own view only doing what he learned to do in his family of origin. This is not to imply that the clinician should view violence lightly or excuse the abusive behavior, but that effective intervention has to be made with a more sophisticated and in-depth understanding than exists in an assumption of individual causation and psychopathology.

The most useful approach for comprehending and treating family violence (including spouse abuse) is one based on understandings derived from systems theory. The clinician should understand, therefore, how the attitudes leading to violence have been learned in the abuser's family of origin and from societal values. Paying heed to the multigenerational nature of most spouse abuse avoids the dilemma of creating family loyalty conflicts that impede therapeutic work by labeling the abuser and by implication his family, "sick." Forming a larger and systemic orientation increases the likelihood of dealing adequately with the violence.

The recognition and treatment of spouse abuse is an appropriate concern for all marital therapists. Marital therapists working in all settings, including private practice, need to be on the alert for and plan to deal with interspousal violence. Instances of such behaviors are not found merely in the cases of those who work for social agencies or specialize in accepting wife-abuse referrals.

TREATMENT ISSUES

Dealing with spouse abuse is not a simple issue, calling as it does upon the clinician to address a number of significant questions. First, is the therapist prepared and required to take a value stance? When it becomes apparent that physical abuse is being perpetrated by one spouse upon another, is the therapist ready to take a stand that such behavior is not tolerable and is to be stopped? Is the therapist prepared to recognize that "a little violence is like a little pregnancy" and that there needs to be a complete prohibition of violence and abusive behavior? This stance involves opposing the norms of both the society and the family in which many clients were reared. Frequently, I take the position with clients that "Nobody deserves to be hit," which creates a very different situation than prevails with a stance of neutrality by the clinician. In my judgment, this is an essential humanitarian position, uttered with "all due respect" for the families from which the clients came, but stated clearly nevertheless. If the clients are bothered by my disclosure of my values and are not ready to accept my position that physical abuse of another individual is not acceptable, I have to be ready to accept the possibility that they may leave treatment. They have to be prepared to accept the fact that I will not acquiesce to the maltreatment of one family member by another.

Second, the therapist cannot maintain a position of neutrality and promise clients that what they reveal is privileged, that the therapist will hold it in a confidential manner. Legally, therapists and other professionals are required in all states to report instances of known or suspected child abuse. Statutory and case law also make it important to report spouse abuse; since the 1976 Tarasoff decision it has been incumbent upon clinicians to warn persons who are at risk physically. The entire context in which therapy is conducted today is such that there is no legal or responsible way for the therapist to indicate to clients that "Whatever you tell me will be held in confidence."

Third, analogous to the situation in which alcoholic consumption is a significant issue, one of the first steps in cases of physical abuse by one spouse of another is cessation of the undesirable behavior. The therapist must make clear that stopping the abuse is a prerequisite to working with the couple. Finding out what is involved in the abuse, where it comes from and why the abusing spouse is physically abusive, is secondary to stopping the battering from occurring.

Fourth, is the spouse abuse that is revealed treatable in the framework of outpatient psychotherapy? Can the abusing spouse put adequate restraints upon herself or himself to stop physically abusing the mate? Is it necessary to put one or both of the spouses in a hospital or, in the case of the abuser, a restrictive jail setting in order to stop the abusive behaviors?

ASSESSMENT OF SPOUSE ABUSE

Assessment of spouse abuse can be done directly or indirectly. The therapist can observe the spouses in assessment sessions and elicit information and reactions to questions. When inquiring about spousal violence the clinician should ask directly about certain behaviors. Following the lead of researchers, one should inquire specifically about slapping, biting, kicking, hitting with the fist, and other specified acts of physical aggression against the spouse. As noted elsewhere (Nichols, 1986b), the use of a genogram can provide one of the quickest ways for the clinician to learn about family patterns such as intergenerational family violence. Questions about how the spouses were disciplined when they were growing up, as well as queries about how their parents related to one another and how they got along with their siblings, may provide additional information on family-of-origin patterns of violent and abusive behavior.

An assessment decision model provided by Rosenbaum and O'Leary (1986) is helpful. The questions to be answered and the decisions to be made include the following: Is violence occurring? If the response is affirmative, is the wife safe? If she is at risk, the therapist should provide referral to a shelter and possibly secure police involvement. Are the children safe? If not, a mandatory call to protective services is indicated. If the wife is currently safe from assault, is she aware of shelter services and other resources if she should need them in the future? If she does not have such information, the therapist should provide it. If the answer to the following three questions—Does the couple wish to remain together? Is remediation a reasonable possibility? Can the violence be controlled?—is "yes," a treatment plan should be selected. This would include conjoint marital therapy, a men's group for violence control, or a combination of conjoint marital treatment plus a group. If the answer to any of the three is "no," then referral is indicated to women's support groups, men's workshops (for abusers), or individual psychotherapy, depending on the specific needs of the couple and the availability of appropriate services.

TREATMENT OF SPOUSE ABUSE

Therapeutic work with spouse abuse involves working with the marital dyad. Although some professionals (Geller & Wasserstrom, 1984) have espoused marital therapy alone as the desired modality for working with spouse abuse, the stance taken here is that marital therapy by itself is not always sufficient to bring about desired changes in marriages where spouse abuse is occurring. Individual and family-of-origin sessions are often an important part of the treatment. The general goals are to change both behaviors and the attitudes that permit and condone violence as a means of problem solving, as well as to provide the support needed by the spouses and other family members.

Stopping the Abusive and Violent Behavior

This is, as emphasized previously, an essential first step. Violence is not something that should be ignored, and "prescribing the symptom" (i.e., directing the couple to increase the behavior) is not a responsible or probably even a legal kind of intervention. Violent and abusive behaviors need to be approached and dealt with directly.

Legal authorities may need to be brought into the picture. Contrary to popular impressions that it doesn't do any good to report wife abuse to the police, there is recent evidence that such action is often effective. National Crime survey data show that calling the police after an act of domestic violence seems to reduce the risk of a husband attacking his wife again within 6 months (the period of the study) by as much as 62% (Longran & Innes, 1986). Changes are occurring in the way in which the police regard domestic violence. The old recommended pattern of merely separating fighting spouses and then leaving the scene is being replaced in police training manuals with a recommendation that all assaults, in the home as well as elsewhere, be treated alike, as assaults (Straus & Gelles, 1986). Other research comparing three different approaches used by the police to handle domestic violence suggests that treating wife beating as a criminal rather than a private matter reduces the extent of repetition (Sherman & Berkman, 1984).

Physically separating the spouses may be indicated as either a temporary or a permanent matter. Shelters for battered women provide a refuge in many larger communities. The first such facility opened in England in 1971. Today there are more than 700 such shelters in the United States. As in the case of reporting abuse to the police, how and when a woman uses a shelter determines its effectiveness in stopping attacks against her. Women who are still highly ambivalent about taking a stand against stopping attacks—for whatever practical or emotional reasons—may be assaulted again, despite the fact that they have sought refuge in a shelter. There are research indications that shelters provide beneficial effects only for those battered women who are already taking control of their lives and hence are not continuing to be dependent on their abusing spouse (Berk, Newton, & Berk, 1986).

Less severe and less physically dangerous abuse may be dealt with by intervening in the spousal system's functioning by more conventional verbal psychotherapy and by restructuring the mate's modes of dealing with problems and tensions. If "people abuse family members because they can" (Gelles, 1985, p. 7), the task of the clinician is to work toward creating conditions so that such people cannot be abusive. This may involve intellectual and emotional changes in some cases, as well as physical and legal in others. Therapeutically, the therapist needs to move as firmly, decisively, and persuasively as possible in raising the cost of being abusive, at the same time, being alert to the damage that her or his actions can do to the self-concept of both the abusing and the abused spouse. The firmness and decisiveness of the therapist's actions needs to be matched by a sensitivity to the fragility of the self-esteem of many of the clients with whom he or she is working.

Changing the Climate

Keeping a balance in dealing with abusiveness and families certainly is not an easy matter. It involves rejecting the rationalizations of an abusive spouse, pointing the spousal system toward more productive ways of relating and problem solving, and supporting the needs and feelings of both parties simultaneously. Variations of the following appear in cases of marital violence:

Husband: She makes me so mad when she won't do what she ought to! I tell her and tell her to put those kids to bed and to keep 'em quiet. She argues with me or just doesn't do it; she doesn't pay any attention. I don't think that the kids get enough sleep. They can't get up in the morning. She lets them do what they want to do. She provokes me. She's got it coming. I can't take it. I can't help myself. I get so worked up that I hit her. I think any man would. Wouldn't you?

Therapist: No. I don't think that anybody deserves to be hit, you, me, or your wife. There are better ways to deal with frustration and upset. You're too smart and capable to be limited to one approach that doesn't work and isn't any good for any of you—yourself, your wife, or your children. You don't have to go out of control. The fact that you generally have been drinking when this happens doesn't let you off the responsibility hook. Let's start looking at how you can control yourself, no matter what the provocation, at home or outside. We'll also look at how your wife can change.

This response by the therapist embodies five concepts frequently given in the treatment literature on marital violence:

1. The abuser alone is responsible for the violence. The victim cannot cause or eliminate the violence.
2. Violence is learned. The abuser learned to be violent, primarily in his family of origin. If the abuser learned to be violent, he can also learn to be nonviolent.
3. Provocation does not equal justification. There are always alternatives to violence. There are no circumstances under which violence between spouses is legitimate.
4. Violence is harmful to all family members, including the abuser. Damage to the victim may be obvious. Effects on the children may be less obvious but equally serious. Violence is illegal, and the abuser can be arrested, tried, and jailed if convicted.
5. Once violence has occurred in a relationship, it will most likely continue unless changes are made (Rosenbaum & O'Leary, 1986, pp. 393–394).

From this kind of confrontive approach one can move to work patiently with the couple to learn new ways of behaving. The first task in the example was to section out the man's responses to his wife and family situation and to recast things in terms of his ability to control his behavior. At this juncture the appeal is to his "macho" side to take on the challenge to change. Some cases profit from a considerable amount of psychoeducational work around self-control and some basic learning of ways for dealing with tensions. For some individuals the very idea that one can control anger and not automatically have to give expression to feelings of upset is a novel concept. The sexism in the man's attitudes and behaviors and in the couples' relationship, which certainly needs to be altered, can be approached later.

Exploration with the man of the instances in which he uses force and hits someone who makes him angry or with whom he has a disagreement frequently is enlightening for him and opens the way to dealing with family-of-origin violence issues. Recognition that he does not hit his boss, or the policeman with a .357 Magnum pistol on his hip who gives him a traffic ticket, or the 275-pound male who crowds ahead of him in a purchasing line, begins to establish the point that one does use discrimination about expression of anger. Control is used in those and other instances. From there it is only a short distance for most persons to the acknowledgment that we truly hit people in the family "because we can." The attempted justification that is frequently encountered (i.e., "Yes, that's true, but . . .") calls for an exploration of the source of the idea that one can selectively hit family members, in my judgment. Family-of-origin issues may be dealt with in conjoint marital sessions, in individual meetings with the man, or in family-or-origin meetings with his entire family or with subsystems. Not all of the family-of-origin roots of violent and abusive behavior involve solely parent-child issues or parental marriages. Recent clinical experience suggests that sibling subsystem sessions in which old issues of childhood and adolescent abusive behavior are reopened and reworked may be quite powerful in breaking cycles and altering the attitudes and behaviors of some men.

Sometimes the parents in a family of origin that tolerated violence when the person was growing up will be disturbed by abusive behavior in the marriage of their daughter or son, so that many such parents can be called on for support by the therapist in stopping the current abuse. Reconciliation of the parents and their point of view with their offspring and their comprehension of what they thought was permissible for them is not easily accomplished, but is worth whatever effort it requires of the clinician.

There are some considerations here regarding marital boundaries. The concern for privacy for the marital couple can be overdone. While the partners need to establish clear boundaries around their relationship, they do not need to be isolated from their families of origin and from the community in which they reside. Both community networks of relationships and ties with their families of origin may be supportive and helpful in some instances. In those cases in which the respective families of origin cannot be counted on to help the couple reduce or eliminate violent and abusive attitudes and behaviors, the efforts of the clinician toward involvement of the partners in interaction with community networks that will reduce isolation may be the course of choice. Reduction of both a perceived sense of isolation and a realistic isolation can be helpful in eliminating abusive behavior.

Resolving Contributory Marital Conflicts

There are marital conflicts that help to produce marital violence or to set the stage for its appearance. Helping both the husband and wife to learn new ways of relating and problem solving often calls for delicate work by the clinician around what they are willing to risk and how much they are able to trust each other. Positive breakthroughs sometimes occur when a wife is able to tell her husband, "I am frightened of you when you get angry. I don't feel like loving you. I don't feel close." Timing is of the essence in determining when such disclosures should be encouraged by the clinician. There should be adequate indication of the husband's reciprocal willingness to risk change for the therapist to be in a responsible position to elicit such statements of vulnerability from the wife. When both partners can be helped to "give" some in the sessions, indicating verbally/behaviorally their openness to new patterns of relating, the clinician can begin to work with them toward taking the steps to "break new ground" and trying to consolidate their gains as they do so.

Anger is a realistic part of marriage. One of the major issues in achieving marital stability has to do with learning how to deal with disagreements and anger without violence. A significant part of the therapeutic work with such couples pertains to their achievement of success in coping with areas of conflict and disagreement. I look for milder areas of conflict at the same time I am working with the processes and issues already mentioned in order to help the couple to achieve agreement or at least neutrality about as many areas of conflict as possible. To the extent that such endeavor is effective, it not only provides success experiences that can be built upon but also reduces the extent of both verbal and physical conflict. Researchers have found that couples with the most conflicts demonstrate the strongest link between verbal blasts and physical blows, that the more conflicts they have, the more likely they are to get into a physical fight (Straus *et al.*, 1980). With many such couples, if we can reduce the number of conflict areas, we stand a good chance of cutting down on verbal and physical abuse.

Changing the marital/family climate also involves changing the rules, that is, altering the attitude that violent behavior is an acceptable means of problem solving. Stated negatively, it is not all right to punish physically; it is not all right to retaliate abusively, physically or otherwise; one does not have the "right" to swear at the spouse or to call them names as a means of expressing dissatisfaction or of trying to get them to conform to one's wishes.

A seemingly casual remark by a therapist such as "You know, I don't think any of us really enjoy being called names—no matter how thick-skinned or sophisticated we are, it does seem to bother us if we're sworn at or called a bitch or a bastard or an asshole" sometimes helps clients to acknowledge that they are not unaffected by the abusive and pejorative behaviors prevalent in their marriage. Therapist encouragement to eliminate such behaviors becomes a part of a change in the behaviors and the rules. Behavioral contracts with a system of rewards for refraining from engaging in verbal abuse often can be paired effectively with communication training that helps the mates to express their wishes and reactions directly and nonabusively.

Direct communication does not imply the need for confrontive exchanges between spouses; assertiveness training for battered wives has in some instances led to unfortunate outcomes when the woman attempted to "stand up to her husband" verbally and received another beating as a result. Rather, it means that the couple should be helped to learn to talk as directly and clearly as they can in a cooperative and problem-solving posture. Although any behavior that challenges the spouse in an abusive marriage may launch an escalation of conflict, as the partners are able to become more secure and increase their sense of self-esteem, they can become more able to deal with differences without being threatened automatically.

Once again, the clinician needs to give attention to the psychological and emotional needs of both spouses in either conjoint or individual sessions. Women who have been battered require assistance in coping with feelings of inadequacy and damaged self-esteem, as well as with feelings of uncertainty and unnecessary guilt in many instances. Males frequently need to learn how to get their emotional requirements met directly and frankly without an overlay of conflictive and physically abusive actions (Nichols, 1986b). Neither husband nor wife needs to end up feeling blamed for what has occurred.

Prevention

Support groups and preventive and treatment programs for both women and men may be helpful in securing change. A large number of treatment programs for men had become available by 1985 (Pirog-Good & Stets-Keally, 1985), and therapeutic programs, including some court-mandated treatment endeavors, have demonstrated effectiveness (Lerman, 1981). Preventive efforts such as the perinatal coaching program of Oakland Family Services (Pontiac, MI) in which young couples are helped to prepare for childbirth and early childrearing by trained volunteers also have made significant contributions to a lessening of the incidence of marital and family violence.

If such groups as Alcoholics Anonymous and Al-Anon are helpful in dealing with alcoholism, auxiliary groups should be no less supportive and helpful in cases of marital violence and spouse abuse. In dealing with situations of this kind, I look for all the assistance that I can get. Simultaneously, I try to use Pollyanna approaches in which all of the constructive steps of the couple are supported and encouraged as honestly as is possible to do so.

Although danger from abusive spouses is seldom a realistic factor for a therapist, solo private practitioners may not have the necessary support to treat abusive marital couples, instead having to refer such couples to clinics where backup support is readily available. The presence of a significant number of persons in a clinic may be a deterrent to abusive or threatening behavior on the part of clients, whereas a solo private practitioner's sparsely populated office may fail to deter such behaviors on the part of clients.

ALCOHOL PROBLEMS

Although five classes of substances—including barbituates, amphetamines, opioids, and cannabis (marijuana), in addition to alcohol—are associated with substance abuse and substance dependency, and several others with abuse only in the DSM-III classifications (American Psychiatric Association, 1980), the concern in this section is primarily with alcohol as a marital problem. This focus is taken because much of what can be said regarding treatment applies as well to substances other than alcohol, and because alcohol seems to appear as an issue in marital cases with far greater frequency than do other substances. Individuals or couples whose difficulties are defined primarily in terms of some form of substance problem are probably more likely to contact a substance abuse clinic or a clinician or program specializing in chemical dependency/abuse treatment than a marital/family therapist.

SOME DEFINITIONS AND DISTINCTIONS

Alcohol appears as an issue in marital cases in a number of different ways. Diagnostically, it can be described in terms of substance *abuse* or substance *dependence*. Dependence is the more serious since it indicates that the individual's body has become accustomed to receiving alcohol and is dependent on it. A tolerance has been developed so that continuing the same amount of alcohol will produce less and less effect or that more and more alcohol is required in order to achieve the same effect. Dependence also means that there will be physical reactions to cessation of the use of alcohol (Levy, 1982). In contrast, the criteria for abuse are a pattern of pathological use and impairment in social or occupational functioning as a result of alcohol use.

To those categories I find it helpful to add one of my own: *problematic use of alcohol*. This refers to the use of alcohol in ways that may or may not fulfill the DSM-III requirements for abuse or dependency, but that are associated with problems in the marriage. This may be fudging a bit technically in some instances, but clinically it makes sense to simply label some uses of alcohol a relationship problem and to deal with those uses from that perspective. I refer to alcohol use which does not cause occupational or social impairment apart from the marriage and to patterns that are specific to the marital interaction. An example of this is the use of alcohol as a way of putting distance between oneself and the partner in some instances. The user may not drink often enough or heavily enough to fit under the heading of an alcohol abuser or dependent. All three types may present to the marital and family therapist, but my experience has been that alcohol often appears as a problem even when it is not severe enough to be designated as abuse or dependency and when it has not been named a primary problem by the couple.

Periodically, one sees a couple in which a partner will hesitantly indicate that they are concerned about their spouse's drinking only to learn that drinking is not that important to the drinking mate. Often he or she will respond, "If it bothers you, I'll stop it—that's no big deal," and then proceed to do so. Those cases are comparatively rare, but they do provide reminders that not all drinking is abusive, chemically dependent, or psychologically important and necessary to the drinker.

Similarly, even for some of those individuals whose drinking is serious, heavy, and prolonged, there is an occasional instance in which they stop drinking "cold turkey" when challenged to do so. Mr. Peterson, for example, consulted a therapist who recommended 2 years of individual psychotherapy for his drinking and for insight into his associated problems. Mrs. Peterson then got him to go to her clergyman who told him to stop drinking, which he did and then remained sober. The marital system adjusted to this change and the Petersons were doing well several years afterward. Not all cases are so amenable to such brief therapy, but they do underline the significant fact that control of drinking rests in the hands of the drinker and her or his marital and family system, not in those of the therapist.

There is a reciprocal relationship between marital problems and difficulties with alcohol. Marital discord can certainly contribute to an increased use of alcohol and even to the appearance of alcoholism, but this does not appear to happen very often. Alcoholism, on the other hand, frequently results in marital discord, and once problem drinking has made its appearance it tends to become a major focus of the life of the marital partners.

There are two broad categories or issues to assess during the period of assessment of marital difficulties and alcohol problems, abuse, or dependency. One pertains to the patterns, role, and meaning of alcohol use within the marriage; the other is concerned with marital problems, including those related to the use of alcohol.

Two important and interrelated questions with respect to alcohol usage are the role of alcohol in the current marital/family system and the history of alcohol problems in relation to the marriage. When did the drinking problems originate, before or after the marriage was begun? If the problems started before the marriage, was the other spouse aware of the problems prior to marriage? Did drinking become problematic after marriage? Answers to these questions may be very important in the treatment and the prognosis for the couple.

Problematic Drinking Prior to Marriage

Three major issues must be considered if the problem drinking was established prior to entry into marriage (Paolino & McCrady, 1977). First, in what system was the problem drinker involved when the problem drinking began—family of origin, previous marriage, or another system such as work group or social peer group? Second, is the drinking still related to that system, maintained and reinforced by it? Third, if problem drinking did predate the marriage, the spouses have never learned how to function as a couple without the presence of problematic drinking.

Preexistence of problem drinking and awareness on the part of the "dry" spouse has several implications for the therapist (Paolino & McCrady, 1977). What were the expectations of the dry spouse regarding marriage? Did he or she expect to change the drinking spouse? Did he or she regard the use of alcohol as being of no consequence? If the dry partner was not aware of the problematic drinking, it seems apparent that there may not have been very good communication between mates, so that the therapist should give close attention to current communication patterns.

Problematic Drinking after Marriage

The situation is somewhat different when problematic drinking appears after marriage. Prior to the onset of drinking the partners have had a

period in which the marriage functioned without the presence of alcoholism—of abusive, dependent, or simply problem drinking. The therapeutic task in such cases is to help the partners return to a form of relating that is similar to that enjoyed before the use of alcohol constituted a
problem in the marriage. Part of the assessment task is ascertainment of
what was occurring in the marriage and in the life of the drinking individual immediately prior to the onset of the drinking. What kinds of
crises and major events were occurring in the individual's life, the marriage, or the extended family of that person? Births, deaths, serious illness, or major losses may be significant (Paolino & McCrady, 1977).
Connections between such events and the onset of problem drinking often
become clear to the clinician before they do to clients and their family
members. Effecting the recognition provides a basis for trying to deal
with such stresses in various ways. As with other problems, establishment of communication and problem-solving skills is indicated.

Another set of issues pertains to the current status of the marital
interaction and the problems. How are the spouses relating and how
much satisfaction and pleasure are they currently receiving? What irrational beliefs need to be corrected? What has happened when the problem drinker has tried to stop or control the drinking on her or his own
or has tried to secure professional assistance (Paolino & McCrady, 1977)?

TREATMENT

The most effective treatment of truly alcoholic marriages in which one
or both partners is alcohol abusive or alcohol dependent has been for me
a family systems approach combined with involvement of the spouses in
Alcoholics Anonymous and Al-Anon for at least the early part of treatment. The drinking is viewed as a problem of the marital/family system.

The Process and Goals of Change

The process of change where a drinking problem is involved has three
stages: (1) an initial acknowledgment that a problem exists and a decision
to make a commitment to change; (2) the actual process of change—
stopping the problematic drinking and stabilizing the marriage for several months; and (3) establishing change over a long period (Paolino &
McCrady, 1977).

One of the early therapeutic tasks, therefore, is to secure a decision
on the part of the problem drinker to moderate or cease the drinking,
which can come about in any one of several ways. Once this has oc-
cured, the clinician is concerned with helping the dry partner to cease

engaging in actions that help to maintain the problem drinking (e.g., nagging the drinker and failing to acknowledge positive steps on her or his part). The longer range goal is to help the partners to reorganize their marital system around a new set of attitudes, values, and behaviors.

Conjoint/Individual Sessions

Conjoint interviews are the modality of choice. It is possible to work with one spouse to bring about some change in some instances, particularly when the couple are still in the "wet" phase of an alcoholic marriage. Getting things "settled down" especially may be facilitated by seeing the "dry" spouse alone if the drinker is not accessible for therapy. The marital system can then be at least temporarily calmed down while one partner begins to try to "settle into" therapy.

A systemically oriented approach described by Berenson (1979) is exceedingly helpful for dealing with some couples. He works explicitly to remain disengaged from the marital system and to get the spouses to take responsibility for their own change. The assignment and reinforcement of the marital/family system as being responsible supports the creation of a therapeutic context in which the therapist can be helpful to the couple. Three possibilities—all actually impossible to effect, says Berenson—are laid out for the dry spouse in an effort to undermine that person's refusal to change. He emphasizes that the only three possibilities for the dry spouse are to continue doing what they are doing, to detach or separate emotionally from the alcoholic spouse, or to physically distance or separate themselves. The purpose is to allow the dry spouse to "hit bottom" and decide to assume responsibility for herself or himself rather than continuing to try to change the mate. All of this is done in a context of support and readiness to help when the dry spouse is ready to face the situation. Equally crucial as dry spouses begin to observe their own functioning, accept responsibility for their contribution to the marital/family functioning, and try to change is the necessity of predicting that the wet spouse will get worse.

I find it helpful in these and other situations to outline a change paradigm in which Partner *B* will attempt to do something to cause Partner *A* to retreat from the new behavior and return to the status quo. "That's predictable. It's to be expected. If you want the change in the marital system that you say you want, you have to be prepared to stay with these new behaviors in spite of what your spouse does. There is a crisis coming. I don't say that lightly or easily, but simply to emphasize that it is predictable and part of the resistance to change that can be predicted."

Once the dry spouse has accepted responsibility for herself or himself and any outcome of that stance and action, the drinking spouse will be more accessible and will hit bottom, according to Berenson (1979). This occurs because the therapist has succeeded in creating a situation in which it is acceptable for therapy to either fail or succeed. Hitting bottom by the wet spouse brings forth another crucial stage, Berenson notes. To move in and encourage the drinker to stop drinking can sabotage all the progress that has occurred, because the drinker has to be genuinely powerless and hopeless in order to stop the drinking. For the drinker to reach this final condition generally brings emotional reactions from others that provide an important supportive context for sobriety.

The concept of the distancer and the pursuer (Fogarty, 1976) has some descriptive and explanatory power for use in alcoholic marriages. The pursuer is seen as the more anxious and uncomfortable of the two mates and thus the one more likely to change. The distancer is viewed as an individual who will keep moving away as long as he or she is pursued and will not change until it becomes apparent that no chase is occurring, which lack faces her or him with the need to get in touch with internal fears of loneliness and of losing the spouse. When the pursuer reaches the point of wishing to let the marriage drop and get out of the relationship the distancer will usually become available for change and retention of the relationship.

If they cannot be used earlier, Berenson (1979) and I prefer to use conjoint sessions once the drinking has moved off center stage. The task is to decrease the emotional distance between the spouses without a resumption of the drinking. This is one of those places where I make it explicit with most couples that we are "breaking new ground" or at least trying to reestablish a more workable relationship without alcohol as a buffer and barrier. A considerable amount of work needs to be done with some couples in order to deal with their apprehensions at the possibility of closeness and intimacy.

According to O'Farrell (1986), once the change in drinking has occurred and the alcoholic problem has been stabilized for some three to six months, the partners face the task of consolidating their gains so that there is not a relapse into problem drinking and so that positive steps are taken toward dealing with residual marital problems. The latter includes handling resentments that have piled up during the years of an alcoholic marital relationship and building skills that the couple lacked earlier.

Assistance should be given the couple not only in dealing with conflicts but also in increasing their positive feelings toward one another and their commitment to the marital relationship. Given the nature of their difficulties, the spouses may need help in dealing with a variety of common relationship issues of marital living (e.g., sex, childrearing, and the normal stresses and crises of the marital life cycle).

Conjoint sessions may come about in other ways besides requesting marital help via the direct contact with a therapist. Kaufmann and Kaufman (1979) found that patients in residential treatment centers for adults eventually requested a change from multiple family therapy to couples' sessions. This tended to occur, according to their observations, when the couple had developed a relationship that could be considered potentially constructive. The partners also felt that they could pursue some issues better without the presence of their children and that they were ready as a couple to take responsibility for the youngsters. Kaufman and Kaufman also warned against the therapist becoming triangulated into the couple's marital system and emphasized the crucial nature of the period in which substance abuse is relinquished and the partners have to find new ways of relating.

Once the drinking has been brought under control, the therapist and the couple also need to establish clear agreements and plans about how the nonabusive-nondependent patterns are to be maintained. Behavioral contracts, possible use of anatabuse, and involvement of the spouses in support groups all may be used. Steps should also be taken to prepare the couple of possible relapses.

Marital Couples Group Therapy

Treatment of alcoholism through the use of couples' groups (Barnard, 1981; Cadogan, 1979; Kaufmann & Kaufman, 1979) is an effective modality and is viewed by some as a treatment of choice. Barnard (1981) has described the goals of such treatment as sobriety, enjoyment of life while sober, reduction of interactional anxiety, support, hope, insight and education, problem solving, communication improvement, overcoming denial, and reducing family pathology. Cadogan (1979) discussed similar goals in working with four to six couples in marital group therapy, adding the reduction of social isolation and the enhancement of feelings of self-acceptance and affiliation when group members find that they are not alone or unique in their difficulties.

Referral and Inpatient Treatment

Some substance abuse cases cannot be managed effectively on an outpatient basis. At the same time, there has been a considerable amount of evidence that 2-week and 28-day "drying out" stints in hospital settings do not necessarily provide any lasting change. My own response has been to search for residential treatment facilities that have good family therapy programs as the basis of their treatment programs. I have simply found that if the inpatient program does not involve the drinker's family in the treatment in a significant fashion, I can have only limited confidence in its ability to help her or him in the vast majority of cases. As a responsible clinician, I would rather give up contact and turn clients over to the inpatient family-system-oriented treatment program than to try to work with a client who has been through an individually oriented detoxification program.

Referral to Alcoholics Anonymous groups for drinkers and to Al-Anon for their spouses is somewhat different in that those groups provide adjunctive help at the same time as clients are being seen in outpatient treatment. From contact with Alcoholics Anonymous and Al-Anon groups over nearly 30 years, I have found it helpful to be aware of what occurs in such groups and to be able to do some interpreting of their activities and role to clients that I am encouraging to get into them. For example, since groups vary widely in their composition and "character" or "personality," I encourage clients that I think can benefit from such involvement to keep looking until they find a group or groups in which they can feel a reasonable affinity with other members. I also point out strongly that "You may not think you are ready for that kind of experience right now, but I would urge you to give it an adequate trial, and we'll talk about it and see if we can help you make it work for you."

Section **III**

Beyond the Dyad

Chapter Nine

Family-of-Origin Issues in Marital Therapy

My office is often filled with "ghosts" and "part-persons." Distortions and split-off parts of fathers, mothers, brothers, sisters, grandparents, aunts, uncles, cousins, and sometimes whole family groups may be bumping around vying for attention. The marital pair with whom I am working may feel supported, confused, frightened, intrigued by the cast of characters they summon onto the stage before and around us. To me it seems to make sense, when those powerful but distorted "ghosts" and "part-objects" are interfering, to replace them with flesh and blood people and real families who can be dealt with directly as whole persons and as families of the present.

Throughout this book the focus has been on the context in which individuals live and function. The point was made early on that the most basic and significant context for understanding individuals and remediating human difficulty is not a person's intrapsychic world, but the world of the family in which the person develops and functions.

The extended family has been described by Laing (1969) as an ongoing play, perpetuating itself over the generations. Actors are born and die. They come and go. The family lasts. Each generation projects onto the next generation a heritage composed of what was projected onto it by prior generations, what prior generations induced in it, and its reactions to those projections and inductions. The family, according to Laing, protects the individual against such terrors as those of personal disintegration, emptiness, despair, and collapse.

The family itself maintains its dynamic balance and is protected against threats of disintegration and chaos by its myths. Family myths, a series of unchallenged beliefs shared by family members concerning each other and their mutual position in family life, serve as family defenses as individual defenses serve the individual (Ferreira, 1963). Myths in nuclear families evidently are formed during the early years of the relationship of the spouses. Ferreira (1963) pointed out, for example, that the idea that having a baby will solve marital problems may evolve into the idea that the parents stay together only for the sake of the children. Such myths are held tightly, even though the individual family member may know that they falsify parts of reality. The behaviors of both family members and those with whom they come into contact are shaped and affected by the myths; the myths of two family systems come into contact and sometimes conflict with the marriage of a man and a woman. How can we work with those conflicting myths unless we can know what they are and have access to them?

MARRIAGE AND FAMILY OF ORIGIN

The major concern in this chapter is with how the continuing ties between individuals in marital relationships and their original kinship unit form an integral part of the spouses' current functioning. What impacts do the connections between the husband and his family of origin and the wife and her family of origin have on their own marital and individual functioning? The idea that one separates from the family of origin and becomes an autonomous individual is erroneous; the continuing ties take two forms: the intrapsychic and internal representations of family figures, attitudes, beliefs, and so on carried by the individual, and the live, active transpersonal transactions that prevail between the individual and members of her or his family of origin.

This focus on the nuclear family of each of the spouses does not imply that the larger extended families of each are of lesser importance. The identification of individuals with their heritage and transgenerational background is notable. One of the major reasons, for example, for the extraordinary interest attracted by Alex Haley's book *Roots* and the television miniseries based on it seemed to be the fact that it stirred deep responsive chords within us about our own roots. The nuclear family is the focus here because it is generally the most readily accessible and most immediately potent part of one's family for doing clinical work. Family-of-origin work certainly can include grandparents of the spouses where they are available, as well as aunts, uncles, cousins, and others in instances where they are thought to have a significant contribution to make to the therapy.

There are several different ways in which a clinician can gather information about the spouses families of origin in marital therapy. Some of these only involve assessment but most also include interventions.

Beavers (1985) has described five methods that he uses in his systems approach to families of origin. These are securing verbal descriptions from his clients, visiting the family of origin, bringing the family of origin in and observing the interaction of the members, inviting parents or siblings to attend a therapy session, and doing a form of data analysis (i.e., integrating the various ways of observing how families interact and sharing conclusions about the goals, processes, and rules for the family of the client).

A significant concept in Beavers' (1977) work and that of Stierlin (1981) is the concept of centrifugal/centripetal force. Families that operate centripetally seek to pull family members toward attachment to the family, in which, in extreme forms, all good things are seen as existing in the family. The centrifugal family does not unite solidly internally, but casts or pushes members outside of the family unit for their attachments and satisfactions. The centripetal or centrifugal forces operating in one's family of origin give important clues as to how one's marriage is likely to function as well as to the kinds of ties that will probably prevail with the family of origin.

Examples of attempts to solve problems of each type of marital relating have been provided by Stierlin (1981). The pathological centripetal couple shows indications of strain, fatigue, and irritation with each other. They deny that there is any problem with the marriage, smile at each other, and use endearments. They fail to mention that their sex life is nonexistent, and if they do mention difficulties with sex, attribute them to headaches, worries over children, fatigue, or some similar external factor, in general expressing only positive feelings and denying problems. Centrifugal couples tend to go their own ways, focusing on their own careers or personal affairs, and not manifesting concern about the other. Many such couples divorce, but if they stay together, it is with the maintenance of separate patterns of living. Both such patterns often involve the parents and their offspring in an overlapping and intermeshing of lives that tend to be problematic and to need assistance.

It should be noted here that there may or may not be significant amounts of correspondence between patterns in the family of origin and current marital behaviors to aid the clinician in understanding and making interventions. Simply put, some persons do replicate dysfunctional marital patterns from their family of origin, while others from disturbed or inadequate families of origin manage to make good marriages and to stay out of clinicians' offices. Similarly, some individuals in families in which the parental marriage was adequate to strong from all accounts do not necessarily fare well in their own marriages. While there often is a reasonable degree of correspondence between the nature and strength of the family of origin and the parental marriage and the marriage and family formed by the offspring, there is enough divergence to conclude that any model that would imply a one-to-one correspondence should be used with caution. The focus here is on ascertaining what correspondence does exist and how such factors need to be altered.

Another pattern of doing family-of-origin work has been offered by Napier (1987). Based on Whitaker and Keith (1981), it includes four facets: (1) direct work with the client's family of origin; (2) "coaching" the client on ways of changing relationship patterns in the family of origin; (3) symbolic reenactment of core childhood issues by using an "empty chair" and other evocative techniques in which the client symbolically deals with family-of-origin persons and issues; and (4) indirect reparenting of the client through the therapist–client relationship. Over the years I have used five major ways of dealing with family-of-origin issues, the descriptions of which follow.

CONJOINT MARITAL THERAPY

Family-of-origin issues are discussed and dealt with in many instances in conjoint marital sessions. This usually begins early in marital treatment when spouses are called on to discuss their expectations of their mate and the marriage. This approach tends to bring out similarities and differences between the values each learned in his or her family of origin. Similarly, it may bring forth discussion and exploration of their relationship with significant figures in their original nuclear and sometimes extended family. How these affect their current relationship and marriage quickly becomes a matter of concern, as does how unresolved issues with their families of origin can be approached.

INDIVIDUAL PSYCHOTHERAPY

There are instances in which a client talks with a therapist about family-of-origin issues in an individual psychotherapy framework. This pattern is used sparingly, primarily when only one person has requested treatment. Occasionally one spouse will wish to return for individual work centered on her or his family of origin after marital therapy has been concluded. He or she may be doing well in the marriage but may feel that there are some residual issues pertaining to the family of origin that need resolution.

COACHING

The pattern of "coaching" clients on how to return home, either physically or through letters and telephone contacts, for the purpose of dealing with family-of-origin issues is one that I have used many times. It appears particularly appropriate as a technique when the issues pertain to differentiating the person from the family. Helping the person to go back home in order to become more free combines well with efforts by the clinician to underline and reinforce the firmness and solidity of the client's existing degree of differentiation. The client who has already made significant steps to establish herself or himself as an adult person and whose issues are essentially concerned with individual liberation uses this approach more easily in my experience than do less differentiated persons. This approach has been described in the pioneering work of Murray Bowen (1978), who developed it early in the history of family therapy and continued to make refinements with it.

A variant of sending clients home with coaching consists of sending them to the graveyard when the parents are no longer living. This can be done for either of two major reasons. One has to do with the need to complete a mourning process that has been truncated or aborted. The failure to complete mourning often is a defense against further loss and frequently is transmitted to other family members, particularly to one's children (Paul, 1967; Paul & Grosser, 1965; Paul & Paul, 1975; Williamson, 1978).

This process can also be dealt with in other ways, including seeing a client with siblings and surviving parent. For example, this was done in one case more than 20 years after the unexpected death of the family's husband/father in a successful attempt to help all parties begin completing their mourning work. The surviving parent who had never remarried was finally ready to accept the loss and to let go of her deceased spouse, consequently releasing emotionally and psychologically her grown children to grieve and to let go and thus become able to make their own attachments. None had been able to sustain relationships with mates. Subsequent work with my client enabled him to become aware that his fear of losing and being left was the driving force in his sometimes frantic latching on to women and his selection of much younger females "so they can't leave me," and to change his patterns considerably.

Another major reason for sending a person to the graveyard is for the purpose of making statements to the deceased parent. Although this is related to completion of the mourning, it seems to possess a dynamic of its own. "I would like to tell my father [or mother] . . ." is the prelude to such a trip for some clients, although in many cases whether they actually make the trip and make the statements to the deceased parent(s) is not essential. The process of deciding what they wish to say and what they wish to change in the incomplete relationship is enough for such individuals to unblock their emotions and to allow them to bring closure on the unresolved relationship. In some respects it is not unlike having the individual "Say what you would like to say to your parent if they were sitting in that [empty] chair."

This kind of intervention is made only after a considerable amount of preparatory work. With a young man who was finally completing his college degree in his thirties, for example, this step was taken after fairly extensive exploration of his feelings that his father had never thought he would "amount to anything," his reactions to feeling that he did not "measure up" to his father's expectations, and discussion of his accomplishments with support by his wife and therapist. At long last, he felt that he could "face" his father as a person of worth and accomplishment. He could finally let go of his father and complete his mourning.

A powerful version of using the cemetary in facilitating differentiation and mourning has been developed by Williamson (1978). He has depicted "new life at the graveyard" as a result of helping clients to make on-site visits to the grave of what he terms a "dead former parent." The rationale, preparation, and subsequent consultation with the client that he uses in the approach have been described by Williamson (1978).

THERAPY WITH FAMILY-OF-ORIGIN MEMBERS

Bringing family-of-origin members in for sessions with their offspring, one's client, is also used in several different ways. Following the Framo (1983) pattern of a pair of 2-hour sessions, usually one on Friday night and the other the next morning, in which one's adult client is seen with members of her or his family of origin, has proven to be a powerful way of resolving issues in many cases. Occasionally, only the client and the parents are seen. In other instances a client and a single sibling or all of the siblings are seen without the parents being present. The patterns are arranged partly on the basis of practicality and availability and partly because of clinical judgments. There are instances, for example, in which it appears to be wiser to bring in only part of a family of origin because of the virulent form that family conflict and estrangement have taken and the readiness or lack of readiness of the client and/or other members to be together in a therapeutic session. Other members can be brought in subsequently.

The major intent is to take the client and the problems back to where they began, to take a direct route to the etiological sources. The experience of dealing with the real figures with whom the conflicts began and with whom current difficulties exist that affect contemporary living is intended to begin freeing the client from the hold of internal representations of those figures. The client begins to face reality through this process. Having moved backward in time, the client can begin to move forward and to deal more realistically with his or her spouse and children (Framo, 1976).

A young man who meets with his family of origin and realizes that his parents actually are physically smaller than he and no longer control him even if they wish to try, begins to change. As he sees that fear and anxiety guide their efforts more than pure power or arbitrariness, his own apprehensions and concerns about being dominated start to diminish.

Family-of-origin work is exceedingly helpful and sometimes necessary in order to deal with other unresolved issues as those pertaining to family justice in addition to those already illustrated or mentioned. Boszormenyi-Nagy and Spark (1973) in a classic work indicated that one's sense of justice plays a major role in determining family relationships. That is, our self-concept and role in family relationships are shaped by our feelings about whether or not we got what was coming to us and gave to others what they had coming to them. Each family member expects fairness and reciprocity. We carry a kind of internal ledger in which there is a balance sheet of what we are owed and what is owed to us by family members. Such "invisible loyalties" help to determine how we treat our spouse and children. For example, we may parentify a child when we feel that we did not get what we deserved from our own parents, expecting the child to repay us for what we missed, according to Boszormenyi-Nagy and Spark (1973).

The effects are also felt by the spouse. According to this orientation, a partner not only will attempt to live up to the normative value orientations of the family of origin but also will try to get their mate to do so. Clinicians frequently see situations in which a spouse develops guilt feelings over disloyalty to her or his parents and consequently rejects the mate; each partner in a couple may attempt to prove unconsciously that they are loyal to their parents by rejecting the spouse and the marriage. Boszormenyi-Nagy and Spark (1973) have also indicated that unconscious attempts to maintain the invisible loyalty to the family of origin by rejecting one's spouse may be a factor in producing impotence, premature ejaculation, or frigidity.

In my judgment, family-of-origin members should be brought in on any occasion that important unresolved issues that affect marital functioning remain and the members can be brought with a good chance of working productively with them. This is a matter of clinical judgment: From what is known of the parents, will they be able to deal with the issues of talking with their children about unresolved matters? Are the siblings willing and able to participate?

FAMILY-OF-ORIGIN SESSIONS

Direct work with the client's family of origin is one of my preferred ways of dealing with certain unresolved issues and reworking relationships between a spouse and her or his family. Results are sometimes dramatic. Seeing his feared father almost literally leap out of his chair and respond as a scared child to mention of his tyrannical father was the turning point in the therapy of one young man, for example. When his father was asked, "What was your father [the client's grandfather] like?" the heretofore-feared father exploded, "He was a Hitler! He was a dictator!" The man went on to describe being intimidated by his "Prussian" father and being driven by fears of failure that led him to work exceedingly hard right up to that very day in efforts to succeed. His son listened with a growing appreciation of his father's fearfulness and with a lessening of his own fears of his father. Seeing his parent as the child of an austere father enabled him to view his own father as a genuine person with concerns of his own for the first time.

What is needed to prepare one's client for family-of-origin sessions? My approach to working with families of clients in family-of-origin sessions is essentially as follows: I urge the husband and wife to bring in their parents and other family members (siblings, usually) for one or two sessions. This expectation is typically established early in treatment. It is made clear that such sessions will include only the members of the original family, and that the spouse will not be involved. Such sessions may include a client and his or her parents, the total family of origin, or merely the sibling subsystem of the original family. The spouse and her or his family of origin will be seen separately. Prior to the scheduled date(s) of the session(s) a considerable amount of attention is given to the questions that the client wishes to address with her or his family of origin. Preparation for family-of-origin sessions also may include a study of family photographs by the therapist and one or both of the clients. This work makes it evident that the locus of responsibility for posing questions and seeking answers and change rests with the client and not with the therapist, although I help clients clarify what they wish to find out and what they wish to have changed by working with them around such questions until they have become clear about their desires.

With Mr. Lee, whose depression and anxiety were affecting his work and his marriage, we evolved three issues that he wished to explore with his parents: What do they see happening to me? What do they expect of me? What are their desires as parents to reduce my level of anxiety and depression (this last issue was something that had been made manifest by the parents through their telephone calls and letters but not explicitly discussed).

The single session held with his parents when they came to town on a vacation trip was carefully structured to make the parents feel comfortable. Straightforwardly I explained that we could use their help in dealing with their son's troubles, that they understood him in ways that nobody else could, and that we appreciated their willingness to be consultants with us. Having made it as clear as possible that we were not blaming or holding them responsible, we began to explore the questions that Mr. Lee and I had established previously. There appeared to be two major outcomes. First, a considerable amount of clarification was obtained for both Mr. Lee and his parents about their respective expectations. It became clear that they essentially understood what was happening with him and would continue to be as supportive as they could be of him. Mr. Lee recognized that they would continue to provide subtle pressures for achievement without being aware of what they were doing, and that they genuinely meant it consciously when they said, "All we want for you is for you to be happy doing whatever you wish to do." Second, the parents relaxed to a noticeable degree their concerns over their son and subsequently diminished their hovering behaviors. This combination of support and loosening of controls provided some of the help that the client needed in order to make his own decisions and thus to lessen his anxiety and the combination of frustration and anger that was contributing to his depression.

Carol and Paul Brown's case (Nichols, 1985a), mentioned in Chapter 1, provided a more complicated family-of-origin situation. It also included issues that were more directly related to Carol Brown's needs for differentiating from her original family.

My interpretation of what was going on with her parents ran as

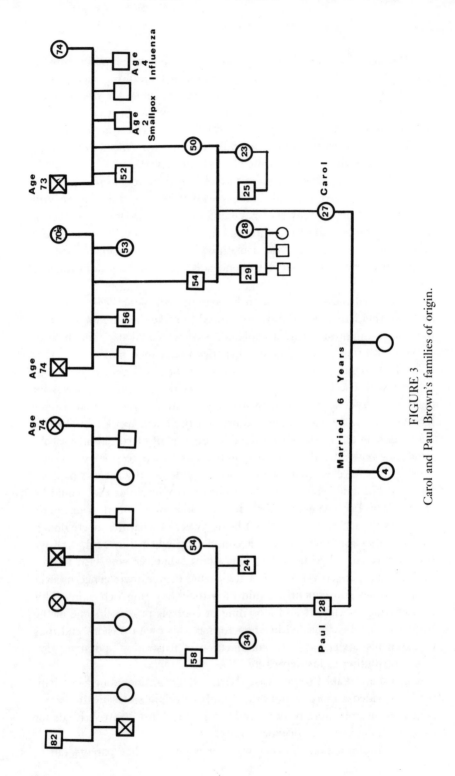

FIGURE 3

Carol and Paul Brown's families of origin.

follows: They protected themselves from a repetition of earlier losses by trying to make certain that their own children did not separate from the family, while at the same time trying to recreate the family that the husband/father had lost by getting their children to serve as parents for them. Not only had the father's family died when he was young, but also the mother had lost three brothers by death during her childhood and had gone through several years in her early teens in which her father was hospitalized with a series of disabling physical and emotional problems.

Carol was seen with her total family of origin. We scheduled a 2-hour Friday night meeting and a follow-up meeting on Saturday morning, modeled after Framo's (1981) pattern. Two preparatory sessions were spent with Carol. Along with examining her fears and dealing supportively with aprehensions about meeting with her total family, we specifically addressed the following questions: What did she wish to learn? What did she wish to accomplish in the meetings? Essentially, she wished to obtain information and understanding about certain times and events that she could not remember, as well as to change her relationship with her parents and brother.

The two meetings were eventful and painful. She did manage to alter her relationship with her brother to a significant degree. Confirmation of the extreme difficulty all three children had experienced in attempting to separate was abundantly clear, evident in the fright and conflict all reported experiencing when they went to college. At the time of the meetings, the youngest was the most tightly bound into the family. The oldest, who had suffered strong feelings of loneliness and depression when he entered college, also was still bonded very firmly to the family, much to the frustration of his wife, whom he had had trouble deciding to marry originally. The girls had married the first males with whom they had become deeply involved emotionally, but after lengthy dating periods. In the sessions the parents, especially the father, made it clear that it was very painful for the children even to talk about separating from the family. He cried as he said, "I don't want to lose you. I don't want you to move away and not be close." The tentacles of guilt induction reached almost visibly toward all three children.

A startling discovery for Carol was the fact that it was not her mother that she feared so much as her father. Her mother did come through in the meetings as an intrusive and controlling person but as less aggressive and more accepting than Carol had perceived to be the case, while her fears of her father were obviously complex. Immediately following the family sessions Carol was flooded with the recall of fearing his angry outbursts, his sharply critical tongue, and most of all, his emotional cut-offs when she was a child. A deep feeling of sadness and aching pain followed her acknowledgement that "my dad did a lousy job of being a father."

The recognition of the paramount role played by her mother's use of denial was also surprising to Carol. Earlier, she had talked about such matters as her mother's need to be right, saying, "You don't criticize my mom or infer that she is wrong; she'll argue it out until she is back on top." From the family sessions it became clear that a wider meaning was present. The mother had established a family rule for the children: "Don't criticize; don't talk about anything in the family in negative terms."

Both Paul and Carol had recognized to some degree—as had Carol's siblings—that her mother was behaviorally communicating, "Don't leave me alone with this man. I can't supply all his emotional needs or meet all his dependency needs." Consciously the mother was saying quite different things, extolling the virtues of family-of-origin life, although putting her own energies into the family she had formed at marriage. Much of the behavior appeared to be motivated by the dual desire to ensure the retention of her husband so that she would not lose another significant male and to keep the children and their male spouses in particular around so that they could serve as a support system and buffer between herself and her needy and increasingly critical, bitter husband.

"Don't leave me alone with this man" was a plea easily identified with by Carol, since her own discomfort at being alone with her father continued to be strong. A major source of the lack of ease seemed to be the bad-mother object-relations role that she evidently fulfilled for him, manifested in his anger and the emotional cut-offs that occurred after he would set her up for such reactions (Dicks, 1967; Fairbairn, 1952). His object-relations splits seemed to put his wife primarily into a good-mother role—although there was some ambivalence in his dealing with her when she did not supply his needs adequately—and his son into a good-father role.

A second part of Carol's discomfort—her apprehension that her father might unload his massive dependency needs on her—became apparent a few weeks later. Originally, her recognition of how she was fearful of her father and his emotional needs began with the comprehension that her increasing uneasiness at being around her mother stemmed from her concern that her mother's denial might break down and that she would be overwhelmed by her mother's dependency needs. At approximately the same time, Carol realized the lengths to which her mother went in protecting herself from being alone with the care of her husband, assuming the role of protecting him and trying to make the children responsible for him. If Mother caved in, Carol feared, she would inherit the responsibility for protecting Father emotionally, of providing the family life that he had lost as a child.

Several factors and experiences had reinforced Carol's apprehensions that responsibility for Father could fall on her if Mother's denial ever collapsed. These included her identification with Mother by extended family members and family acquaintances, Mother's preparation of her for such a caretaking role, an experience in her early teens in which Father jokingly introduced her as his wife at a social function, and her role as "the family star"—as the child who always performed well and who, in the words of her father, "was running the school when she was in the sixth grade".

Over the years the family had not been aware of Carol's fearfulness: Prior to the family sessions, the parents evidently had not comprehended that she had been fearful at each step of the way toward adulthood. Fears of separation had dogged her from the time of entering kindergarten, and the pattern had been repeated when she became fearful when her older daughter reached the same point. As a result of the family sessions, Carol's fears of being separated, of going out into the world, took on new meaning. She recognized how she already had taken some responsibility emotionally for her father and had been carrying his fears of being separated and abandoned. As this became evident, Carol's fears of going to kindergarten, of being left outside on the first-grade playground after recess and lunch, of going to college (where she had become physically ill to the point of vomiting at the start of each term), and other fears became more explicable and, eventually, more expendable. She began to realize that there had been no realistic danger to her welfare in the past, thus releasing some sizable amounts of tension. Part of the releasing process involved breaking current reinforcers of her fears; she noted, for example, that she had "kind of peaked in high school and gone downward after that." I pointed out that she had literally left home after high school and that she had received a double message—as had her siblings—about going to college: Get a college education, but don't go away and separate from the family. She was still getting the same kind of message: Be married and have children, but don't go away and separate from the family.

All of the findings and subsequent reactions to the family sessions were shared by Carol with Paul, and were dealt with in conjoint interviews (Nichols, 1985a, pp. 219–222). Eventually the Browns moved to another state, thus providing themselves with less opportunity for contact with Carol's family and more control over their daily life.

OTHER PATTERNS AND ISSUES

There are still other ways of conducting family-of-origin sessions. Nerin (1986), for example, conducts family reconstruction workshops in which individuals work on unresolved issues from their families of origin without the family members being present. His experiences with a large number of persons indicate that it is possible and important to confront and deal in such a format with matters from one's family of origin that have remained as unresolved issues from earlier in one's life. It is difficult to understand, however, how sessions without the presence of family-of-origin members could have the same immediacy and perhaps the same results as sessions in which face-to-face contact is possible. Moreover, since the uncovering and working through of family secrets is sometimes a significant part of the kind of family-of-origin sessions that I have described, it seems unlikely that, given Nerin's framework, important family secrets could be uncovered and dealt with. For this to occur, some informed person from the family of origin or extended family of the individual would need to be present to provide information about the secret, to reveal it or confirm a client's suppositions about what had happened in the family in the past. Among the kinds of secrets that are commonly revealed are information about mental illness, abortion, incest, criminal conviction, desertion, extramarital affairs, and out-of-wedlock pregnancies and births.

Secrets have been described in terms of individual secrets, internal family secrets, and shared family secrets by Karpel (1980). One person keeps a secret from the other family members in the case of an individual secret, while at least two people keep a secret from at least one other person in an internal family secret. This pattern creates subgroupings within the family, in contrast to shared family secrets, which are known by all family members who agree to keep the information from those outside the family. In an excellent article, Karpel (1980) has discussed different stances toward secrets and has emphasized the ethical issues in dealing with them.

A FINAL POINT

Using family-of-origin sessions often has powerful and effective results, though there is no magic in them. Rather than clearing up all of a client's problems, the use of such sessions can be primarily expected to open the way for working on and working through these problems in subsequent therapeutic sessions. Whatever "freeing up" occurs as a result of family-of-origin meetings—or other forms of family of origin work, for that matter—the client still has work to do in using the new freedom or understandings in her or his marriage and contemporary living. My hope, in other words, is not that working with the family of origin will "fix up" the individual and the marriage, but that such an endeavor will make the individual more available for working and living in the present, in his or her marriage and in the world. Therapists have long sought ways—including such violent modes as electroconvulsive shock treatment—of breaking up old patterns in order to make persons more accessible to treatment and to change. The family-of-origin way seems to be not only more humane but also more effective, both making the person available for more work and producing change during the experience of the family-of-origin work.

Chapter Ten

Marital Break-up: Therapy with Divorcing Spouses

- "We've talked about divorce, but decided to give it one more chance. Both of us want to continue the marriage if we can."
- "I don't know what I want to do. I don't know whether I want to work on the marriage or not. I don't know why I'm here. Henry has come because he wants to keep trying [with the marriage]."
- "George told me the other day that he wanted a divorce. I begged him to see somebody with me and see whether we could salvage things. That's why we're here. I want to work things out."
- "Neither of us knows what we want to do. There's been so much trouble, so many problems. We don't know whether we want to try to save the marriage or what."
- "Some days I want a divorce and some days I don't. I keep changing my mind. And so does she."
- "We have finally decided that getting a divorce is the best thing to do. We do have three children and we want to do what is best for them when we do break up. Can you help us with this?"

MARITAL THERAPY OR DIVORCE?

Marital therapists starting work with a couple cannot always be certain what clients are seeking, even when they secure some statement of the complaints during the initial telephone contacts. After the clients enter their office it becomes imperative to determine, as noted earlier, what they are seeking. Are they in fact seeking treatment? Are both partners seeking the same thing?

Marriage can be a most intense form of object relationship and an exceedingly strong form of family relationship. It also is the most vulnerable: The attachments leading to marriage are voluntarily formed and can be voluntarily broken, and as most adults and many children in the United States are probably aware, a marriage can be ended by divorce. Although it takes the commitment or at least the acquiesence of two partners to enter and maintain a marriage, it only takes one spouse under the laws of many states to end a marriage. Under the operation of these no-fault statutes, it essentially requires only one partner to decide that "the objectives of matrimony no longer exist," "the marriage is moribund," or the marriage is "irretrievably broken." Marriage, still an attractive status for most persons, can be legally ended easily today in this society when compared with the past.

The possibility of divorce is thus something that can be considered by all couples, though how many actively do so is an unanswered and probably unanswerable question. In Chapter 5 of this book and elsewhere (Nichols & Everett, 1986) the stance of marital partners with regard to the question of divorce has been described as preambivalent, ambivalent, or postambivalent. Preambivalent couples or individuals are those who have never seriously considered divorce as a personal alternative. Ambivalent couples or individuals are those who are undecided and wavering back and forth between wishing to end the marriage or continue it. Postambivalent couples or individuals have made a decision— some having decided to end the marriage and thus not being open to any reconsideration, others having decided to continue the marriage.

Couples present to the clinician with all of the patterns illustrated in the quotes given above, plus various combinations of those patterns in changing forms. The four major patterns are: (1) both partners wish to continue the marriage and to work on it; (2) one wishes to continue and to work on it and the other is uncertain whether he or she wishes to continue; (3) one wishes to continue and the other does not; and (4) both are undecided (Nichols and Everett, 1986).

Sorting out the reasons clients are present and what they wish to do is at least as important as determining the nature of their problems and their disorders and symptomatology in all cases. Where one or both marital partners are seriously considering or have decided upon divorce, establishing the answers to what they are seeking is even more imperative. Are the conditions available for the establishment of a therapeutic alliance and a good-faith effort to help them either work on the marriage or to separate and terminate the marriage as humanely as possible?

Not infrequently, one spouse has already decided to terminate the marriage and is primarily seeking to place the spouse with a therapist. Whitaker and Miller (1969) pointed out three ways in which one partner may attempt to alleviate guilt feelings over a unilateral decision to divorce the spouse: The person may encourage the rejected spouse to return to their family of origin; encourage them overtly or covertly to take a lover; or provide them with a therapist. Gardner (1976) added a fourth: The partner seeking out of the marriage may try to give his or her spouse money. In my clinical experience, the action of "dropping the rejected spouse on a therapist's doorstep" generally occurs within the first one to three sessions. The partner who has definitely or essentially decided to leave the marriage before the therapist is contacted does not maintain the fiction of working on resolving problems very long in most cases. Exceptions have occurred in cases where it emerged that the departing partner was biding for time in order to hide assets or for some similar purpose. The essential clue for the therapist that a good-faith effort to work in treatment is not being made is usually the evasion of the reluctant partner when efforts are made to effect change.

DIVORCE AS A PHENOMENON AND PROCESS

Divorce has become a major sociocultural phenomenon. Approximately 1,200,000 couples are involved in divorce and most in child custody decisions and struggles each year in the United States (Glick, 1979). Divorce in which the custody of children and the possession of property and resources are at stake is still the occasion for considerable conflict between two parting spouses in many instances. All divorces, even with no-fault laws, which do not require assignment of blame and proof of fault, are still potentially open to conflict over the property division. Where there are children, there may be struggles over custody as a direct issue or the children may be used as pawns in property and personal conflict issues between the parents. The rise of family mediation in which divorcing partners use the services of a mediator to settle division and ownership issues around children and property is a direct sociocultural response to a large social need.

Despite recent efforts to pass more realistic laws and to provide more humane ways for marital partners to end their marriage, divorce continues to be a painful, often confusing, and generally disruptive experience in the lives of the adults and children directly affected by the process. For many of those involved, the experience is not merely painful but also quite traumatic, at least for the early period of time surrounding and soon after the marital breakup.

Evidence seems solid that separation/divorce is a stressor of the first order (Bloom, White, & Asher, 1979). "Separation distress" (Parkes, 1973) results primarily from the loss of the attachment to the other person. It includes focusing attention on the image of the lost object (person), feelings of guilt for having caused the loss, and such "alarm reaction" feelings as restlessness, fear, panic, sleeping and eating disorders, and an acute alertness to the possibility of the lost person returning. One of the difficult things for separating/divorcing individuals to comprehend and cope with is the fact that strong attachment feelings for the lost person may be present long after love has been eroded and disappeared (Weiss, 1975).

Family system theory should sensitize the clinician to the fact that the family continues while the marriage ends. The result of divorce is marital break-up and family reorganization. The parents continue to be parents and the children continue to be part of the biological families from which their parents came. Systems and family therapy theories have been accused of being more likely "to intervene to modify the system than to unbalance or terminate it" (Jacobs, 1986, p. 196). If that charge means that a systems approach is not open to ending *families* and family relationships, it is correct. If it means that systems-oriented therapy and therapists try to hold *divorcing couples* together even when the partners wish to divorce, it appears to be without foundation.

As noted above, divorce is a time of break-up for the marriage and a period of transition for the family system as a whole. It brings about an alternative form of family life cycle and individual and marital life-cycle tasks that are different from those tasks necessary to continuing a marriage until it is broken by the death of a spouse. What happens with the adults is also different from what happens with the children, but inseparable from those results. The outcome for the children depends in part on their youngsters' ages, developmental stages, and adjustment prior to the break-up, as well as on what happens with the adults and how they respond.

The specific focus in this chapter is on dealing with the needs of the divorcing adults from the period of break-up through the early adjustment stage. Attention is not given here to the therapeutic needs of children or to preparation of the adults for remarriage, as important as both of these sets of needs are; the treatment needs of children (Nichols, 1984, 1985b, 1986a) and the therapeutic challenge of stepfamilies (Nichols, 1980;

Nichols & Everett, 1986) have been addressed elsewhere. Those areas are omitted here not because they are insignificant but because of the concern with focusing specifically on the marital partners, as has been the case throughout this book. Much more comprehensive treatments of "divorce therapy" are found in works by Rice and Rice (1986) and Sprenkle (1985).

DIVORCE, LIFE CYCLES, AND THE ADJUSTMENT OF ADULTS

The full cycle for those individuals who marry, have children, divorce, and remarry involves the following typical stages: Dating/Courtship, Marriage, Discord and Separation, Divorce, Single-Parent Living (or Single-Living for the noncustodial parent), Resocialization, Dating/ Courtship, and Remarriage (Nichols & Everett, 1986). "Living together" as a prelude to marriage is subsumed under the Dating/Courtship category.

During marital break-up and divorce, what occurs has been described variously. Piercy and Sprenkle (1986) have conceptualized stages of (1) predivorce decision making, (2) divorce restructuring, (3) postdivorce recovery, and (4) remarriage. Carter and McGoldrick (1980) described a divorce phase consisting of the decision to divorce, planning the break-up of the system, separation, and the divorce; and the postdivorce family, which may include a single-parent family and noncustodial single-parent living. For those persons who remarry, Carter and McGoldrick set forth the steps of entering a new relationship, conceptualizing and planning a new marriage, and the actual remarriage and reconstitution of the family.

For the divorcing adults, Weiss (1975) has pictured the divorce process as involving stages of transition and recovery. These cover the time between the marital separation and when the persons have established a stable and strong identity and are themselves again. Transition is considered to last for approximately 8 months to a year. By the end of 2 to 4 years the person typically has moved through the stress, disorganization, and reactive feelings resulting from the break-up and has achieved a balanced, manageable pattern of living.

Kaslow (1981) has proposed a "diaclectic" model of stages in the divorce process. Three divorce stages are named: a predivorce deliberation period, a during-divorce litigation period, and a postdivorce reequilibration period. Each of those stages has two major sets of feelings typically experienced by the divorcing persons and two corresponding sets of "requisite actions and tasks." The feelings during the predivorce deliberation period, for example, range from disillusionment, dissatisfaction, and alienation through feelings of chaos and low self-esteem. Requisite actions and tasks during the postdivorce reequilibration stage include achieving a resynthesis of identity and completing the psychic divorce. Kaslow emphasizes that the stages of divorce do not unfold in an invariant sequence, that there may be moves forward and backward, with couples reconciling and "giving it one more try," for example.

DEVELOPMENTAL TASKS FOR
DIVORCING SPOUSES

Developmental tasks for adults in the process of marital break-up and early postdivorce adjustment as conceptualized here include the following:

Tasks of the Decision to Divorce Stage

1. Accepting the reality that a separation/divorce is occurring (regardless of how or by whom the decision is made).
2. Coping with initial emotional/psychological reactions.
3. Performing the initial planning for the contemplated actions.

Tasks of the Separation/Divorce Stage

1. Making the necessary practical arrangements for living for oneself (and one's children), and practical arrangements for divorce and divorce settlement.
2. Informing pertinent parties (children, relatives, friends).
3. Restructuring relationships with spouse and children.
4. Adapting to new living patterns.
5. Seriously beginning the mourning process (bereavement and grief).
6. Coping with other emotional/psychological reactions to separation/divorce.

Tasks of the Postdivorce Stage

1. Completing the mourning process.
2. Achieving a stable identity as a single, formerly married person.

3. Achieving a new perspective on life and an appropriate orientation to the future.
4. Completing the restructuring of relationships with children, former spouse, and family.
5. Securing appropriate stabilization of one's social network.

A few comments are in order regarding the developmental tasks as they are outlined above. Bohannon (1970) described what he termed six "stations of divorce," which are actually overlapping experiences for the divorcing spouses: the emotional divorce, the legal divorce, the economic divorce, the coparental divorce, the community divorce, and the psychic divorce. The last element which is concerned with the problems of regaining individual autonomy, is the portion that would normally be expected to take the longest to achieve. It is closely associated with what I have described as the tasks of achieving a stable identity, a new perspective on life, and an appropriate orientation regarding the future. Securing a community divorce is related to the achievement of a new social network in the postdivorce adjustment period. An additional point to be noted is that the framework described here includes no reference to securing therapy, a consideration during the period of divorce that may be acutely necessary for some couples, while others may weather the transition from married to divorced without therapeutic help and do so very well. While I may think that all persons could probably profit from such professional help if they were open to it, seeking and using therapy does not quality as a developmental task.

Another perspective that has some utility is provided by Rice and Rice (1986), who propose a model of family life-cycle development based on the concepts of identity and intimacy. Communion is considered to be the key task in achieving intimacy and separation to be the key task in achieving identity. The basic themes of identity and intimacy occur again and again throughout the life cycle, but they have different meanings in the various periods of an individual's life. The normal role and place of intimacy/communion and identity/separation in seven chronological periods from birth through senescence, along with the effect of divorce on each of those aspects of human development, is described by Rice and Rice in an interesting attempt to explain the impact of divorce on both children and their parents. I think that their framework can be characterized as essentially complementary to the model described here.

Lastly, the effects of divorce on the participants are strongly affected not only by their prior development, strengths, and personal adaptation, but also by sociocultural factors, the nature of their social supports including extended family relationships, economic and other resources, and a variety of idiosyncratic or "situational" factors. Among the latter are matters such as whether an individual desired the divorce or had it thrust upon him or her, whether it was expected or arrived "like a bolt out of the blue," and whether he or she is able to feel treated fairly by his or her spouse.

THERAPEUTIC INTERVENTIONS

Therapists intervene in the divorcing process where and when they can. Most descriptions of "divorce therapy" appear to be statements of what would be considered ideal rather than what typically occurs with divorcing couples.

THE DECISION TO DIVORCE STAGE

When spouses are considering divorce, it would appear desirable from the therapist's viewpoint to be able to involve both partners in an ongoing and careful exploration of the issues involved in making a rational and responsible joint decision about continuing or dissolving their marriage. This has been described as the therapist's task during this stage (Piercy & Sprenkle, 1986), especially since taking this role can be a powerful form of assistance for the troubled couple when they are available for such help. The opportunity to fulfill that role arises in one of three ways. First, a couple may contact a therapist with the specific request for help with deciding whether to continue their marriage or to divorce. Second, on some occasions the experience of marital therapy will expose how far apart the partners are, how little satisfaction the marriage is providing, and the limited possibility that they are going to change and solve their major problems. These revelations face the mates with the possibility of either denying what emerges or considering divorce and evaluating the consequences of taking that course of action. Third, some couples that contact a therapist after having made a decision to divorce may be desirous of reviewing the decision with the assistance of the clinician. Clinical and supervisory experience has demonstrated for me the reality that both marital partners are likely to be present for a serious examination process in only a minority of cases.

Similarly, a good case can be made from a systemic perspective for involving not only the divorcing couple but also children and the partners' respective families of origin in therapeutic and psychoeducational work during certain parts of the separation/divorce and postdivorce period. Again, the best efforts of clinicians to secure such systemic involvement seem to be successful only part of the time.

For those cases in which a definite decision is made to end the marriage after some extended time in marital therapy, one or both partners may decide that they do not wish to go on working with the clinician. Occasionally, clients have the perception that marital therapists only work with marriage as an ongoing relationship, while at other times, one client may be unable or unwilling to continue working on the process of getting apart with the least damage possible. When the mates decide that they are going to divorce and conclude that they have no further need or desire to work with the therapist, the clinician may hold a contrary opinion of their needs based on sound clinical assessment. Nevertheless, if the clients feel themselves to be ready to terminate, there is no ethical alternative except to present one's perceptions of their needs with an accompanying statement showing respect for their right to make such a decision. I consider it professionally ethical and clinically responsible to make an accurate statement about their needs and those of their children and to make a strong recommendation that they use professional help of whatever kind indicated, if continued help does indeed seem advisable. This includes offering to help them find other competent clinicians if for any reason they might be willing to consider dealing with someone new in order to implement their new decision. Although it is important to make it clear that they are not being dropped, it seems of equal importance to clarify that my recommendations are not being made from a self-serving position; the major concern is that they get the help that in my judgment they require.

There are a few cases in which the splitting marital partners do not need much assistance in evaluating the possible consequences of divorcing. The most solid examples would be those in which the marriage for all practical purposes died some time earlier, and the clinician is needed primarily to help the partners recognize that they both know that the marriage is dead and that they both wish to take the necessary steps to bury it. A considerable amount of the partners' emotional work in dealing with their loss may have taken place already. There does remain, however, need for assistance in coping with their continuing feelings of attachment to the family and the patterns of daily living, and in coping with other developmental tasks of marital break-up.

Whether the decision to end the marriage is made outside or inside the context of professional consultation or therapy, it seldom is desired equally by both spouses. Some research studies have determined that ending the marriage is desired equally by both mates in only about 15% of the divorces undertaken in this country (Berman & Turk, 1981; White & Bloom, 1981), which means that in most divorces one partner frequently feels abandoned and has to adjust to an unwanted parting with the spouse (Sprenkle & Cyrus, 1983).

The clinician ends up working with one partner in many instances, not necessarily by choice but because the opportunity is lacking to work with both. A considerable amount of the therapeutic work consists of helping that individual—usually the partner who does not wish to end the marriage—to deal with their feelings and reactions to what is occurring.

The most destructive unilateral ways in which one spouse ends the marriage appear to be those in which the other mate learns second-hand or after the decison has been made that they are being divorced. This takes the form of being served with divorce papers without prior warning, being told by someone else that his or her spouse has decided to divorce, being told by the spouse that he or she is leaving or moving away to a new job location and that he or she is not going, or being joined for one or two sessions with a therapist and told there that he or she is being divorced. The feelings of helplessness, abandonment, anguish, shock, inadequacy, worthlessness, and even chaos that flood the shocked partner often threaten to be engulfing. The news may be met with denial, emotional and physical withdrawal, and on occasion a begging of the departing spouse to reconsider. Even though a clinician may hold the opinion that the unilateral decision should not have been a surprise to the unsuspecting spouse—that there were signs "all over the place" that the break-up was coming—the reality is that few individuals appear able to function as normative textbook cases of "fully actualized persons" in their intimate relationships so that they monitor all cues and process all data and are not shocked by such rejection.

THE SEPARATION/DIVORCE STAGE

Separation and divorce are included together because in some cases the "real divorce" is felt to occur when the physical separation takes place, the legal divorce often being experienced as anticlimatic. This appears to have been enhanced with the advent of no-fault divorce in which a "cut and dried" formality may be enacted ritualistically in a few minutes in an almost empty courtroom. In other cases in which there is a bitter custody or property battle, the lengthy struggle makes the legal divorce much more painful and "the final step" in ending the marriage for the partners.

At least from the time Goode (1956) did his pioneering research on the effects of divorce on women, there has been research and clinical evidence that the physical separation, the "splitting" time, is one of the most difficult periods in the divorce process. The clinician's work at this stage calls not only for therapeutic attention to the emotional needs of the partners but also for psychoeducational endeavors aimed at helping them to learn what reactions can be expected and how each partner can cope with them. What is normal, "par for the course," during the separation period?

Typical emotional reactions during the separation/divorce stage include some of those mentioned previously, along with anger, depression (which frequently can be accurately portrayed as "anger turned inward," as well as reaction to loss), hopelessness, loneliness, and others. Some may experience relief either as a major response or as a part of what they perceived as a paradoxical mixture of reactions. It is during this period also that clients may face the most acute problems with disruptions in eating and sleeping routings. Some may request and some may actually need medication as a bridge across the acute phase of their upset and pain.

Suicide thoughts and threats may be forthcoming with some persons during the early stage of separation. Similar reactions of an even more serious nature (i.e., actual attempts at suicide) may emerge a little later with those individuals who are highly resistant to the marital termination when their attempts to get their spouse to reconsider are unsuccessful. The same kinds of steps that clinicians ordinarily take with suicide threats and possibilities are indicated in such situations. Additionally, the therapist works on helping the client to recognize the transitional nature of what is occurring and on helping to provide effective support. Such support includes not only the aid of the clinician but also of appropriate individuals in the person's social network. When the person is ready for divorce adjustment group experiences, they also can be helpful.

During this period I work carefully with clients to learn what and whom they find helpful and supportive and to use all of the support that seems indicated. Some clients wish to keep most of their emotional reactions to themselves and to deal with them in therapy. Others find it necessary to talk with a sibling, parent, or friend, as well as to use the support and help of the therapist.

One of the more difficult things for many clients to do is to face the fact that their spouse is different than they had thought. Either the spouse, who has behaved in ways that clearly indicate to an outsider a lack of integrity and concern for the client, has changed or the client had been mistaken in her or his perceptions of the spouse. Once the client has been able to face the fact that the spouse has, for example, lied, been generally deceitful, and broken trust, he or she becomes able to accept the ending of the marital relationship and to proceed with adjustment to the situation. As one woman put it, "When I walked into the restaurant and saw him with his girlfriend, I knew that he had lied once again. That was it." Another indicated, "I have had to face that fact that he's not a nice person. I think that he was at one time, but he isn't now. You can't do the things he does and treat people the way he has treated me and be anything other than a bastard." In some instances it is exceedingly important to help the client make a distinction between what happened during "the good years" or "the good times" of the relationship and what has happened recently. The clinician may need to underline the fact that "You did have some good times in your marriage. Those good times and good qualities can be retained as good memories. They are not erased by the recent pain, unhappiness, and rottenness. You do need to recognize and to keep remembering that both parts have been present."

Another point frequently needs to be emphasized with the client who is struggling with the spouse's accusation that "You caused me to get into an affair. If you had [been different in whatever specified ways], I wouldn't have done it. Don't blame me; you're as much to blame or more than I am. Frankly, it's your fault anyway." That point is that the client does need for her or his sake to recognize and accept whatever responsibility she or he had for marital difficulty and marital failure, but that she or he is not responsible for what her or his spouse did. The clinician's affirmation that, "Yes, there were problems in the marriage. You had a part in that, as we have been trying to understand. Your [spouse] was upset and dissatisfied, true. However, there were several other ways in which he or she could have dealt with the situation. That was her or his choice and action, not yours," needs to be repeated on occasion as part of stopping a client's unhealthy self-blaming behaviors.

Clients need help in dealing with their children at all phases of the divorce process. This is one place that the therapist probably has more leverage than at most others in seeking cooperation between the divorcing spouses. Asking both of the partners to meet with the therapist for the purpose of working on issues affecting their children has more chance of success than many clinicians seem to realize. Contact by the clinician in which it is made clear that the children and not the adults or their relationship are the focus frequently results in reasonably fruitful sessions.

Psychoeducational work with most of the clients with whom I work during this phase involves two major areas. One has to do with the reactions that individuals experience when the physical separation occurs: I describe the reactions that are normal when we move out of our usual environment or have someone or something taken out of our usual environment. The dynamic of "interhabituation" in which we are accustomed to having someone or something in the environment and daily life patterns operates when a loss of that person or thing occurs, so that even if it is something that irritates or bothers us, something as mundane as an ugly chair or the messy habits of another person, we miss it for a time when it is gone." Examining with the clients what they are experiencing and helping them to learn immediate ways of coping is important. No less important in my experience is the task of helping them to understand what is occurring and the normality of certain of their reactions.

Dealing with the mourning process is the other major area in which psychoeducational work is exceedingly helpful during the separation stage. Two decades ago I used the concept of bereavement and grief as a major part of establishing one of the early programs providing divorce adjustment groups (Nichols, 1977). We found that all three major categories of participants in such groups—the "contemplators," "the waiters" (who were waiting for their divorce to be legally completed), and "the reactors" (who were divorced)—benefited from understanding their situation in terms of loss and mourning. Although the loss (bereavement) and grief (emotional reaction to the loss) may pertain to the loss of the object (spouse), loss of the intact marriage, the loss of hopes and dreams, and the loss of the former support system, most of the focus is on the loss of the object.

A useful model for understanding acute grief reactions can be put together from works dealing with the reactions of survivors to loss (e.g., Lindemann, 1944; Parkes, 1973; Oates, 1955). As described elsewhere in more detail (Nichols & Everett, 1986), the process involves five phases that may be telescoped into a short period of time or spread out for some individuals. Briefly, the stages and reactions are:

1. An initial reaction of shock, followed by numbness, when informed of the loss.
2. A period of denial, often accompanied by a range of agitated

behaviors including difficulties in settling down physically and sleeping.

3. A breakdown of denial and an eruption of surprising emotional rections, often including crying, anger, rage, bitterness, guilt, and feelings of going crazy.

4. A period of talking and thinking about the loss, of turning over the memories, and often of trying to determine whether one could have done anything to make events turn out differently.

5. An eventual acceptance by most persons of the loss and an acceptance of living in the present and facing the future, accompanied occasionally by painful reminders that he or she no longer has a mate present, but essentially marked by emotional investment in new objects and pursuits.

Use of such a framework with clients involves realistically informing them that "Knowing what is likely to happen and knowing what you are going through does not necessarily lessen the pain or make things easier, but it does help you avoid making things worse. If you can understand that feeling like you are numb or unreal or perhaps going crazy is a normal part of reaction to loss and that you are going through a process that has a beginning and an end makes it more possible to deal with the loss and the situation as well as you can. It also helps to know that, as simple as it sounds, your best ally is time. The acute and worst part of this does pass."

During the process of coping with loss in a normal fashion, the client gradually becomes free of the intense emotional attachments to the spouse/former spouse, reinvests those released energies, and reorganizes her or his world in order to deal with the spouse/former spouse in new ways. Where there are children, of course, the continuing coparental tasks and relationships generally keep the divorced partners dealing with each other for a period of years, if not throughout their lives.

Pathological grief reactions to loss by divorce, as in losses of an important other person by death (Brown & Stoudemire, 1983), include delaying or distorting the process. The person who shows no reactions to loss, the individual who "over grieves," and the former spouse who develops a major depression or other distortion of the process of grieving all are exhibiting pathological grief. Slight delays in the grief process are not uncommon. The impact of the loss of the person depends on several things, including an individual's general strength and coping ability, the manner in which the loss occurred, and the general resources that he or she has for dealing with the situation.

THE POSTDIVORCE STAGE

The therapist's role during the postdivorce stage has been described as that of facilitating the growth of the divorced persons as autonomous individuals who form stable life-styles, helping them to develop social relationships that are independent of the former love relationships, and, often, helping them deal with issues pertaining to their children (Piercy & Sprenkle, 1986). To this should be added the task of helping the clients to complete the mourning process. Even though the time of separation may be regarded as the "real divorce" by some clients, it does not appear to be any more possible to complete the mourning until after the marriage is legally ended than it does to "really get on with one's life" in other aspects of adjustment and living.

Ending the marriage legally and getting into the postdivorce period may also be a definitive marker that for some persons effectively ends any lingering or recurrent fantasies about reconciliation. For still others, and particularly for children, reconciliation fantasies may reach an eventual demise when one of the former spouses remarries. Examining with the client her or his fantasies about reconciliation is a task that emerges during the postdivorce stage as well as during the separation period prior to the legal divorce. Couples often reconcile temporarily. When the question of reconciliation arises with one spouse, the therapist needs to inquire carefully as to the reasons the matter has arisen and to seek to determine the realities in the situation. Is reconciliation looking desirable because of loneliness? Is reconciliation a desire of both spouses? Reexamining with the client the reasons the separation/divorce was inaugurated and the developments that have occurred subsequently typically helps the client to get things into an appropriate perspective.

Feelings may arise, recede, and arise again during the stages of marital breakup and early adjustment. The partners may move back and forth, or up and down, in the reactions to breaking up and adapting. They may be swayed by the reactions of their children, family, or friends, and ebb and flow in the expression of reactions, feeling anger and bitterness at one point and tolerance and ambivalence at others. Anxiety that leads to rage or momentary panic may emerge during the course of working out legal details and effecting new adjustments in living and child custody and visitation.

Clinicians need to be well informed about the realities of life faced by their clients in the postseparation, postdivorce stages. The negative economic consequences of divorce on women and children (Weitzman, 1985) and some of the difficulties men face in living alone are only two such realities. Differences between being alone and loneliness (Peplau & Perlman, 1982), the importance of "letting go" of the former spouse and the marriage, and the possibilities of greater cooperation than is generally considered possible between formerly married persons in dealing with the ongoing needs of their children are other such matters.

A FINAL NOTE

Increasingly, it seems, therapists find themselves working with clients who are going through a second, third, or subsequent divorce. Some of those divorcing persons are truly individuals who do not learn from their experiences. Some, a very small proportion, fit the pattern frequently described in psychoanalytic literature of individuals driven by unconscious motives who repetitively marry the same kind of person in efforts to solve psychoneurotic conflicts. More frequently, clinical experience indicates that sociocultural factors play a large part in marital fragility. The fact that it is not necessary to remain in an unsatisfactory relationship and the absence of values supporting a norm of "till death us do part" rather than individual psychopathology account for a notable proportion of the divorces in today's serial monogamy.

Some individuals do learn from failure in their first marital attempt; again, from clinical experience and casual observation this appears to be a not insignificant number. Although the proportion of failures in a second marriage is higher than in a first, a large number of persons make a second marriage that is more enduring and more satisfying than the first. Speculation that this sometimes occurs because of greater maturity and more effective choice is probably accurate, although the idea that some succeed in a second marriage because they are determined to make it work also probably has some basis in fact.

A pattern of three marriages is not uncommon. Examination of those that I have seen clinically indicates that frequently the pattern begins with a marriage that was entered into at a young age and/or a long-term marriage ended by divorce or the death of the mate and a second marriage that was undertaken hastily. The second marriage typically lasted only a short time before it was recognized by the client to be "a mistake from the beginning." The third marriage in this pattern from clinical cases was generally entered into after the client had taken sufficient time to adjust to being alone following the ending of the second marriage, and consequently the client had made a more appropriate choice.

Epilogue

Chapter Eleven

Learning from Experience and Research

Family and marriage, marriage and family—these are interrelated primary concerns when we as therapists practice marital therapy. How do each of these in their manifold expressions and interactions affect the marital partners with whom we work? How do they keep changing and how do we keep learning about them? How do we continue learning about and improving our clinical work? My suggestion is that marital therapists need to give a significant amount of attention to learning from the experience and observation of their own clinical work—including learning from their failures in treatment—and from the empirical research of others.

Awareness of the nature of the marital relationship and a comprehension of its relation to the family systems of the partners have both been emphasized throughout this book as being essential to informed therapeutic work with couples. The tributaries concept of individual and marital development described and illustrated graphically in Figure 1 (Chapter 1) has been an approach that I have used, with some modification, since I formally began teaching about families more than 25 years ago. In this conceptual framework each partner is understood as developing in her or his family of origin, with all of the genetic, emotional, psychological, interactional, and social components that the family embodies and in the sociocultural settings in which the family resides. Both partners continue to develop as they start their own relationship and form their own marriage and nuclear family. The pictorial representation is not complete: The channels (or "streams" in the tributary metaphor) loop back from the individuals and their marriage and nuclear family to their families of origin and thus provide the feedback loops that operate in family systems. The processes are not simply one-way or linear but circular; family affects marriage and marriage affects family.

This powerful stream—family and marriage, marriage and family, rather than techniques, is what marital therapists need to study. Whatever time is left over perhaps could be given to studying the techniques of others, but that ranks low in the hierarchy of priorities, compared to learning about the content of marriage and family and the effectiveness of one's clinical endeavors. My concern is that practice should always be based on sound theoretical underpinnings, that theory and substantive knowledge should inform practice, and that practice should inform and provide guidance for research and theory. Current emphasis on the demonstration of techniques in the family therapy field often seems to skew the priorities.

LEARNING FROM RESEARCH

Some of the content areas in marriage and family that therapists need to study and update their knowledge about include mate selection, ethnicity, marital and family violence, divorce processes, remarriage, and stepfamily functioning, as well as materials on various forms of marital and family interaction. The family studies materials of such publications as the *Journal of Marriage and the Family* and *Family Relations* provide current research and theoretical updating, as do some other journals.

Major family studies publications are abstracted quarterly in the *Sage Family Studies Abstracts*, available in many college and university libraries. An annual inventory of family studies and research, edited by Professor David H. Olson of the University of Minnesota, provides another guide to available materials. Monographs on a variety of family studies topics appear annually as well.

A growing number of family therapy journals such as *Family Process, Journal of Marital and Family Therapy, American Journal of Family Therapy, Contemporary Family Therapy, Journal of Sex and Marital Therapy, Journal of Divorce, Journal of Psychotherapy and the Family*, and others provide not only clinical and theoretical materials but also reports of empirical research. The major focus of early research on marital and family therapy was on outcome. Gurman and Kniskern (1981), who have extensively summarized and evaluated outcome research, concluded by the early part of this decade that there was no further need or justification for review of the outcome materials. Instead, they called for focusing on what needs to be studied in the future and on identifying the most relevant of the clinical questions that need to be answered. A focus on process research (what goes on during treatment) has been marked out (Pinsof, 1981) as the next major area for family therapy research. It is in delineating and posing questions for such research that clinicians can make a significant contribution to the further development of the field.

Some of the findings from reviews of the research literature on marital and family therapy deserve mention at this point. Gurman and Kniskern (1978b), for example, found several therapist variables that stood out in the literature as apparently contributing to deterioration in marital and family therapy. Negative outcomes are more likely to occur when the therapist provides little structure or guidance in early sessions; confronts sensitive affective issues early in treatment; labels unconscious motivations in the early stage instead of providing support, gathering information, or stimulating interaction; and permits without challenge references that accept or promote sex-role stereotypes.

As Gurman and Kniskern (1981) described the "flip side" or positive meaning of those findings, there is a growing body of empirical evidence suggesting a connection between a therapist's relationship skills and treatment outcome. It is important to be active, to provide structure, and to be respectful of tenuous defenses early in therapy. Securing positive outcomes, according to Gurman and Kniskern (1981), depends not merely on "the reasonable mastery of technical skills"—which may be enough to prevent deterioration—but on developing "more refined" relationship skills. This suggests that the therapist must become adept at relationship skills, something that, in my observation, seems to develop not only from the therapist's personality attributes but also from the attainment of experience in working with clients. Research still needs to be directed toward answering questions concerning the specific therapist relationship skills that work positively or negatively across different kinds of therapy and those that are uniquely important within different approaches (Gurman & Kniskern, 1981).

Questions that have been generated by Coleman (1985) in collaboration with Gurman from a study of a dozen cases of "failure in marital therapy" include the following: What is happening in the therapist's own life and experience and what kinds of marital/family experiences has he/she had that may affect the approach taken to the clients? What kinds of values and attitudes does the therapist bring to the case? What relationship may exist between the values and attitudes of the therapist and the clients? Can the issue of therapist "burnout" be addressed and assessed empirically? Can we determine what kinds of effects therapist burnout has on treatment?

Another research question stemming both from the Gurman and Kniskern reviews and from clinical experience pertains to the question of client variables in premature termination or other less-than-ideal outcomes in therapy. What kinds of contributions do clients make to discontinuation or negative outcome in marital therapy? Coleman (1985) has raised several questions concerning the motivation and "consumerism" of clients. Probably the most important question, and the most difficult, to make operational for marital therapy research is that of the extent to which the partners appear to be real therapy "customers." While such a question is important in individual psychotherapy or in total family therapy, it appears to be even more important in marital therapy, because, as I have repeatedly emphasized, the marital relationship is voluntary in nature, and there is the perennial issue of whether both partners wish to continue in the marriage as well as to work on their problems.

Interestingly, Coleman's (1985) findings from the failure cases regarding the role of inadequate assessment (83% of the failures were related to assessment deficiencies) and referral factors closely parallel points made earlier in this book. Certain kinds of referrals have limited chance for successful treatment outcome. For example, cases in which there has been contamination by the referring source so that the expectations are unrealistic or the clients are still so attached to therapeutic ideas or orientations (e.g., psychoanalytic, individual intrapsychic) from previous therapeutic experience that they are not able to focus on transactional issues and motivations may not have high chances for marital therapy success. Coleman (1985) found with the case studies that a cluster of variables was associated with poor treatment prognosis. These included a long history of problems and a persistent major symptom, a previous history in treatment generally based on the individual rather than on the family system, a relatively severe diagnosis, and being guided into treatment by an external source rather than being self-referred and self-motivated.

LEARNING FROM EXPERIENCE

There appear to be essentially three ways in which a clinician can learn from experience. One has to do with learning from what works, which is the pragmatic method involving the accrual of experience and the refinement of the ability to recognize what appears in therapeutic sessions. As this occurs, the therapist is able to assess the meaning of the phenomena that appear and to make appropriate responses to them. As the clinician acquires such abilities, he or she is able to look at what is happening and to listen to what is being said and to "know" that something is missing (e.g., that a fact is being omitted), or to make a bold move toward engaging a client in the treatment process with the assurance that the move will be received positively rather than negatively. Another part of this is the confidence on the part of the therapist that if a given move does not work well, all is not lost; one can still deal effectively with the clients and keep them engaged in the therapeutic alliance and thus in treatment. This is known to the therapist in part because he or she "has been there before" and knows both intuitively and empirically that the action has a good chance of succeeding. Still another part of learning from experience pertains to attaining the ability to project the effects of therapeutic endeavor into the future. I refer to this with students as learning that "the meat will continue to cook" or "the toast will continue to brown after being removed from the heat," a metaphorical way of saying that things will continue to happen after the clients have left the treatment session.

A second method is associated with learning from failure. Having tried something that fails—or having failed to do something—the clinician experiences the pain of failing. This pain can be excruciating and can cause one to reexamine not only therapeutic approaches and interventions but also one's epistemological assumptions (Tomm, 1985). Failing, either as a result of an error of commission or of omission, faces the professional person with the possibility of either learning or not learning from the experience.

The third method has to do with the assumption of a learning position based on assuming personal authority. A combination of learning from what works and learning from failure partially underlies the step of taking the posture of personal authority on the part of the therapist, a step that comes about when the clinician manages to drop old authorities as reference points and to make decisions for her- or himself. One thus becomes one's own personal authority and does not have to constantly look backward over the shoulder in order to try to ascertain what one's teacher, supervisor, or guru would do or recommend in that situation. In my observations, young therapists have to shed the effects of being supervised in "live" supervision or doing cotheraphy with their teacher/ supervisor and become emotionally and intellectually free enough to recognize that they do not yet have their own therapeutic knowledge, style, and power, in order to begin growing and becoming mature therapists. What seemed so potent and magnificent in the mentor generally does not translate into the same thing with the disciple (Sugarman, 1987).

One needs to "graduate" from the role of student at the feet of or in the workshop of a master or professional "parent." In brief, just as one has to "leave home" and work out new patterns of dealing with one's parents so that they become "former parents," (Williamson, 1981), one has to "leave home" from one's therapeutic training or emotional adherence to a "school" of therapy and work out new patterns of dealing with one's teacher/supervisor/mentor/guru so that he or she becomes a "former parent."

My own quantum leap forward in education, training, and growth came one day during the second year of graduate school when I recognized that the individual standing behind the lectern lecturing was not brighter than I or otherwise superior to me, that he had not descended from either Mt. Sinai or Mt. Olympus with engraved tablets or other gifts of wisdom and authority. Rather, he was a few years older and more knowledgeable in some ways than I. From that day forward, I essentially stopped following or struggling against the inculcated pattern of "pleasing teacher" and tackled the material in my courses with the objective of learning what I thought was important and being responsible for mastering and using it. That is what I have attempted to get my family therapy students to do—to take responsibility for their own learning with my guidance. I have often said to students, "I don't need disciples; I have children of my own, and we have enough to do to work out their maturation and our mutual letting go so that they can leave home and be their own person without me taking on other children. I'll help you learn and I'll do my best to help you get the tools to learn, to be a professional and a therapist, but the major responsibility for learning is yours." Similarly, I do all that I can to help couples get to the point of helping themselves, to become informed and to understand as much as possible about what is happening in therapy and in their lives, so that they can be appropriately responsible and feel responsible for their own change. This has worked well with both students and clients.

My contention is that unless the therapist is able to mature to the point of forming her or his own therapeutic orientation and attaining "personal authority," it is unlikely that the clients of that therapist will be able to be free enough to take responsibility for themselves. Reverting to the "clearing out of the stream" metaphor referred to earlier, I wish the couples with whom I work to get to the point where they are capable of helping themselves, of being able to rely on their joint personal authority. For this to be possible, not only must I be free enough to function on my own, assessing the difficulty and moving to make interventions on the basis of what I perceive is before me in terms of what they need (instead of what I have seen others do) but also I must be mature enough to grant the clients with whom I work the freedom to function as best they can on their own. This involves the recognition that change is not in the therapist's hands but in the clients'. I take a large part of the responsibility for the therapeutic process, but this involves doing my best to help the clients change, make decisions, take risks, and—it is to be hoped—solve problems and grow. It does not involve taking the responsibility for the change of others.

Just as I intend to keep learning and understanding as long as I am able to do so, I extend the same right to my clients. Just as my formal education was intended to form a beginning from which I obtained a base of knowledge and secured tools for learning, I hope that therapy serves a similar purpose for clients. When they leave, I hope that they take with them more than change secured through whatever means; I want them to leave in possession of some understanding and some tools for further learning and problem solving on their own.

This is stated with a full recognition that the couples and individuals with whom one works vary widely in their ability to take responsibility for themselves; some are much more cooperative and much more open to treatment and change than others. Nevertheless, the point made earlier bears reiteration: Many persons will be cooperative if they understand what is going on and what is being asked or expected of them.

Being a therapist means that one has to learn to live with a considerable amount of frustration, uncertainly, and ambiguity. Those conditions are part of the therapeutic world; they go with the territory. In the early part of one's education, training, and clinical experience, it is necessary to learn to live with anxiety. As experience accrues and one becomes more experienced and more comfortable with what occurs, anxiety about going into the room with clients and about what transpires in therapy sessions tends to lessen. The task as one continues to perform any endeavor for an extended period of time—including things as widely disparate as practicing therapy or playing professional basketball—is to retain one's intensity, one's sharp edge.

At any stage of one's therapeutic career, being a therapist means that clients may leave one's office with the outcome uncertain. Sometimes the therapist may not know the outcome until next week, next year, if ever. On occasions when clients leave treatment prior to the time that the therapist thinks they should, the therapist's perception is that the endeavor failed. It may have. It may not have. The effects may continue long after therapy sessions have ended. The presenting symptoms may be partially altered at the time of termination and may or may not continue to change and disappear after contact with the therapist has been severed.

One of the kinds of experiences that continues to accumulate as one totals up years as a therapist is that of learning that things are not necessarily as they seem at the end of the treatment contact with clients. Cases that seemed to be failures will on occasion turn out to have been effectively worked with and helped, even though such did not appear to be the situation at the time of termination. Sometimes one learns directly, as with an "impasse" case that appeared hopelessly deadlocked and going nowhere at termination. Four years later one of the spouses called to bring the therapist up to date and to express appreciation for the help that, with the incubative effects of time, led to major breakthroughs and important changes for the couple. In other instances, couples whose treatment appeared to be less helpful than the therapist would wish refer other persons for therapy with glowing testimonials. Only a long-range perspective allows one to balance out what appears to be with what turns out to be the case in reality.

AN OPEN-ENDED ENDING

Learning about marriage and marital therapy is a continuing process. Marriage, once again, is the focus, not therapy as such, and certainly not the techniques of any given therapeutic approach. We as persons and we as professionals have only begun to scratch the surface of comprehending the complex, changing, highly voluntary, and vulnerable relationship that is marriage. Given the elusive and volatile nature of the marital status in a rapidly changing society, it is almost as if we are dealing with mercury: We can describe certain properties of the phenomenon but find that it scoots away when we attempt to put our finger on it and to pin it down solidly. We need to learn more about the thing with which we are attempting to deal, and not about ways to dealing with things, in order to comprehend its nature and characteristics and to work with it in an effective manner. We also need to accept the fact that as we think that we are getting close to comprehending it, marriage changes.

There are other issues in working with marriage, not the least of which are keeping up with changes in male–female relationships and attempting to rid oneself of sexism—whether one is a man or a woman. In the approach taken in this book it is assumed that the therapist should try to treat women and men equitably. It also is assumed that all of us have some unconscious sexism, racism, and other kinds of learned biases that may crop up in our work with other human beings. The major hope is that any inequities that occur can be spotted and eradicated from the therapeutic relationship and process.

In keeping with the changing nature of marriage and the corresponding demands for flexibility and adaptability on the part of the martial therapist, this book does not end but continues. . . .

References

Ackerman, N. W. (1966). Family psychotherapy: Theory and practice. *American Journal of Psychotherapy. 20,* 405–414.

American Association for Marriage and Family Therapy (1983). *Family therapy glossary.* Washington, DC: Author.

American Psychiatric Association. (1980). *Diagnostic and statistical manual of mental disorders* (3rd Ed.). Washington, DC: Author.

Anderson, C. A., Reiss, D. J., & Calahane, F. (1986). Marital therapy with schizophrenic patients. In. N. S. Jacobson & A. S. Gurman (Eds.), *Clinical handbook of marital therapy* (pp. 537–556). New York: Guilford Press.

Anderson, C. A., & Stewart, S. (1983). *Mastering resistance: A practical guide to family therapy.* New York: Guilford Press.

Balint, M. (1965). *Primary love and psychoanalytic technique.* New York: Liveright.

Bank, S. P., & Kahn, M. D. (1982). *The sibling bond.* New York: Basic Books.

Barnard, C. P. (1981). *Families, alcoholism, and therapy.* Springfield, IL: Charles C Thomas.

Barrett, M. J., Skyes, C., & Byrnes, W. (1986). A systemic model for the treatment of intrafamily child abuse. *Journal of Psychotherapy and the Family, 2*(2), 67–82.

Baruch, G. K., & Brook-Gunn, J. (1984). *Women in midlife.* New York: Plenum Press.

Bateson, G. (1980). *Mind and nature.* New York: Bantam Books.

Beavers, W. R. (1977). *Psychotherapy and growth: A family systems perspective.* New York: Brunner/Mazel.

Beavers, W. R. (1985). *Successful marriage: A family systems approach to couples therapy.* New York: W. W.Norton.

Beavers, W. R., & Kaslow, F. W. (1981). The anatomy of hope. *Journal of Marital and Family Therapy, 7,* 119–126.

Berenson, D. (1979). The therapist's relationship with couples with an alcoholic member. In E. Kaufman & P. Kaufmann (Eds.), *Family therapy of drug and alcohol abuse* (pp. 233–242). New York: Gardner Press.

Bergler, E. (1948). *Divorce won't help.* New York: Hart.

Berk, R. A., Newton, P. J., & Berk, S. F. (1986). What a difference a day makes: An empirical study of the impact of shelters for battered women. *Journal of Marriage and the Family, 48,* 481–490.

Berman, E. M. (1986, May). Personal communication.

Berman, E. M., & Lief, H. I. (1975). Marital therapy from a psychiatric perspective. *American Journal of Psychiatry, 132,* 583–592.

Berman, E. M., Miller, W. R., Vines, N., & Lief, H. I. (1977). The age 30 crises and the 7-year-itch. *Journal of Marital and Sex Therapy, 3,* 197–204.

Berman, W. H., & Turk, D. C. (1981). Adaptation to Divorce: Problems and coping strategies. *Journal of Marriage and the Family, 43,* 11–38.

Bernard, J. (1972). *The future of marriage.* New York: World Publishing.

Bloom, B. L., White, S. W., & Asher, S. J. (1979). Marital disruption as a stressful life event. In G. Levinger, & O. C. Moles, (Eds.), *Divorce and separation* (pp. 184–200). New York: Basic Books.

Blumstein, P., & Schwartz, P. (1983). *American couples.* New York: William Morrow.

Bohannon, P. (Ed.). (1970). *Divorce and after.* Garden City, NY: Doubleday.

Boss, P. G. (1983). The martial relationship: Boundaries and ambiguities. In H. I. McCubbin & C. R. Figley (Eds.), *Stress and the family. Vol. I. Coping with normative transitions* (pp. 26–40). New York: Brunner/Mazel.

Boszormenyi-Nagy, I. (1965). A theory of relationships: Experience and transaction. In I. Boszormenyi-Nagy & J. L. Framo (Eds.), *Intensive family therapy* (pp. 33–87). New York: Harper & Row.

Boszormenyi-Nagy, I., & Spark, G. M. (1973). *Invisible loyalties.* New York: Harper & Row.

Bowen, M. (1978). *Family therapy in clinical practice.* New York: Jason Aronson.

Brown, J. T., & Stoudemire, G. A. (1983). Normal and pathological grief. *Journal of the American Medical Association, 250 (3),* 378–382.

Browne, A., & Finkelhor, D. (1984). *The impact of child sexual abuse.* Unpublished manuscript, University of New Hampshire, Durham.

Cadogan, D. A. (1979). Marital group therapy in alcoholism treatment. In E. Kaufman & P. Kaufmann (Eds.), *Family therapy of drug and alcohol abuse* (pp. 187–200). New York: Gardner Press.

Carter, E. A., & McGoldrick, M. (1980). The family life cycle and family therapy: An overview. In E. A. Carter & M. McGoldrick (Eds.), *The family life cycle: A framework for family therapy* (pp. 3–20). New York: Gardner Press.

Clark, T. E., & Nichols, W. C. (1983). *Marital and family therapy: A definition.* Unpublished paper.

Clayton, R. R., & Voss, H. L. (1977). Shacking up: Cohabitation in the 1970s. *Journal of Marriage and the Family, 34,* 273–281.

Coleman, S. B. (Ed.). (1985). *Failures in family therapy.* New York: Guilford Press.

Combrinck-Graham, L. (1985). A developmental model for family systems. *Family Process, 24,* 139–150.

Coyne, J. (1986). Strategic martial therapy for depression. In N. S. Jacobson & A. S. Gurman (Eds.), *Clinical handbook of marital therapy* (pp. 495–511). New York: Guilford Press.

Cromwell, R. E., Olson, D. H., & Fournier, D. G. (1976). Tools and techniques for diagnosis and evaluation in marital and family therapy. *Family Process, 16,* 1–49.

Cuber, J., & Harroff, P. (1966). *Sex and the significant American.* Baltimore: Penguin Books.

Davis, W. S. (1983). *A test of the predictability of collusion, ambivalence, and idealization in the mate selection process.* Unpublished doctoral dissertation, the Florida State University, Tallahassee.

deShazer, S. (1982). Diagnosis = Researching + doing therapy. In B. P. Keeney (Ed.), *Diagnosis and assessment in family therapy* (pp. 125–132). Rockville, MD: Aspen.

deShazer, S. (1985). *Keys to solution in brief therapy.* New York: W. W. Norton.

Dicks, H. V. (1963). Object relations theory and marital studies. *British Journal of Medical Psychology, 36,* 125–129.

Dicks, H. V. (1967). *Marital tensions.* New York; Basic Books.

Duhl, B. S., & Duhl, F. J. (1981). Integrative family therapy. In A. S. Gurman & D. P. Kniskern (Eds.), *Handbook of family therapy* (pp. 483–513). New York: Brunner/Mazel.

Dyer, E. F. (1963). Parenthood as crisis: a re-study. *Marriage and Family Living, 25,* 352–355.

Ehrenwald, J. (1963). *Neurosis in the family and patterns of psychosocial defense.* New York: Harper & Row.

English, H. B., & English, A. C. (1958). *A comprehensive dictionary of psychological and psychoanalytical terms.* New York: Longmans, Green.

Erikson, E. H. (1950). *Childhood and society.* New York: W. W. Norton.

Fairbairn, W. R. D. (1941). A revised psychopathology of the psychoses and psychoneuroses. In W. R. D. Fairbairn (1952), *Psychoanalytic studies of the personality* (pp. 28–58). London: Routledge & Kegan Paul.

Fairbairn, W. R. D. (1952). *Psychoanalytic studies of the personality.* London: Routledge & Kegan Paul.

Fairbairn, W. R. D. (1963). Synopsis of an object-relations theory of the personality. *International Journal of Psycho-Analysis, 44,* 224–225.

Feldman, L. B. (1976). Goals of family therapy. *Journal of Marriage and Family Counseling, 2,* 103–113.

Feldman, L. B. (1986). Sex-role issues in marital therapy. In N. S. Jacobson & A. S. Gurman (Eds.), *Clinical handbook of marital therapy* (pp. 345–359). New York: Guildford Press.

Ferreira, A. J. (1963). Family myth and homeostasis. *Archives of General Psychiatry, 9,* 457–463.

Finkelhor, D. (1983). Common features of family abuse. In D. Finkelhor, R. J. Gelles, G. T. Hotaling, & M. A. Straus (Eds.), *The dark side of families: Current family violence research* (pp. 17–28). Beverly Hills, CA: Sage Publishing.

Finklehor, D. (1985). Sexual abuse and physical abuse: Some critical differences. In E. H. Newberger & R. Bourne (Eds.), *Unhappy families* (pp. 21–30). Littleton, MA: PSG Publishing.

Fisher, L. (1979). On the classification of families. *Archives of General Psychiatry.* In J. G. Howells (Ed.), *Advances in family psychiatry, Vol I.* (pp. 27–52). New York: International Universities Press.

Fisher, R., & Ury, W. (1981). *Getting to yes: Negotiating agreement without giving in.* Boston: Houghton Mifflin.

Fogarty, T. F. (1976). Marital crisis. In P. J. Guerin (Ed.), *Family therapy theory and practice* (pp. 325–334). New York: Gardner Press.

Foster, S. W. (1986). Marital therapy of eating disorders. In N. S. Jacobson & A. S. Gurman (Eds.), *Clinical handbook of marital therapy*, (pp. 575–593). New York: Guilford Press.

Framo, J. L. (1965). Rationale and techniques of intensive family therapy. In I. Boszormenyi-Nagy & J. L. Framo (Eds.), *Intensive family therapy* (pp. 143–212). New York: Harper & Row.

Framo, J. L., (Ed). (1972). *Family interaction: A dialogue between family researchers and family therapists.* New York: Springer.

Framo, J. L. (1976). Family of origin as a therapeutic resource for adults in marital and family therapy: You can and should go home again. *Family Process, 15,* 193–210.

Framo, J. L. (1981). The integration of marital therapy with sessions of family of origin. In A. S. Gurman & D. P. Kniskern (Eds.), *Handbook of family therapy* (pp. 133–159). New York: Brunner/Mazel.

Framo, J. L. (1983). *Workshop on Couples Therapy.* Bay City, MI: Michigan Psychological Association.

Friedman, L. J. (1980). Integrating psychoanalytic object-relations understanding with family systems interventions in couples therapy. In J. K. Pearce & L. J. Friedman (Eds.), *Family therapy: Combining psychodynamic and family systems approaches* (pp. 63–79). New York: Grune & Stratton.

Fry, W. F. (1962). The marital context of an anxiety syndrome. *Family Process, 1,* 245–252.

Gardner, R. A. (1976). *Psychotherapy with children of divorce.* New York: Jason Aronson.

Gehrke, S., & Moxom, J. (1962). Diagnostic classification and treatment techniques in marriage counseling. *Family Process, 1,* 253–264.

Geller, J., & Wasserstrom, J. (1984). Conjoint therapy for the treatment of domestic violence. In A. R. Robards (Ed), *Battered women and their families: Intervention strategies and treatment programs* (pp. 33–48). New York: Springer.

Gelles, R. J. (1985). Family violence: What we know and can do. In E. H. Newberger & R. Bourne (Eds.), *Unhappy families* (pp. 1–8). Littleton, MA: PSG Publishing.

Giovacchini, P. (1976). Symbiosis and intimacy. *International Journal of Psychoanalysis, 5,* 413–436.

Glick, P. C. (1955). The life cycle of the family. *Marriage and Family Living, 17,* 3–9.

Glick, P. C. (1979). Children of divorced parents in demographic perspective. *Social Issues, 35,* 170–182.

Goethals, G. W., Steele, R. S., & Broude, G. J. (1976). Theories and research on marriage: A review and some new directions. In H. Grunebaum & J. Christ (Eds.), *Contemporary marriage: Structure, dynamics and therapy* (pp. 229–273). Boston: Little, Brown.

Goldner, V. (1985). Feminism and family therapy. *Family Process, 24,* 31–47.

Goldstein, R., & Swift, K. (1977). Psychotherapy with phobic patients: The marriage relationship as the source of symptoms and the focus of treatment. *American Journal of Psychotherapy, 31,* 285–292.

Goode, W. J. (1956). *After divorce.* New York: Free Press.

Goodrich, W., Ryder, R. G., & Rausch, H. L. (1968). Patterns of newlywed marriage. *Journal of Marriage and the Family, 30,* 383–389.

Gottlieb, A., & Pattison, E. M. (1966). Married couples group therapy. *Archives of General Psychiatry, 14,* 143–152.

Greenberg, L. S., & Johnson, S. M. (1986). When to evoke emotion and why: Process diagnosis in couples therapy. *Journal of Marital and Family Therapy, 12,* 19–23.

Greene, B. L. (1970). *A clinical approach to marital problems: Evaluation and management.* Springfield, IL: Charles C Thomas.

Greene, B. L., Lee, R. R., & Lustig, N. (1973). Transient structured distance as a maneuver in marital therapy. *The Family Coordinator, 22,* 15–22.

Greene, B. L., Lee, R. R., & Lustig, N. (1975). Treatment of marital disharmony where one spouse has a primary affective disorder (manic-depressive illness): I. General overview—100 couples. *Journal of Marriage and Family Counseling, 1,* 39–50.

Greenspan, S. I., & Mannino, F. V. (1974). A model for brief intervention with couples based on projective identification. *American Journal of Psychiatry, 131,* 1103–1106.

Grotstein, J. S. (1981). *Splitting and projective identification.* New York: Jason Aronson.

Guntrip, H. (1969). *Schizoid phenomena, object relations, and the self.* New York: International Universities Press.

Gurman, A. S. (1973). The effects and effectiveness of marital therapy: A review of outcome research. *Family Process, 12,* 145–170.

Gurman, A. S. (1978). Contemporary marital therapies: A critique and comparative analysis of psychoanalytic, behavioral, and systems theory approaches. In T. J. Paolino & B. S. McCrady (Eds.), *Marriage and martial therapy* (pp. 445–556). New York: Brunner/Mazel.

Gurman, A. S. (1982). Behavioral marriage therapy in the 1980s: The challenge of integration. *American Journal of Family Therapy, 10,* 86–96.

Gurman, A. S., & Kniskern, D. P. (1978a). Research on marital and family therapy: Progress, perspective, and prospect. In S. L. Garfield & A. E. Bergin (Eds.), *Handbook of psychotherapy and behavior change: An empirical analysis* (2nd ed., pp. 817–901). New York: Wiley.

Gurman, A. S., & Kniskern, D. P. (1978b). Deterioration in marital and family therapy: Empirical, clinical, and conceptual issues, *Family Process, 17,* 3–20.

Gurman, A. S., & Kniskern, D. P. (1981). Family therapy outcome research: Knowns and unknowns. In A. S. Gurman & D. P. Kniskern (Eds.), *Handbook of family therapy* (pp. 742–775). New York: Brunner/Mazel.

Gurman, A. S., Kniskern, D. P., & Pinsof, W. N. (1986). Research on the process and outcome of family therapy. In S. L. Garfield & A. E. Bergin (Eds.), *Handbook of psychotherapy and behavior change* (pp. 525–623). New York: Wiley.

Hafner, R. J. (1977). The husbands of agoraphobic women and their influence on the treatment outcome. *British Journal of Psychiatry, 129,* 378–383.

Hafner, R. J. (1986). Marital therapy for agoraphobia. In N. S. Jacobson &

A. S. Gurman (Eds.), *Clinical handbook of marital therapy* (pp. 471–493). New York: Guilford Press.

Haley, J. (1963). Marriage therapy. *Archives of General Psychiatry, 8,* 213–234.

Haley, J. (1976). *Problem-solving therapy.* New York: Harper Colophon.

Hammond, D. (1984). Assessment and therapy of sexual dysfunctions. In R. G. Stahmann & W. J. Hiebert (Eds.), *Counseling in marital and sexual problems* (3rd ed., pp. 217–235). Lexington, MA: D. C. Heath.

Heiman, J. R. (1986). Treating sexually distressed marital relationships. In N. S. Jacobson & A. S. Gurman (Eds.), *Clinical handbook of marital therapy* (pp. 361–384). New York: Guilford Press.

Hobbs, D. F. (1965). Parenthood as crisis: A third study. *Journal of Marriage and the Family, 27,* 367–372.

Hobbs, D. F., & Cole, S. P. (1976). Transition to parenthood: A decade replication. *Journal of Marriage and the Family, 38,* 723–731.

Holm, H. J. (1982). The agoraphobic married woman and her marriage pattern: A clinical study. In F. W. Kaslow (Ed.), *The international book of family therapy* (pp. 388–413). New York: Brunner/Mazel.

Jackson, J., & Grotjahn, M. (1959). The concurrent psychotherapy of a latent schizophrenic and his wife. *Psychiatry, 22,* 153–160.

Jacobs, J. W. (1986). Divorce and child custody resolution: Conflicting legal and psychological paradigms. *American Journal of Psychiatry, 143,* 192–197.

Jacobson, N. S. (1979). A review of the research on the effectiveness of marital therapy. In T. J. Paolino & B. S. McCrady (Eds.), *Marriage and marital therapy* (pp. 395–444). New York: Brunner/Mazel.

Jacobson, N. S., & Gurman, A. S. (Eds.) (1986). *Clinical handbook of marital therapy.* New York: Guilford Press.

Jacobson, N. S., & Margolin, G. (1979). *Marital therapy.* New York: Brunner/Mazel.

Kantor, D., & Kuperman, W. (1985). The client's interview of the therapist. *Journal of Marital and Family Therapy, 11,* 225–244.

Kaplan, H. S. (1974). *The new sex therapy: Active treatment of sexual dynsfunction.* New York: Brunner/Mazel.

Kaplan, H. S. (1979). *The new sex therapy: Vol. II: Disorders of sexual desire.* New York: Brunner/Mazel.

Karpel, M. (1980). Family secrets: I. Conceptual and ethical issues in the relational context. II. Ethical and practical considerations in therapeutic management. *Family Process, 19,* 295–306.

Kaslow, F. W. (1981). Divorce and divorce therapy. In A. S. Gurman & D. P. Kniskern (Eds.)., *Handbook of family therapy* (pp. 662–696). New York: Brunner/Mazel.

Kaslow, F. W., & Lieberman, E. J. (1981). Couples group therapy: Rationale, dynamics, and process. In G P. Sholevar (Ed.), *The handbook of marriage and marital therapy* (pp. 347–362). New York: Medical and Scientific Press.

Kaufman, E., & Kaufmann, P. (1979). *Family therapy of drug and alcohol abuse.* New York: Gardner Press.

Kernberg, O. (1974). Mature love: Prerequisites and characteristics. *Journal of the American Psychoanalytic Association, 34,* 743–758.

Kluckhohn, C. & Murray, H. A. (1956). Personality formation: The determinants. In C. Kluckhohn, H. A. Murray, & D. M. Schneider (Eds.), *Personality in nature, society, and culture* (2nd ed., pp. 53–67). New York: Alfred A. Knopf. New York.

Kris, E. (1934). *Psychoanalytic explorations in art.* New York: International Universities Press.

L'Abate, L., & McHenry, S. (1983). *Handbook of marital interventions.* New York: Grune & Stratton.

Laing, R. D. (1969). *The politics of the family and other essays.* New York: Pantheon.

Lansky, M. R. (1986). Marital therapy for narcissistic disorders. In N. S. Jacobson & A. S. Gurman (Eds.), *Clinical handbook of marital therapy* (pp. 557–574). New York: Guilford Press.

Lantz, J. E. (1986). Family logotherapy. *Contemporary Family Therapy, 8,* 124–135.

Lasswell, T. E., & Lasswell, M. E. (1976). I love you, but I'm not in love with you. *Journal of Marriage and Family Counseling, 2,* 211–224.

Lederer, W. J., & Jackson, D. D. (1968). *The mirages of marriage.* New York: W. W. Norton.

LeMasters, E. E. (1957). Parenthood as crisis. *Marriage and Family Living, 19,* 352–355.

Lerman, L. G. (1981). *Prosecution of spouse abuse: Innovations in criminal justice response.* Washington, DC: Center for Womens Policy Studies.

Lester, G. W., Beckman, E., & Baucom, D. H. (1980). Implementation of behavioral marital therapy. *Journal of Marital and Family Therapy, 6,* 189–199.

Levinson, D. J. (1977). The mid-life transition: A period of adult psychosocial development. *Psychiatry, 40,* 99–112.

Levinson, D. J. (1986). A conception of adult development. *American Psychologist, 41,* 3–13.

Levinson, D. J., with Darrow, C. N., Klein, E. G., Levision, M. H., & McKee, B. (1978). *The seasons of a man's life.* New York: Alfred A. Knopf.

Lewin, K. (1948). The background of conflict in marriage. In K. Lewin, *Resolving social conflicts* (pp. 84–102). New York: Harper & Row.

Liberman, R. P. (1970). Behavioral approaches to family and couples therapy. *American Journal of Orthopsychiatry, 40,* 106–118.

Liddle, H. A. (1982). On the problem of ecclecticism: A call for epistemological clarification and human-scale theories. *Family Process, 21,* 243–250.

Lindemann, E. (1944). Symptomatology and management of acute grief. *American Journal of Psychiatry, 101,* 141–148.

Longran, P. & Innes, C. (1986). *Preventing domestic violence against women.* Washington: Bureau of Justice Statistics Bulletin.

Luther, G., & Loev, I. (1981). Resistance in marital therapy. *Journal of Marital and Family Therapy, 7,* 475–480.

Madanes, C. (1984). *Behind the one-way mirror: Advances in the practice of strategic therapy.* San Francisco: Jossey-Bass.

Mahler, M. S., Pine, F., & Bergman, A. (1975). *The psychological birth of the human infant.* New York: Basic Books.

Mannino, F. V., & Greenspan, S. I. (1976). Projection and misperception in couples treatment. *Journal of Marriage and Family Counseling, 2,* 139–143.

Margolin, M. (1985). Building mutual trust and treating sexual disorder. In

A. S. Gurman (Ed.), *Casebook of marital therapy* (pp. 271–301). New York: Guilford Press.

Martin, P. A. (1976). *A marital therapy manual*. New York: Brunner/Mazel.

Martin, P. A., & Bird, H. W. (1953). An approach to the psychtherapy of marriage partners. *Psychiatry, 16*, 123–127.

Mayo, J. A. (1979). Marital therapy with manic-deprssive patients treated with lithium. *Comprehensive Psychiatry, 20*, 419–426.

Merton, R. (1968). *Social theory and social structure*. New York: Free Press.

Miller, J. G., & Miller, J. L. (1980). The family as a system. In C. K. Hofling & J. M. Lewis (Eds.), *The family: Evaluation and treatment* (pp. 141–184). New York: Brunner/Mazel.

Minuchin, S. (1974). *Families and family therapy*. Cambridge, MA: Harvard University Press.

Minuchin, S. & Fishman, H. C. (1981). *Family therapy techniques*. Cambridge, MA: Harvard University Press.

Minuchin, S., Rosman R., & Baker, L. (1978). *Psychosomatic families: Anorexia nervosa in context*. Cambridge, MA: Harvard University Press.

Mittelman, B. (1944). Complementary neurotic reactions in intimate relationships. *The Psychoanalytic Quarterly, 13*, 479–491.

Mittelman, B. (1948). The concurrent analysis of married couples. *The Psychoanalytic Quarterly, 17*, 182–197.

Model, S. (1981). Housework by husbands: Determinants and implications. *Journal of Social Issues, 2*, 225–228.

Murphy, J. M. (1976). A tandem approach: Marriage counseling as process in tandem with individual psychotherapy. *Journal of Marriage and Family Counseling, 2*, 13–22.

Murstein, B. I. (1976). The stimulus–value–role theory of marital choice. In H. Grunebaum & J. Christ (Eds.), *Contemporary marriage: Structure, dynamics and therapy* (pp. 165–186). Boston: Little, Brown.

Napier, A. Y. (1976). Beginning struggles with families. *Journal of Marrriage and Family Counseling, 2*, 3–12.

Napier, A. Y. (1987). Early stages in experiential marital therapy. *Contemporary Family Therapy, 9*, 23–41.

Neill, J., & Kniskern, D. P. (Eds.) (1982). *From psyche to system: The evolving therapy of Carl A. Whitaker*. New York: Guilford Press.

Nerin, W. F. (1986). *Family reconstruction: Long day's journey into light*. New York: W. W. Norton.

Nichols, M. (1984). *Family therapy: Concepts and methods*. New York: Gardner Press.

Nichols, W. C. (1977). Divorce and remarriage education. *Journal of Divorce, 1*, 153–161.

Nichols, W. C. (1980). Stepfamilies: A growing family therapy challenge. In L. Wolberg & M. Aronson (Eds.), *Group and family therapy 1980* (pp. 335–344). New York: Brunner/Mazel.

Nichols, W. C. (1984). Therapeutic needs of children in family system reorganization. *Journal of Divorce, 7*(4), 23–44.

Nichols, W. C. (1985a). A differentiating couple: Some transgenerational issues in marital therapy. In A. S. Gurman (Ed.), *Casebook of marital therapy* (pp. 199–228). New York: Guilford Press.

Nichols, W. C. (1985b). Family therapy with children of divorce. *Journal of Psychotherapy and the Family, 1(2)*, 55–68.

Nichols, W. C. (1986a). Sibling sybsystem therapy in family system reorganization, *Journal of Divorce, 9(3)*, 13–31.

Nichols, W. C. (1986b). Understanding family violence: An orientation for family therapists. *Contemporary Family Therapy, 8*, 188–207.

Nichols, W. C., & Everett, C. A. (1986). *Systemic family therapy: An integrative approach*. New York: Guilford Press.

Oates, W. E. (1955). *Anxiety in christian experience*. Philadelphia: Westminster Press.

Oberndorf, C. P. (1934), Folie à deux. *International Journal of Psychoanalysis, 15*, 14–24.

O'Farrell, T. J. (1986). Marital therapy in the treatment of alcoholism. In N. S. Jacobson & A. S. Gurman (Eds.), *Clinical handbook of marital therapy* (pp. 513–535). New York: Guilford Press.

O'Leary, K. D., & Turkewitz, H. (1978). The treatment of marriage and marriage disorders from a behavioral perspective. In T. J. Paolino & B. S. McCrady (Eds.), *Marriage and marital therapy* (pp. 240–297). New York: Brunner/Mazel.

Oltsmann, R. F., Broderick, J. E., & O'Leary, K. D. (1977). Marital adjustment and the efficacy of behavior therapy with children. *Journal of Consulting and Clinical Psychology, 18*, 3–28.

Paolino, T. J., & McCrady, B. S. (1977). *The alcoholic marriage*. New York: Grune & Stratton.

Papp, P. (1980). The Greek chorus and other techniques of family therapy. *Family Process, 19*, 45–57.

Parkes, C. M. (1973). *Bereavement*. New York: International Universities Press.

Paul, N. L. (1967). The role of mourning and empathy in conjoint marital therapy. In G. H. Zuk & I. Boszormenyi-Nagy (Eds.), *Family therapy and disturbed families* (pp. 186–205). Palo Alto, CA: Science and Behavior Press.

Paul N. L., & Grosser, G. (1965). Operational mourning and its role in conjoint family therapy. *Community Mental Health Journal, 1*, 339–345.

Paul, N. L., & Paul, B. P. (1975). *A marital puzzle: Transgenerational analysis in marriage counseling*. New York: W. W. Norton.

Peplau, L. A., & Perlman, D. (Eds.). (1982). *Loneliness: A sourcebook of current theory, research and therapy*. New York: Wiley.

Phillips, C. E. (1973). Some useful tests for marriage counseling. *The Family Coordinator, 22*, 43–53.

Piercy, F. P., & Sprenkle, D. H. (1986). *Family therapy sourcebook*. New York: Guilford Press.

Pinsof, W. M. (1981). Family therapy process research. In A. S. Gurman & D. P. Kniskern (Eds.), *Handbook of family therapy* (pp. 699–741). New York: Brunner/Mazel.

Pinsof, W. M. (1983). Integrative problem-centered therapy: Toward the synthesis of family and individual psychodynamics. *Journal of Marital and Family Therapy, 9*, 19–35.

Pinsof, W. M., & Catherall, D. R. (1986). The integrative psychotherapy alliance: Family, couple, and individual therapy scales. *Journal of Marital and Family Therapy, 12*, 137–151.

Pirog-Good, M., & Stets-Kealey, J. (1985). *Domestic violence victimization: A mul-*

tiyear perspective. Paper presented at the annual meeting of the American Society of Criminology, San Diego, CA.

Pittman, F. S., & Flomenhaft, K. (1970). Treating the doll's house marriage. *Family Process, 9,* 143–155.

Ravich, R. L., & Wyden, B. (1974). *Predictable pairing.* New York: Wyden.

Rice, J. K., & Rice, D. G. (1986). *Living through divorce: A developmental approach to divorce therapy.* New York: Guilford Press.

Rapoport, R. (1964). The transition from engagement to marriage. *Acta Sociologica, 8,* 36–55.

Robinson, L. R.(1979). Basic concepts in family therapy: A differential comparison with individual treatment. In J. G. Howells (Ed.), *Advances in family psychiatry, I* (pp. 428–435). New York: International Universities Press.

Rollins, B. C., & Feldman, H. (1970). Marital satisfaction over the family life cycle. *Journal of Marriage and the Family, 32,* 20–28.

Rosenbaum, A., & O'Leary, K. D. (1986). The treatment of marital violence. In N. S. Jacobson & A. S. Gurman (Eds.), *Clinical handbook of marital therapy* (pp. 385–405). New York: Guilford Press.

Rosenzweig, H. D. (1985). Sexual abuse: Some practical implications of our knowledge. In E. H. Newberger & R. Bourne (Eds.), *Unhappy families* (pp. 47–62). Littleton, MA: PSG Publishing.

Rossi, A. S. (1968). Transition to parenthood. *Journal of Marriage and the Family, 30,* 26–39.

Russell, C. A., Olson, D. H., Sprenkle, D. H., & Atilano, R. B. (1983). From family symptoms to family system: Review of family therapy research. *American Journal of Family Therapy, 11*(3), 3–13.

Ryder, R. G. (1970a). Dimensions of early marriage. *Family Process, 9,* 51–68.

Ryder, R. G. (1970b). A typology of early marriage. *Family Process, 9,* 385–402.

Sager, C. J. (1966a). The treatment of married couples. In S. Arieti (Ed.), *American handbook of psychiatry, Vol 3* (pp. 213–224). New York: Basic Books.

Sager, C. J. (1966b). The development of marital therapy: An historic review. *American Journal of Orthopsychiatry, 36,* 456–467.

Sager, C. J. (1967). Transference in conjoint treatment of married couples. *Archives of General Psychiatry, 16,* 185–193.

Sager, C. J. (1974). Sexual dysfunction and marital discord. In H. S. Kaplan, *The new sex therapy* (pp. 501–516). New York: Brunner/Mazel.

Sager, C. J. (1976). *Marriage contracts and couple therapy.* New York: Brunner/Mazel.

Satir, V. (1967). *Conjoint family therapy.* Palo Alto, CA: Science and Behavior Books.

Scharff, D. E., & Scharff, J. S. (1987). *Object relations family therapy.* New York: Jason Aronson.

Schover, L. R., Friedman, J. M., Weiler, S. J., Heiman, J. R., & LoPiccolo, J. (1982). Multiaxial problem-oriented system for sexual dysfunctions. *Archives of General Psychiatry, 39,* 614–619.

Seagraves, R. T. (1982). *Marital therapy: A combined psychodynamic-behavioral approach.* New York: Plenum.

Segal, H. (1964). *Introduction to the work of Melanie Klein.* New York: Basic Books.

Sgroi, S. M. (1982). *Handbook of clinical intervention in child sexual abuse.* Lexington, MA: Lexington Press.

Sherman, L. W., & Berkman, R. A. (1984). The specific deterrent effects of arrest for domestic assault. *American Sociological Review, 49*, 261–272.

Sherman, R., & Fredman, N. (1986). *Handbook of structural techniques in marriage and family therapy*. New York: Brunner/Mazel.

Sieberg, E. (1985). *Family communication: An integrated approach*. New York: Gardner Press.

Skynner, A. C. R. (1976). *Systems of family and marital psychotherapy*. New York: Brunner/Mazel.

Slipp, S. (1984). *Object relations: A dynamic bridge between individual and family treatment*. New York: Jason Aronson.

Sonne, J. C., & Swirsky, D. (1981). Self-object considerations in marriage and marital therapy. In P. Sholevar (Ed.), *The handbook of marriage and marital therapy* (pp. 77–101). New York: SP Medical and Scientific Books.

Spanier, G. B. (1983). Married and unmarried cohabitation in the United States: 1980. *Journal of Marriage and the Family, 45*, 277–288.

Spark, G. M. (1977). Marriage is a family affair. *The Family Coordinator, 26*, 167–174.

Speck, R., & Attneave, C. (1973). *Family networks*. New York: Pantheon.

Spitz, R. (1945). Hospitalism: an inquiry into the genesis of psychiatric conditions in early childhood. In *Psychoanalytic studies of the child* (Vol. 2, pp. 113–117). New York: International Universities Press.

Spitz. R. (1965). *The first year of life*. New York: International Universities Press.

Sprenkle, D. H. (Ed.). (1985). *Divorce therapy*. New York: Haworth Press.

Sprenkle, D. H., & Cyrus, C. L. (1983). Abandonment: The stress of sudden divorce. In C. R. Figley & H. I. Mccubbin (Eds.), *Stress and the family. Vol. II. Coping with catastrophe* (pp. 53–75). New York: Brunner/Mazel.

Steinglass, P. (1978). The conceptualization of marriage from a systems perspective. In T. J. Paolino & B. S. McCrady, (Eds.), *Marriage and marital therapy* (pp. 298–365). New York: Brunner/Mazel.

Stewart, R. H., Peters, T. C., Marsh, S., & Peters, M. J. (1975). An object-relations approach to psychotherapy with marital couples, families, and children. *Family Process, 14*, 161–178.

Stierlin, H. (1981). *Separating parents and adolescents*. New York: Jason Aronson.

Stock, W. (1985). The influence of gender on power dynamics in relationships. In D. C. Goldberg (Ed.), *Contemporary marriage: Special issues in couples therapy* (pp. 62–99). Homewood, IL: Dorsey Press.

Straus, M. A. (1977). A sociological perspective on the prevention and treatment of wifebeating. In M. Roy (Ed.), *Battered women* (pp. 194–239). New York: Van Nostrand Reinhold.

Straus, M. A., & Gelles, R. J. (1986). Change in family violence from 1975 to 1985. *Journal of Marriage and the Family, 48*, 465–479.

Straus, M. A., Gelles, R. J., & Steinmetz, S. K. (Eds.). (1980). *Behind closed doors: Violence in the American family*. New York: Doubleday Anchor Press.

Sugarman, S. (1987). Teaching symbolic-experiential family therapy: The personhood of the teacher. *Contemporary Family Therapy, 9*, 138–145.

Sullivan, H. S. (1953). *The interpersonal theory of psychiatry*. New York: W. W. Norton.

Sullivan, H. S. (1954). *The psychiatric interview*. New York: W. W. Norton.

Thibaut, J. W., & Kelley, H. H. (1959). *The social psychology of groups.* New York: Wiley.

Thomas, A. (1956). Simultaneous psychotherapy with marital problems. *American Journal of Psychotherapy, 10,* 716–727.

Todd, T. C., & Stanton, M. D. (1983). Research on marital and family therapy: Answers, issues, and recommendations for the future. In B. B. Wolman & G. Stricker (Eds.), *Handbook of marital and family therapy* (pp. 91–115). New York: Plenum.

Tomm, K. (1985). Struggling with the threat of suicide. In S. B. Coleman (Ed.), *Failures in family therapy* (pp. 300–329). New York: Guilford Press.

Trepper, T. S. (1985). The apology session. *Journal of Psychotherapy and the Family, 2*(2), 93–101.

von Bertalanffy, L. (1968). *General systems theory.* New York: Braziller.

Wachtel, E. F., & Wachtel, P. L. (1986). *Family dynamics in individual psychotherapy: A guide to clinical strategies.* New York: Guilford Press.

Walker, L. E. (1979). *The battered woman.* New York: Harper Colphon.

Warkentin, J., & Whitaker, C. A. (1967). The secret agenda of the therapist doing couples therapy. In G. H. Zuk & I. Boszormenyi-Nagy (Eds.), *Family therapy and disturbed families* (pp. 239–243). Palo Alto, CA: Science and Behavior Books.

Watson, A. S. (1963). The conjoint psychotherapy of marital partners. *American Journal of Orthopsychiatry, 33,* 912–922.

Watzlawick, P., Beavin, J. H., & Jackson, D. D. (1967). *Pragmatics of human communication.* New York: W. W. Norton.

Watzlawick, P., Weakland, J., & Fisch, R. (1974). *Change: Problem formation and problem resolution.* New York: W. W. Norton.

Weiss, R. L. (1978). The conceptualization of marriage and marriage disorders from a behavioral prspective. In T. J. Paolino & B. S. McCrady (Eds.), *Marriage and marital therapy* (pp. 165–239). New York: Brunner/Mazel.

Weiss, R. L., Hops, H., & Patterson, G. R. (1973). A framework for conceptualizing marital conflict: A technology for altering it, some data for evaluating it. In L. A. Hamerlynck, L. C. Handy, & E. J. Mash (Eds.), *Behavior change: Methodology, concepts, and practice* (pp. 304–342). Champaign, IL: Research Press.

Weiss, R. S. (1975). *Marital separation.* New York: Basic Books.

Weitzman, L. J. (1985). *The divorce revolution: The unexpected social and economic consequences for women and children in America.* New York: Free Press.

Whitaker, C A. (1958a). *Psychotherapy of chronic schizophrenic patients.* Boston: Little, Brown.

Whitaker, C. A. (1958b). Psychotherapy with couples. *American Journal of Pschotherapy, 12,* 18–23.

Whitaker, C. A. (Speaker). (1971). *Dr. Carl Whitaker* (Audio Cassette Recording). Chicago, IL: Instructional Dynamics Incorporated.

Whitaker, C. A. (1976). The hindrance of theory in clinical work. In P. J. Guerin (Ed.). *Family therapy theory and practice* (pp. 154–164). New York: Gardner Press.

Whitaker, C. A., & Keith, D. V. (1981). Symbolic-experiential family therapy. In A. S. Gurman & D. P. Kniskern (Eds.), *Handbook of family therapy* (pp. 187–225). New York: Brunner/Mazel.

Whitaker, C. A., & Miller, M. H. (1969). A reevaluation of "psychiatric help" when divorce impends. *American Journal of Psychiatry, 126,* 611–618.

White, S. W., & Bloom, B. L. (1981). Factors related to the adjustment of divorcing men. *Family Relations, 30,* 349–360.

Wile, D. B. (1981). *Couples therapy: A nontraditional approach.* New York: Wiley.

Willi, J. (1982). *Couples in collusion.* New York: Jason Aronson.

Willi, J. (1984). *Dynamics of couples therapy.* New York: Jason Aronson.

Williamson, D. S. (1978). New life at the graveyard: A method of individuation from a dead former parent. *Journal of Marriage and Family Counseling, 4,* 93–101.

Williamson, D. S. (1981). Personal authority via termination of the intergenerational hierarchical boundary: A "new" stage in the family life cycle. *Journal of Marital and Family Therapy, 7,* 441–452.

Williamson, D. S. (1982). Personal authority via termination of the intergenerational hierarchical boundary: Part II. The consultation process and the therapeutic process. *Journal of Marital and Family Therapy, 8*(2), 23–37.

Williamson, D. S. (1984). Extramarital involvements in couple interaction. In R. F. Stahmann & W. J. Hiebert (Eds.), *Counseling in marital and sexual problems: A clinical handbook* (3rd ed. pp. 147–160). Lexington, MA: D. C. Heath.

Wills, T. A., Weiss, R. L., & Patterson, G. R. (1974). A behavioral analysis of the determinants of marital satisfaction. *Journal of Consulting and Clinical Psychology, 42,* 802–811.

Wynne, L. C. (1965). Some indications and contraindications for exploratory family therapy. In I. Boszormenyi-Nagy & J. L. Framo (Eds.). *Intensive family therapy* (pp. 289–322). New York: Harper & Row.

Wynne, L. C. (1983). A phase-oriented approach to treatment with schizophrenics and their families. In W. R. McFarlane (Eds.), *Family therapy in schizophrenia* (pp. 251–265). New York: Guilford Press.

Wynne, L. C. (1984). The epigenesis of relational systems: A model for understanding family development. *Family Process, 23,* 297–318.

Wynne, L. C., McDaniel, S.H., & Weber, T. T. (1986). *Systems consultation: A new perspective for family therapy.* New York: Guilford Press.

Yankelovich, D. (1981). *New rules.* New York: Random House.

Zinner, J. (1976). The implications of projective identification for marital interaction. In H. Grunebaum & J. Christ (Eds.), *Contemporary marriage: Structure, dynamics and therapy* (pp. 293–308). Boston: Little, Brown.

Zemon-Gass, G., & Nichols, W. C. (1981). *Changing marital developmental tasks: Continuing family therapy issues.* Unpublished manuscript.

Zemon-Gass, G., & Nichols, W. C. (1988). Gaslighting: A marital syndrome. *Contemporary Family Therapy, 10.*

Zuk, G. H. (1986). *Process and practice in family therapy* (2nd ed.). New York: Human Sciences Press.

Zunin, L., & Zunin, N. (1972). *Contact: The first four minutes.* New York: Ballantine.

Index